T0272416

HEIRLOOM SKILLS

A COMPLETE GUIDE TO
MODERN HOMESTEADING

ANDERS RYDELL & ALVA HERDEVALL

TRANSLATED BY ELLEN HEDSTROM

Skyhorse Publishing

Contents

Preface

To be honest, there's not much modern about modern homesteading. Most of the content in this book is about knowledge from the past, the crafty tricks and hints that have been used for generations—sometimes many generations.

By "modern" we mean using knowledge and methods from the past and making them work in a modern context, in day-to-day life in the 2020s. Of course, not everything was better in the past, but the methods of housekeeping usually were. The aim was to use items that were readily available and to recycle and reuse them, and these methods, techniques, and materials stand the test of time in addition to being natural and decomposable. They also make use of things that won't cause harm to you or your environment. Essentially, we're talking simple, natural ingredients that go a long way such as a few eggs, some beeswax, and a good bacterial culture.

We hope this book will inspire you and whet your appetite to increase your own skills.

Modern homesteading should not be confused with living self-sufficiently and surviving without buying or swapping items. Modern homesteading means something entirely different to us. It's not about producing everything from scratch or isolating yourself from the community and not consuming anything; it means a simpler and somewhat more basic way of life.

A large part of it is making things from scratch, preferably using produce that we've grown ourselves or made, or that someone in our community that shares our philosophy has produced. We would never use pesticides on anything in our own garden so why would we accept products from someone who does?

For us, modern homesteading means living in harmony with nature and the change of seasons. We won't buy tulips during the fall or eat "fresh" strawberries on New Year's Eve. We do, however, love placing a bunch of home-grown tulips on the table in May or biting into a strawberry in June.

Modern homesteading is all about understanding the raw ingredients, learning to value them and use them responsibly. It's about appreciating things that are good quality and made with love. It's reusing and recycling, mending and making do, and throwing away as little as possible. We may not grow the wheat, but we grind the flour. We don't grow the coffee beans but we roast them, and while we don't own a cow, we'll happily churn some butter.

Most of all we appreciate everything that we produce ourselves. This appreciation does not come for free; the love is not unconditional and everyone who lives this way of life will eventually discover this. However, it's the tears, the dedication, and the time spent that make those tomatoes taste all the sweeter.

To have the opportunity to grow our own food, to keep chickens, ducks, and bees, and to have fruit trees and berries to tend to, is a responsibility that at times weighs heavily on us, but it is also hugely rewarding and a real luxury. We nearly always get back more than we give and not a day passes that we don't feel deeply grateful for this.

Our Modern Homesteading Manifesto

Live Like a Farmer

We often get asked, "How self-sufficient are you?" We don't really know how to answer that as this has never been the end goal. Of course, we could manage for a short while, maybe even a long time if we had to, but we usually answer, "As much as we have time for, can manage, and feel like doing."

Anyone can spend time as a modern homesteader according to their own ability. Maybe you have a farm, a backyard, a balcony, or even a windowsill in an apartment. The important thing is not how much you do but that you make something of what you have, and this is our basic philosophy.

We don't own a lot of land, we don't have woodlands, fields, or pastures but we do have a larger than average garden and the trick is to treat it as if it is a farm. We're always looking for new spots to plant trees and bushes, grow flower beds and vegetables, and build barns and pens for new animals. We build and extend using broken up stone and cut down trees and even home-grown soil. Each year our lawn gets smaller, which doesn't just benefit us, but the biodiversity in our yard.

Think Ecological

In our household, the things that hold the most value are not the individual plants, trees, bushes, or animals, but rather the circular systems and the natural interactions between them, as this is where the magic happens. An apple falls from the tree and we eat it, the core gets given to the chickens that give us eggs, meat, and fertilizer. Egg shells and chicken bones get composted and together with the fertilizer form the basis of new nutrient-rich soil, meaning new apples, berries, vegetables, and flowers.

We constantly strive to create and close these systems and discover new layers to enrich them. The beauty in viewing our land this way is that we value everything around us. A tangle of nettles gives us nourishment, the dandelions on the lawn become honey, and those Spanish slugs are turned into foie gras.

A working system means that each component is valuable and has a purpose, and everything you choose to add to a system becomes important. At some point, that orange peel you threw on the compost will make its way back to your mouth, which is why it's important to think about how it's produced.

Take Care of the Smallest Animals

It's not really our hens, ducks, bees, flowers, and plants that keep our circular system going, but the very smallest of our animals; the millions of bacteria, microbes, and yeasts that surround us and even live inside us. Children who grow up on farms have been found to be less likely to have allergies and asthma due to the bacteria, dust, and dirt that they are exposed to.

One of the most important things to learn with this lifestyle is to appreciate and nurture this invisible world and learn to live in harmony with it; for example, not cleaning too much and using the right sort of products. A large part of our work is promoting the processes that allow bacteria, yeast, and other microorganisms to work and thrive. It can be anything from composting to having nutrient-rich soil in your kitchen garden, from ensuring your hens have a healthy gut bacterium to lactic acid bacteria in bees as well as our own fermentations. Without our smallest friends we would have neither bread, beer, nor honey so they really are our true heroes.

Time—It's All Relative

"How do you find the time?" is the question we get asked the most. How do you find time to run your own household with plants, animals, and selling goods (and write a big book about it) while working full-time and running a family? Our secret is simple: we don't. At least we don't find time for everything we would like do, and that is completely fine.

It's all about prioritizing, which means we are usually outside, always have the kids with us, and try to work from home. Finally, the most important thing is, we do it because it is important to us and we enjoy it.

The Basic Ingredients

Getting the most out of modern homesteading doesn't

mean growing hundreds of different vegetables; it's more about focusing on foods that you would like to eat, things you need, and what will pique your interest. These kinds of products are usually versatile. For example, some products can be used in countless ways like eggs, honey, and beeswax, and this book will show you lots of examples of how these miracle ingredients can be used.

Goals & Motivations

If you would like to increase the amount of homesteading you do, it can be helpful to think about your goals and motivations. For us it's about being able to control what goes into our products, from the raw ingredients to the finished goods. By making things ourselves and keeping an ecological perspective, we reduce our carbon footprint and at the same time promote resilience within our family.

Dreaming about growing your own plants and keeping bees and other animals is fun, but it also means responsibility, which usually involves long-term commitment.

The road to modern homesteading is not always straight; the winding journey is filled with happiness and joy, but also at times mishaps and failures.

It requires a big dose of patience and humility. After all, a tree doesn't grow in a day and neither does a modern homesteader.

Good luck and welcome to the world of heirloom skills and modern homesteading!

Alva and Anders

Fresh Cut Flowers

Each season brings its own flowers. Spring brings bulbs with crisp, green leaves filled with chlorophyl. Then comes summer, with an explosion of flowers like a slow, scented firework display when we fill our home with bouquets as fluffy as clouds. Finally comes fall, with its pale, dull tones rumbling into the end of the season, but there is beauty even here, with pompous sunflowers and a landscape of eternal blooms, petals, and infructescence, replacing the blooms from the summer.

Growing flowers is an important part of our lives. These days it's hard for us to imagine a spring without tulips, a summer without peonies and dahlias, and a fall without asters. Despite drying them and making soaps, scented oils, and bath salts, we can't preserve our flowers in the same way that we do with vegetables, so we began sharing our excess with neighbors, friends, and people in our community. Filling our flower stall and welcoming people to pick their own is one of the highlights of the season.

A Modern Flower Philosophy

Filling one's home with fresh flowers all year round is wonderful but sadly not great for the environment. Before we grew our own flowers, we'd buy a bunch every Friday, especially during the cold and dark season when the longing for summer was the greatest. Deep down we knew that it was the height of stupidity and the more we learned about the flower industry, the more we realized that those flowers we placed on the table every Friday were an environmental disaster, often grown under poor working conditions.

In order to produce a large amount of fresh cut flowers commercially all year round in Northern Europe, large greenhouses are used, which use a lot of energy to keep them warm. The majority of fresh flowers are grown in countries where the workforce is often uneducated, poorly paid (usually women), and working with pesticides inside large greenhouses. Pesticides can have devastating consequences for the health of the workers, but also for the flowers and environment. Flowers already covered in pesticides are treated with chemicals to preserve them during transport and once they reach your hometown are in a mummified state. This is the reason some roses never bloom at home as the plant is full of toxins and has simply died.

That the flowers we gave as gifts to those we loved the most could be something so devastating was a sad realization, but at the same time we didn't want a home without flowers. We had to find a new way and started to view flowers in the same way we do vegetables; flowers are seasonal and buying a rose or tulip in the middle of winter is neither natural nor sustainable.

In 2013 a movement was started in the US by Debra Prinzing that became known as the Slow Flowers movement. It was a reaction to the way in which modern society consumes cut flowers, which is completely disconnected from what growing flowers is all about. The ethos behind the Slow Flowers movement derives from "the slow movement" which advocates for a lifestyle where quality comes before quantity. In the food arena there has been a reaction against fast food, mass production, and over-consumption.

The same principle can be applied to flowers. It's about buying and growing flowers that are suited to the climate and season where you live. The way in which you grow flowers needs to be environmentally friendly, ecologically sound, and sold locally. In Sweden an organization called *"Snittblomsodlare"* (Cut flower farmers) work with spreading knowledge about small scale, local flower farmers and environmentally friendly, locally grown seasonal flowers. Sadly, these only make up a fraction of the flowers that are sold.

Of course, the best thing to do is to grow your own fresh flowers; it doesn't get more local than that. Letting the flowers follow the seasons is a good idea—it means we have to wait a bit longer until we can place a bunch of tulips or dahlias on the table, but in the winter dried flowers take the place of the fresh ones.

Giving away a bouquet of fresh flowers that you have grown yourself is a real pleasure, or you can just let them fill your own home. We have made fresh flowers into a lifestyle—we sell them, give them away, place them in our home, add them to food, and make soap and creams from them, and it brings us a lot of joy.

FRESH CUT FLOWERS

Bulbs & Tubers

Tulips & Narcissus

Planting tulips and narcissus is rewarding and, as spring nears, we long for these first blooms.

PLANTING Tulip bulbs should be planted in the fall from September until first frost. Place them somewhere the sun will shine in spring, at a depth three times their size. It's easiest to dig in a flat area, place them on the ground, and cover with soil. We plant our tulips close together with around ¾ to 1 inch between them (2–3 cm). It means they can support each other as they grow. Go for perennials, such as the Darwin hybrids, preferably the older varieties that haven't been overly cultivated to ensure they bloom year after year.

SOIL & NUTRIENTS Tulips prefer soil that drains well; otherwise the bulbs rot. Many people fertilize with bone meal due to it being long lasting. We prefer nitrogen fertilizers using chicken or horse manure when planting in the fall, and chicken or horse manure with nettle water during the spring.

HARVEST & DISPLAY We harvest our tulips with the bulb still attached. Partly because we think they look lovely arranged in a vase or tied together upright on a plate, but also because they last twice as long in a vase this way. Cut tulips and narcissus prefer cold water changed daily. Let the tulips wilt completely, place the bulb in the sun to dry, and store in a dark, cool space until it is time to plant them again in the fall.

PESTS Deer love tulips but hate narcissus, meaning we can grow our narcissus without any cover. Our tulips on the other hand are grown behind a 6½-foot (2-meter)-tall net. We have tried most things to keep them away, from gadgets that send out soundwaves to sheep's wool and wolf urine on a stick, but nothing has worked except the net.

Dahlias

THE dahlia is the queen of summer, a cut flower that just keeps on giving from June until the frost gets it.

SPROUTING For more resilient flowers, you can pre-sprout the tubers during the spring. Plant one tuber per pot and cover with soil. The cut side should face down and the eyes should face up. Don't water until you see shoots poking up from the soil. When the plant has grown a few inches, pinch the tips (above the other sets of leaves) to encourage branching and strength.

PLANTING Dahlias prefer sun. Plant your sprouting plants outside, placing them slightly deeper than they grew in the pots to give you a more stable plant. Dahlias need support as they grow to stop them getting too heavy and breaking. Tie them up with jute twine or use plant supports out of metal. You can also place them close together so that they support each other.

SOIL & NUTRIENTS Dahlias prefer a loamy, well-drained soil. As they bloom over a long period of time, they require a lot of nutrients. Make sure you fertilize the soil substantially before you plant them outside and then regularly use a nitrogen fertilizer as they flower, stopping when the flowering ends during late fall.

WATER Dahlias are some of the thirstiest flowers there are, but don't leave the tuber to stand in water as it will rot.

HARVEST & DISPLAY Cut the stems above a set of leaves. Some dahlias get stems with several buds; if you want a flower with a long stem, you can remove all the buds except the big one. They will last a week if you add fresh water daily and cut the stem every second day

PESTS All types of snails seem to love dahlias. If you have a lot of snails where you live, we recommend you sprout your dahlias to give them an advantage over snail attacks. Earwigs also have a weakness for hiding among the petals to have a snack. A tip to combat earwigs is to rub the stalks with some beeswax balm.

HIBERNATION Once the dahlias stop flowering in late fall, let them wilt and absorb the nutrients they need into the tuber. You can then remove these, dry them, and store over winter in a dark, cold space free of frost and not too dry, for example in a root cellar.

Dahlia "Arabian Night." Harvest regularly to ensure an abundant flowering.

PROPAGATING The easiest way to get more plants is to divide the tubers, but you can also take seeds or cuttings. It's easiest to divide a tuber in spring before you pre-sprout them. Make sure you get a stem, lateral bud (eye), and root on each bit you divide. Some larger tubers will almost divide by themselves during the winter and all you need to do is carefully separate them, or perhaps use a sharp knife.

For seeds, allow the flower to wilt, the petals to fall off, and the seed pod to turn brown. Dry the seed pod indoors and carefully remove the seeds into a coffee filter or a seed bag. Note that your new dahlia is not genetically identical to the mother plant and will therefore look completely different. If you want seeds from a double dahlia, remove some of the inner petals to avoid honey and bumble bees. Alternatively, you can pollinate using a brush.

You can try and cross-pollinate two of your favorite types by removing the petals before they bloom so no insects can get at them. Isolate them in a bag and then brush them with a soft brush once they are ready.

FRESH CUT FLOWERS

From Flower to Seed

Always read the packet to see how to store the seeds before you sow them and what temperature and light is needed for your seeds to grow. All too often we've been in a hurry and just guessed, only to end up with five weedy flowers poking out from the hundreds of seeds we've sown.

Direct Sowing

The quickest way to plant a flower is to drop a seed straight into the soil. We learn by trial and error year by year with different types of seeds. A small, fragile shoot is vulnerable to insects, drought, and frost, so just because it's an easy way to sow doesn't mean you can get away with not tending to it just like the majority of flowers.

Pre-Treatment

TEMPERATURE We grow our seeds in a fairly warm environment, around 68–75°F (20–24°C). Once the shoots come up, we place them in a slightly cooler space indoors at around 64°F (18°C).

LIGHT EXPOSURE Some summer flowers need more light, and should not be covered with soil, or just a very thin layer, such as snapdragons, cosmos, poppies, verbena, summer rudbeckia, and zinnias, which are small seeds. Other seeds prefer dark and should be covered with a good layer of soil. These seeds are often slightly larger, such as annual phlox, sunflowers, and sweet peas.

STRATIFICATION Seeds from countries that have cold winters need a period of cold in order to grow, such as perennials and roses. Stratification of seeds means placing them in a cold, damp, and dark spot for a period of time. By mimicking nature your seeds will think it's spring and start to sprout. Place the seeds in a bag with some damp sand or vermiculite (a mineral that retains damp) for 2 weeks to simulate late summer when the seeds absorb water, then place in a fridge for around 6 weeks to simulate winter. The seeds that germinate need to be sown right away, so check the seeds regularly.

COLD STRATIFICATION You can also let nature do the stratification by sowing the seeds outside during the winter, under a roof, in a garage or a cold greenhouse. Add a layer of snow now and again but watch out so the soil doesn't get too damp.

SEED STARTER When a seed germinates, it doesn't need as many nutrients as when it starts to shoot. That's why you use a seed starter mix to start off with. You can switch to a richer soil when you repot them. Apart from the seed starter needing less nutrients, it also needs to be a finer texture and well drained to let water through. If there are lumps in the soil, the roots can't get established. If the soil is too damp, there is a risk of mold. If you want to make your own seed starter, remove any gravel from the soil and add a third of fine sand if you wish.

SOIL BLOCKERS We make frequent use of our soil blocker, a type of soil press to make soil cubes (soil blocks) for sowing and repotting. The cubes come in three different sizes where the smallest one fits the middle-sized one, and the middle-sized one fits the largest one. In this way, once the plant has outgrown its cube, you simply lift it into the next size and slot it in like a puzzle piece. These soil blocks have lots of benefits, the most obvious one being avoiding plastic pots. Another one is the effective use of space if placed close together on a tray or in a trough. Combined with clever storage and good lighting, this method is a winner if you want to avoid transforming your entire home into a plant shop.

A plant gets its nutrients and water via its roots. In a plastic pot the roots will try and grow outwards but be blocked by the walls. If the plant stands for too long before being planted outside, the roots will keep growing round inside the pot, resulting in a tight tangle. If the tips of the roots can't get through the soil, they thicken and branch out, making the situation worse. When it's time to plant outside, the tips of the roots have a hard time finding a way out of the mess and into the rich soil. The end result is a plant that stops growing completely unnecessarily. Soil blocks contain only soil, meaning the roots can easily make their way out once planted out.

BROADCAST SEEDING Apart from soil blockers, broadcast seeding is the way we usually sow our summer flowers.

There is little effort involved as the seeds are spread widthways in a trough, container, pot, or tray.

PRUNING We prune all our flowers except sunflowers. Once the plant has started to grow and look good, you need to grab some scissors and chop it off. It feels really strange at first and the flower looks dull, but it's the only way to get big, bushy plants. Once the plant reaches around 8 inches (20 cm) in height, it is time to trim it. Cut just above the second or third set of leaves on the main stem. As the plant continues to grow, it splits into two new stems, which generates double the blooms.

LIGHTING In areas where daylight hours are short for much of the year, seeds sown indoors early in the year need artificial lighting. We use fluorescent lighting specifically for plants that can be attached to make a long row. We attach the lights so that the fixture hangs underneath the shelving. We tie them so that they shine close to the soil when the seeds start to sprout and then gradually raise them up.

WATERING Whether you use soil blocks or other methods, seeds get moisture from above while they sprout and grow roots. After this they get their water from beneath on a tray to build long, strong roots. The soil should feel damp all the way through but not wet and heavy.

Soil Blockers

Repotting

Soil

All plants need nutrients such as nitrogen, phosphorus, and potassium. Whether you buy or make your own soil it needs to contain these. In store-bought soil, peat levels are often high. Peat retains moisture, which is good for growing plants, but there is some debate over whether peat is a sustainable product. So instead of peat, a loamy soil is preferable, such as garden compost.

The pH level of the soil doesn't need to be exact but should be around 5–6. Coniferous plants and berries as well as some perennials such as hydrangea prefer a more acidic soil with a lower pH level. The easiest way to make soil more acidic is to add some soil and pine needles from the forest. On the other hand, if you want a more alkaline soil with a higher pH level, you will need to add lime.

Fertilizers

Once the plant has used up the nutrients in the soil you will need to add some form of fertilizer. The easiest way is to add a liquid such as compost tea or liquid manure (see Compost & Fertilizer, page 107). You can even buy organic liquid fertilizer; pick one which is both organic and plant-based, such as liquid seaweed extract.

Pricking Out

When your seedlings are ready to be repotted, the easiest method is pricking out. Start by separating the small plants from each other without damaging the roots, then make a hole in the soil with a stick. You can buy special pricking sticks, but a pen or chopstick works just as well. Gently push down the roots of the plant and then the plant, using the stick to make sure it goes in deep to give it stability.

Watering

Always water your plants from the bottom to give them lovely long well-developed roots that grow downwards.

Suggestions for fresh cut flowers:

Fresh greens	Annuals	Perennials
allgold	amaranth	alpine bistort
astilbe	Australian straw	Asian bleeding
basil	flower	heart
beech	bishops flower	carnation
cistus	black-eyed Susan	coneflowers
cherry tomato	blushing bride	dahlia
common holly	California poppy	feverfew
common ninebark	Chinese aster	forking larkspur
coral bells	common baby's	garden phlox
eucalyptus	breath	globe thistle
European	cosmos	great burnet
hornbeam	daucus carota	great masterwort
forsythia	globe flower	hortensia
garden lady's	large pink	honeysuckle
mantle	pot marigold	iris
glossy privet	sea lavender	martagon lily
guelder rose	showy baby's	peony
honeysuckle	breath	rose
laurustine	snapdragon	sea holly
malus	snow maiden	
mint	straw flower	Grass
mock oranges	sunflower	foxtail millet
oregano	sweet pea	hare's tail
Reeve's spirea	yarrow	oat
smoke tree	zinnia	quaking grass
thicket shadbush		wheat
tartarian		
honeysuckle		
vine maple		

Planting Out

Hardening Off

When the spring sun starts to shine, it is easy to become enthusiastic about creating your dream garden, so it's important to sit on your hands and channel that energy into something else. While there is still a risk of overnight frost, there is no point in even thinking about planting out your small, tender seedlings. You can get information on local weather patterns and when the risk of night frost has passed in your area, so keep an eye on the local weather forecast around this date. It is also a good idea to have some jute or a fiber roll ready for any unexpected weather change.

About a week before planting out, the plants need to get used to colder weather. This can be done by placing them outside during the day and then bringing them back inside at night. Start with a few hours outside on the first day and then gradually increase the time.

Placement

Think about where you are going to place your summer flowers. It's a bit like putting together a bouquet. Check the seed packets to see how high the flowers will grow but halve the distance between the plants as this is merely a recommendation for larger, commercial settings. If you plant the flowers close together, it stops weeds taking hold and you can get more flowers and longer stalks in the same space. In addition, the taller flowers can support each other so they don't break or grow sideways. Choose a sunny spot with some protection from the wind. It's best not to mix perennials and annuals too much as there is a risk you may rip up the perennials while weeding. Think about what varieties and colors you want to grow together. Choose flowers that are taller or stick out in some way to create something eye catching. Or you might want something that climbs a tower or trellis together with some lower flowers which is both beautiful and functional. Sweet peas on a trellis also protects against the wind and sun.

Soil

Whether we are growing food or plants we also grow our own soil. All organic material rich in carbon goes back onto the soil to improve and fertilize it. Remove the leaves from stalks as soon as you harvest and place them around the flowers.

Fertilizer

We have a golden rule not to use fertilizer with nitrogen after midsummer. This is even more important when it comes to flowers as too much nitrogen means an overproduction of leaves but no flowers. Use nettle water (nitrogen) regularly throughout May and June until midsummer (June 21st). After this use comfrey water (potassium and phosphorous). A recipe for fertilizer tea can be found in the chapter on compost and nutrients on page 107.

FRESH CUT FLOWERS

Picking & Arranging Flowers

Let your imagination flow when you pick and bind your bouquets and create your flower arrangements. Cut your fresh flowers during the dampest part of the day to make them last longer.

Go out early in the morning or late at night and pick what you need using a sharp pair of flower scissors or shears. You also need a bucket of water to place them in while picking as fresh flowers need a lot of water. When harvesting tulips with the bulb we place them horizontally in a wheelbarrow or cart. Whether you harvest in the morning or at night, they will last a lot longer in a vase if you leave them in a cool place with lots of water. We are lucky to have a large root cellar where we place finished bouquets wrapped in paper or the wheelbarrow with tulips. Large flower sellers have cold rooms to store cut flowers and some nurseries and flower shops have flower fridges about the size of a beer fridge. As you are unlikely to be able to fit the flowers in your fridge, you can place them in a shady spot overnight or for a few hours in the morning, depending on what time you harvest.

Color & Shape

There's really no hard and fast rule when it comes to being creative; sometimes having a plan for your creative expression is good, other times being a bit more haphazard works. If you are new to this, it can be worth following some guidelines and as you develop you can start to experiment and be more elaborate.

Begin by considering what vibe you want to convey. Is it a bright and breezy bouquet or an over-the-top dramatic arrangement? A harmonious summer posy or a wild and wonderful creation? Where will you place it? The kitchen table or the bedroom window? How will you arrange it? A vase, a pot, or a plate? Now you can start to consider which flowers will contribute what, so that when you come to pick your flowers you have an idea of all the components in the completed bouquet.

Colors in a bouquet can work together in three ways; gradient, contrasting, or a monochrome color scheme. A bunch of flowers with a gradient color scheme has several similar colors such as yellow and orange. A contrasting scheme has clearly contrasted

but complementary colors such as red and green. If you have too many contrasting colors it can be hard on the eyes though and feel too busy. In a monochrome bouquet, the flowers all have the same color in different shades, also called tone on tone. It gives a calming and harmonious appearance. We often use tone on tone in

bouquets and arrangements with one or two gradients of color, but you also need to consider if the colors are warm or cool. Warm colors work best with other warm colors, and the same goes for cool colors.

The shape of the bouquet or arrangement as well as the individual components also affect the overall impression. A large, bushy bunch gives a wild and free look while a staighter arrangement gives a more low-key impression. A balanced bouquet mixes calming shapes with unstructured ones, large unruly flowers with small ones, and distinctive structures with more subtle ones.

FRESH CUT FLOWERS

FRESH CUT FLOWERS

TYING A BOUQUET

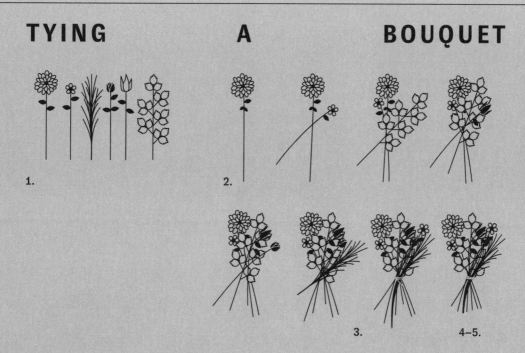

1.

2.

3.

4–5.

We usually tie our bouquets using four different components.

THE FOCAL POINT—this draws the eye in and is usually a large flower with a calming shape such as a dahlia, asters, or a peony.

SUPPORTING FLOWERS—flowers that support and enhance the focal flower both with color and shape, for example phlox, yarrow, or carnations.

THE ACCENT—flowers or grass that stick out with their contrasting shape or color, such as amaranth, globe flower, wild carrot, or hare's tail grass.

FOLIAGE—twigs or leaves that give volume such as raspberry, common ninebark, or smoke tree.

Instructions
Use a floral knife or similar sharp knife, string, scissors, and a vase filled with water.

1. Lay the flowers in front of you.
2. Place the longest stem in your hand, then place another stem on top of it at a 45-degree angle so they form an X. Hold the X between the thumb and the index finger in your left hand. Using your right hand, place the next stem over the top stem. If you arrange the flowers at different levels, the bouquet will feel more alive—the more variety in length, the wilder the appearance. Repeat and turn the bouquet counter-clockwise as you add more stems, foliage, and flowers. Keep adding flowers at an angle and check them from above now and again. If needed, release your grip slightly to slide a stem in from the top into the spiral.
3. Bind the flowers with string, such as jute, twist it round a few times, and tie a knot.
4. Trim the stems and cut at an angle to create a larger surface for water intake.
5. The bouquet is done and should be able to stand without support.

FRESH CUT FLOWERS

Creating a Flower Arrangement

An arrangement is created in the opposite way from a bouquet, as you build it from the outside in, or from the bottom up. It is easier to plan the shape, density, and placement of stems for a specific container. The arrangement can be made low and horizontal to be placed on a dinner table, large and bushy to create a centerpiece, or small and dainty to be placed on a desk. We love arranging lots of small vases together to create a focal point and the children enjoy helping out with swapping out the flowers as they wilt, adding a few surprise weeds which makes it even more fun.

An arrangement consists of components in several layers.

FOLIAGE, LAYER 1—this forms the base of your arrangement and sets the foundation for the shape. Use foliage that adds volume and gives stability to the flowers such as ninebark or raspberry.

FOLIAGE, LAYER 2—this layer is added to the base to create further volume. Use foliage that is slightly lighter than that in the base and cut slightly shorter. We prefer mint, amaranth, and lady's mantle.

FOLIAGE, LAYER 3—the third layer should add some life and movement to the arrangement. Use foliage with a bit more structure and shape. This layer can be bushier and contain fruit, berries, or seed pods. We like hawthorn, cherry tomatoes, flax, false goat's beard, or honeysuckle.

SUPPORTING FLOWERS, LAYER 4—these are flowers that add color and shape and enhance the focal flower such as sweet pea, teasel, and snapdragon.

FOCAL FLOWERS, LAYER 5—this is the focal point that catches the eye and is usually a large flower with a calming shape such as a rose, hydrangea, or tulip.

ACCENTS, LAYER 6—flowers or grass that stand out as a contrasting shape or color, such as great burnet, setaria, or quaking grass.

Instructions:

You need a floral knife or other sharp knife, some chicken wire, a flower frog (sort of like a sturdy pin cushion that you put the stems into) and a pot or a vase filled with water.

1. Lay the flowers in front of you.
2. Place a flower frog at the bottom of your pot or vase.
3. Cut a square from the chicken wire to fit your pot or vase and fold it at the edges so it takes the shape of an upside-down bowl. Press it into your vase to add support to the flowers that will be placed in the flower frog.
4. Fill the vase almost to the brim with water.
5. Add the first layer of foliage, twig by twig until you get the shape and size you need.
6. Add the second layer of foliage by placing the twigs in the same way on top of the first layer.
7. The third layer can be added where you think it gives the best effect. It can spill out from the edges or stick out horizontally, whatever you prefer.
8. Next add the supporting flower and the focal flowers.
9. Finally, add a few accents above all the other layers, letting them hover above the rest of the arrangement.

Binding a Wreath

You will need a frame in a material of your choice (you can make one by twining branches of woodbine, willow, or vine), string, and scissors.

Instructions:

1. Lay the foliage in front of you.
2. Depending on the thickness you want, you can add a layer of just foliage to start with.
3. Make a small bunch in your left hand and cut the stems.
4. Place the bunch against the frame and press it into the frame with your left thumb in the desired position.
5. Wind the string around the frame and flowers once.
6. Make a new bunch and place it so it overlaps with the previous one and hides the stems.
7. Repeat until you have covered the frame.

FRESH CUT FLOWERS

FRESH CUT FLOWERS

DRYING

When flowers are at their most beautiful, it's easy to feel like you never want the season to end. Instead of feeling melancholy, harvest them to make them last longer and adorn your home during fall and winter with different types of dried flowers. Some types of grass change completely when dried and curl up like corkscrews. Preserved flowers are flowers with paper like petals that keep their color for a long time once dried. Keep harvesting throughout the season for drying. Flowers picked to be preserved can keep blooming, so don't wait too long; bunches that are starting to wilt are perfect for drying.

Instructions:
Hang fresh flowers in bunches upside down, preferably in a dark, dry place to stop them fading or getting moldy.

Examples of flowers that work well dried:

Fern	Great burnet	Wheat
Timeless rose	Hydrangea	Seed pods, e.g
Straw flower	Sea lavender	poppy
Sunray	Drumsticks	
Honeywart	Starflower	

Sourdough & Baking

Our kitchen dates back to the eighteenth century and is without a doubt the room in our house with the most history. The spartan country kitchen has inspired us to source other originals. The cold floor is covered in rag rugs and the wood burning stove roars and crackles. Behind the iron range is old baking oven originating from the latter part of the nineteenth century. It has been bricked up but it still gives an air of working hands, bird song through the window, and the smell of freshly baked bread.

Of all the bubbling jars in our kitchen, the one that receives the most love is our sourdough starter. All our breakfasts involve some type of bread, and these healthy bacteria are also used when we bake buns, pizzas, and pancakes. If one of the kids is in a "I don't like it" or "I don't want it" phase, we can rest assured that they'll at least get some home-baked bread made with our own milled whole wheat flour inside them.

The first thing we did when we started our modern homesteading journey was to replace storebought bread. Although maybe just the word "bread" will suffice as storebought bread is really no more than just flavored air. Factory-made bread that calls itself sourdough does not get a slow rise, uses commercial yeast, and only has added sourdough to give it that tangy taste. In addition, it often contains unnecessary additives and sugar. Sourdough bread from a local baker is an alternative for those who live in bigger cities, but it is also a financial drain on bread-loving families.

When we first started making sourdough bread, we found it incredible that the only thing we needed was water, flour, and a bit of salt—nothing else.

During Viking times, only unleavened bread made with barley malt was made in Sweden. Not until the country was converted to Christianity did the monks introduce woodfired baking ovens in monasteries around the country. During the nineteenth century almost every home and bakery featured a brick oven. Towards the end of the century these were slowly replaced by cast iron ranges. During the twentieth century making bread was moved from the home in favor of industrial production, meaning the skill of baking dating back a thousand years was lost. It is really only in more recent times that we have started to appreciate baking our own bread again.

There are probably as many ways to make sourdough bread as there are people baking it. We like to think that there is no right or wrong way to do it, as long as it tastes good. As with any fermentation process, there are levels of obsession you can apply and just like anything else, experience makes a difference. Sourdough baking is no exception, but we do want to reiterate how easy it is to bake sourdough bread on a regular basis. Making bread using your sourdough starter a regular part of life forces you to get into a routine which in turn gives you experience. Once you understand your sourdough you can start experimenting with different ingredients and techniques.

Creating a Routine

Baking sourdough bread is a slow process that requires patience. At first, it requires careful planning, but in time it will become a routine. Baking for us has become almost meditative. On a practical level, we split the process into several smaller steps so the hands-on work is not too taxing. We bake once or twice a week and during periods when we are both away, we plan our baking for the weekend.

Our Routine: Day 1

7.00 Get up, remove the sourdough starter from the fridge and place it on the countertop. Eat breakfast with the kids.

8.00 Take the kids to daycare.

8.30 Make the sponge (preferment) with the starter (mother dough) and start work.

11.00 Grab a coffee and mix flour and liquid for the autolyze which takes about an hour. If we don't have time for this step, we skip it.

12.30 At some point during lunch, the sponge starts to bubble and doubles in size meaning it is ready to use. We add the sponge (making sure to keep 3 ½ oz (100g) in a jar in the fridge) to the autolyze and fold in the salt. Leave it to rise on a stool next to the desk.

1:00–3:00 Fold the dough four times in this period.

3.30 Get the kids.

4.30 Shape the bread, place in proofing baskets, and pop in the fridge until the next morning, or place the whole dough in the fridge if making bread rolls the next morning.

Day 2

6.30 If we are making bread rolls, we get up before the kids wake, turn the oven on, shape the rolls, and bake.

8.00 If we are making loaves, we turn the oven on and pop a cast iron dish in it. Place the proofing baskets on the kitchen counter while the oven heats up. Bake in the cast iron dish.

What Is Sourdough?

Sourdough is a dough mixture containing wild yeast and lactobacillus. When the flour and water mix, microorganisms, yeast, and bacteria create a chemical reaction releasing carbon dioxide. The carbon dioxide is retained by the gluten in the dough, creating bubbles. When you mix your sourdough, a selection of good bacteria in your flour and the air around you mix, meaning your sourdough is unique. Sourdough baked from scratch rises for around 16–24 hours. This slow process allows the bacteria to break down the phytic acid in the flour, which does not happen in bread that has a fast rise. Phytic acid stops the body from absorbing important nutrients and minerals such as iron, zinc, and calcium.

Flour & Grinding

Grinding your own flour adds another dimension to baking with the sound of grains being crushed by the stones and the feel of the golden flour between your fingers. The taste and smell are vastly different from the usual bland, white flour and have a lot more character and depth. Depending on how coarse or fine you grind the flour and whether you sift it, the flour will change the structure of the bread. A coarser flour gives a coarser texture, and the bread will be moister as it binds more liquid.

We always use organic flour when we bake; apart from the obvious benefits, organic flour contains more microorganisms, meaning a better fermentation process. We used to buy 50lb sacks of flour from well-known organic mills but now we buy sacks of whole wheat kernels (wheat berries) from the same providers.

Flour is fresh produce, and it doesn't get fresher than grinding your own. The older the flour, the less nutrients it contains. We use a millstone to grind our own flour from wheat berries to retain the fiber, vitamins, and minerals from the bran and germ. A roller-milled flour doesn't use the whole grain—instead, it separates out everything, leaving just the endosperm. Because the germ contains fat, removing it also removes some of the taste.

Ultimately, a fresh stone ground whole wheat flour gives your bread the best taste and most nutrients. However, bread using 100% whole wheat flour can feel dense, so we tend to add some variation to our breads and sometimes add some sifted flour. We have an electric flour sifter that we can add on top of our little stone mill. You can also sift by hand, but it can be time consuming and you may end up with a thin layer of flour dust all over the kitchen.

SOURDOUGH & BAKING

Hydration & Bakers Percentage

Baking is part intuition and part mathematics. There is no right or wrong, but in order to have control over your dough and have the ability to modify recipes, you need to understand the relationship between the flour and the liquid, which is known as hydration. A more hydrated dough (a wetter dough) is harder to handle but results in a moist bread with larger holes (open crumb).

In the world of baking, they use a system where the amount of flour is always 100% and the rest of the ingredients are given as a proportion to the flour, known as baker's percentage. If you bake with 2½ lb flour (1000g), 1½ lb liquid (700g) and ½ oz salt (15g) you have 70% liquid (700/1000g). Some people also count the sourdough as part of hydration although we don't. It is usually calculated as 50/50.

The example below is shown as a baker's percentage. Depending on the flour, you can adjust the ratios to increase hydration for protein-rich flours. We tend to adjust the hydration depending on the amount of whole wheat and coarseness of the flour, adapting as we go along. A dough that contains more whole wheat flour needs more hydration than a dough made of sifted flour.

A dough made from sifted flour or mixed wheat and spelt usually has around 66% hydration. A dough with half whole wheat and half sifted flour uses around 75% hydration, and in a dough using only whole wheat flour, we can add up to 80% hydration.

Baker's Percentage Example

100%—3.3 LB (1,500 G) FLOUR
66%—33 FL OZ (990 G) WATER
15%—7.9 OZ (225 G) SOURDOUGH
2%—1 OZ (30 G) SALT

How to get the percent from the ingredients:
weight of ingredients / weight of flour × 100

How to get the weight of the ingredients:
the percentage of the ingredients × weight of flour

Temperature & Humidity

Just like all living things, your sourdough is affected by its environment, and you will need to find your perfect spot for your bread to rise through trial and error.

A sourdough prefers a humid (60–80%) and warm spot (77–82ºF, 25–28ºC) avoiding drafts. We usually place the sponge in the bowl that is part of our dough mixer and cover half of it with a plastic lid. In the summer we then let it rise in a ceramic bowl with a glass lid while in winter we place it in a greased plastic container to create a warm and moist environment. Both the sourdough starter and your sponge will rise a lot faster in a warm spot rather than a cold one. You'll also notice a difference between a warm summer day and a cold winter one.

Apart from temperature, humidity will also affect the rising process. Humidity levels are also expressed as a percentage and varies according to the temperature. In the winter when the cold air outside drifts inside your house and warms up, the humidity levels sink, creating dry air. This is another reason why the rising process is harder during wintertime.

Lower humidity during rising gives a better crust while higher humidity during baking also gives a better crust.

Sourdough Starter

The Boudin Bakery in San Francisco has used the same starter since the bakery opened in 1849. In 1906 the city was hit by a devastating earthquake resulting in a fire at the bakery. The owner, Louise Boudin, risked her life and ran into the burning building and managed to rescue a small bit of the starter. In other words, the starter is regarded as precious by its owner!

Your starter is uniquely adapted to your environment, and you may only even need to make it once in your life, and who knows, you may even pass it on to the next generation. You do need to care for it though and this is easiest done by simply baking with it once a week.

If you don't use it regularly, you need to keep it going by feeding it, meaning you add flour and water to it. Your starter will become more potent the more you use it. Practically speaking, the more it develops, the less of it you will need in relation to flour and liquid.

You can start a sourdough by using an activator, for example raisins, apples, kefir, or honey. This increases the ratio of yeast cells to lactic acid bacteria, which gives you a lighter (and less acidic) starter, meaning the dough will rise faster.

Day 1
Mix 1¾ oz (50 g) flour, preferably a mix such as rye and wheat or wheat and spelt, with 1.7 fl oz (50 g) water in a glass jar. Loosely add a lid without tightening it to get air in with natural bacteria to get the yeast spores going. Leave in a warm, moist place, around 77–88°F (25–30°C) for 24 hours.

Day 2
You should now be able to see traces of activity in the shape of small bubbles and there should be a fresh, yeasty smell coming from it. If you want, you can taste it! Feed the starter with 1¾ oz (50 g) different flour types and 1.7 fl oz (50 g) water. Mix it with a fork or small whisk getting some air into it, add the lid (without tightening it), and return to the warm spot. If there has been no activity after 24 hours, leave it for a bit longer until it starts to bubble, feed it, and then move to the step below.

Day 3
You should now see lots of bubbles. Remove half the starter and feed it with 1¾ oz (50 g) of mixed flours and 1.7 fl oz (50 g) water. Add the lid (without tightening it and return to the warm spot.

Day 4
By now it should be bubbly and very active with a yeasty smell and your starter is now ready to bake with, or place in the fridge until you are ready to use it.

Baking with Your Starter
Make sure you have enough sponge to make your bread by feeding the starter before you start. Don't take it all though—make sure you always keep around 3½ oz (100 g) in your jar. Don't make the mistake we did, though! When our second child was a baby, we managed to bake using a five-year-old starter through sheer sleep deprivation!

1. Reviving Your Starter (the Night before If Needed)
If you haven't used your starter for more than a week it will need to be revived. If this isn't the case and your starter is bubbly and lively, you can skip this step:

Remove everything except around 1 oz (25 g) of starter. Feed it with 1¾ oz (50 g) flour and 1.7 fl oz (50 g) water. Mix well and leave out at room temperature until it starts to bubble. A healthy and mature starter should start to bubble 2–3 hours after it has been revived.

2. Sponge—around 4–6 Hours
You need to feed your starter enough to both make a sponge and also have enough left in your jar for the next time you bake. The amount of sponge you use depends on how soon you want to bake, the temperature and humidity in the room, and the potency of your starter. We usually start with 3½ oz (100 g). The amount of flour and water you use to feed it depends on how many loaves you want and the size of the loaf. Before you start feeding the starter, think about the amount you need. For two loaves you need around 2.2 lb (1000 g) flour and around 20 baker's percentage of sponge, so around 7 oz (200 g). But you also want to keep around 3½ oz (100 g) of your sponge for your starter, so feed it with 5½ oz (150 g) flour plus 5 fl oz (50 g) water according to the instructions below:

Remove a jar of lively starter from the fridge.

Place around 3½ oz (100 g) in a larger jar (the sponge should grow to at least twice the size).

Feed with 5½ oz flour plus 5 fl oz water and mix with a fork. The sponge should not be too runny, more like a thick pancake batter! If it is too thick it won't rise properly and if it's too runny it runs the risk of turning sour.

Leave in room temperature with a loose lid until it has risen to its highest point, which is usually when it has doubled in size and has a fresh, healthy odor. This usually takes around 4–6 hours. If you leave it for too long it will start to sink and your dough will not rise properly.

You can check to see if your sponge is ready by placing a bit in a glass of water. If it floats it has enough air in it and is active and ready to be used.

If you don't use your starter every week, you need to feed it. We usually keep a maximum of 3½ oz (100 g) starter in the fridge. Pour out ¾ leaving just under 1 oz (25 g) and feed with 1¾ oz flour and 1.7 fl oz water. Sometimes the starter splits and starts to smell of alcohol. In this case, follow the instructions for reviving your starter. If you go on holiday and want to stop baking for a while, you can dry out your starter. Spread it out on some baking paper and dry in room temperature. Then place it in a jar with a lid. When you want to reactivate your starter, mix the dry bits with lukewarm water. You can even freeze your starter.

If you miss the point at which your sponge has peaked, it will go from a fluffy mousse to a sloppy mess that won't float in water. However, you can still save it. Add equal parts water and flour (around 1 tbsp), mix it up, and wait for around one hour and it should start bubbling up again.

3. Autolyze—around 1 Hour

About an hour before you make your dough (once your sponge has risen about 50 percent in size) it's time for autolyze. This process allows the flour to absorb the liquid and produce gluten in peace and quiet without the sponge or salt. If you are in a hurry, you can skip this stage and just mix all the ingredients except salt which can hamper the gluten building process.

Mix the flour and liquid in a separate bowl without kneading.

4. Rising—around 4 Hours

After around 1–3 hours of autolyze, you can mix the sponge and autolyze. Wet your hands when working with the dough.

Mix the sponge and autolyze.

Fold the salt into the dough.

Leave the dough to rise one last time (bulk fermentation) for one hour in a bowl or container with a lid.

Stretch and fold the dough over itself a few times while turning it until you get a ball shape. Alternatively, you can lift the dough in the middle and fold it underneath itself (coil fold). Do this four times over the next 2 hours during fermentation.

Leave to rise 1 more hour at room temperature.

5. Cold rising over night

BREAD ROLLS: Place the whole dough in a bowl in the fridge for 12–36 hours.

LOAVES: Place the dough on a floured surface. Shape the loaves and place in proofing baskets.

Place a tea towel over them and place in the fridge for 12–36 hours.

Baking

BREAD ROLLS: Preheat a baking steel or tray on the highest temperature for at least half an hour. Turn out the dough on a floured surface and cut into pieces and place them on the tray or place on a peel to slide onto the steel in the oven. Sprinkle some water at the bottom of the oven and bake at 480ºF (250ºC) for around 12 minutes.

LOAVES: Preheat a baking steel at the highest temperature for at least half an hour or in a cast iron pot with a lid (Dutch oven) at 480ºF (250ºC) for 1 hour. Turn the proofing baskets over onto baking paper cut to size for the pot (or grease the pot using a neutral oil). Sieve some flour over the bread, score it, and carefully lift it with the baking paper to place it in the pot. Reduce the temperature to 446ºF (230ºC), sprinkle some water in the bottom of the oven, and bake with the lid on until the bread reaches an internal temperature of 205ºF (96ºC) for white bread and 208ºF (98ºC) for rye bread. After 10 minutes release some of the steam, and then do this again 1–2 times during baking.

If you place your bread in the oven with the fold facing up, it opens up like a flower bud and gives your bread a rustic feel.

If you place it with the fold facing down, score the bread to allow it to expand. We like to make decorative scores of different lengths and depths to give different results. If we make a pattern, we will do a light scoring, and to stop them from cracking too much we place longer, deeper scores along the sides or around the loaf. If we succeed, the center of the loaf lifts up like a flat, patterned surface.

A hot oven with high humidity at the start of the bake ensures it stays together and rises. Condensation on the surface also means the bake is more even and gives a smooth, shiny crust. Open the oven door slightly to release the steam a few times during the bake. Dryer air at the end of the bake gives a crisp crust. Some ovens have a steam function, but we usually just sprinkle some water at the bottom of the oven. You can also place a vessel with water at the bottom while preheating the oven.

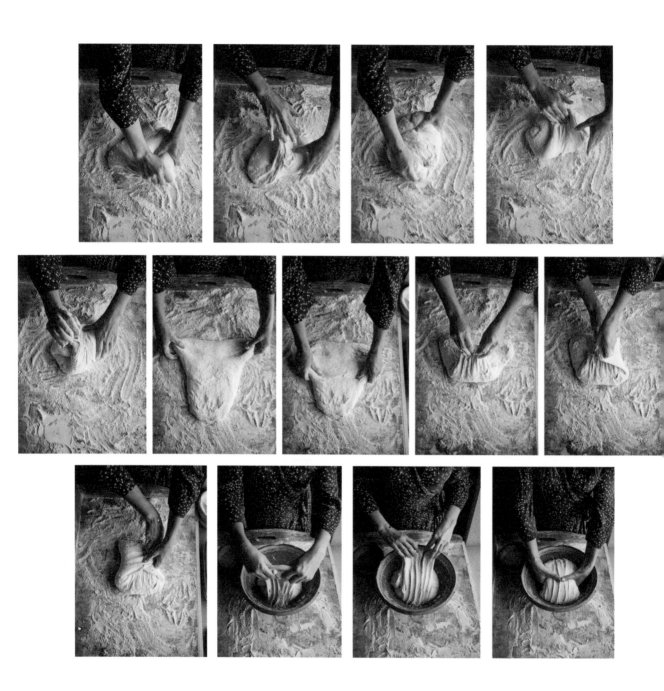

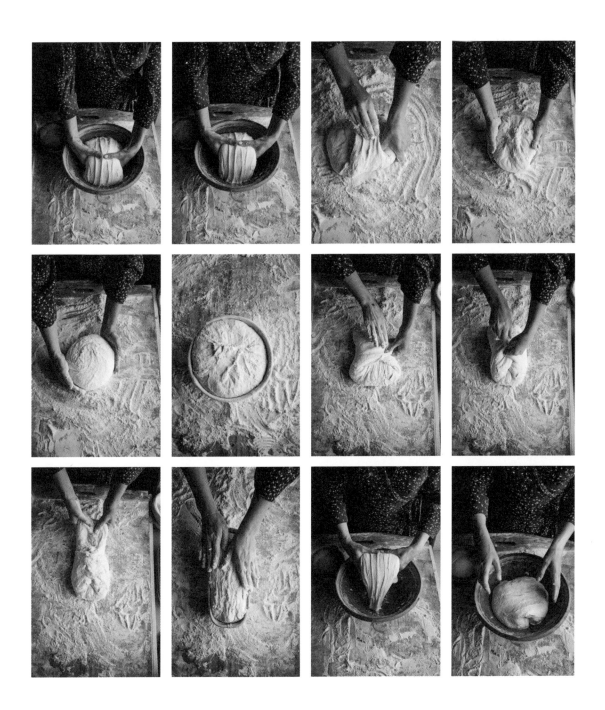

SOURDOUGH & BAKING

OUR BREAD ROLLS   AROUND 25 ROLLS

We bake these rolls a lot and you can make them in all sorts of variations with toppings or fillings. The great thing about rolls is you don't need proofing baskets but can take them straight from the bowl. They are also quicker to bake than a large loaf, making them perfect for breakfast.

2¾ cups (650 g) water
24.7 oz (700 g) whole wheat flour
10½ oz (300 g) rye flour
7 oz (200 g) sponge, see page 41
1 oz (25 g) sea salt
Optional: spelt flakes, sesame seeds, pumpkin seeds,
    poppy seeds, sunflower seeds, or cheese to garnish

Day 1

Mix water, flour, and rye flour and leave to autolyze for an hour.

Mix the sponge with a wooden spoon or run it briefly in a dough mixer on a low speed. Sprinkle the salt on the dough. Stretch and fold the dough over itself for two full turns so the salt blends with the dough. Leave to rise for 1 hour in a bowl or container with a lid.

Stretch and fold the dough over itself a few times, turning it round until it forms the shape of a ball, or lift the dough in the middle and fold it under itself (coil fold). Do this four times over the next 2 hours.

Leave to rise for 1 more hour without folding it and then place in the fridge overnight.

Day 2

In the morning, preheat a baking streel or tray at the highest temperature for 30 minutes, then reduce the temperature to 480°F (250°C).

Tip the dough onto a floured surface and cut into pieces to make the rolls big enough. If you want, you can add seeds, flakes, or cheese. Bake for around 12 minutes until the inner temperature is 205°F (96°C).

Spelt Bread with Buttermilk

This bread is perfect if you've recently churned milk and have fresh buttermilk. The buttermilk contains acid which reduces the formation of gluten and gives a soft bread with small air bubbles. It also tastes wonderfully caramelized.

<u>Makes 1 loaf</u>
7 oz (200 g) sponge, see page 41
3⅓ cup (800 g) buttermilk at room temperature
21 oz (600 g) whole wheat flour
14 oz (400 g) spelt flour
¾ oz (20 g) sea salt

Mix all the ingredients except salt. Use a wooden spoon or dough hook to combine the ingredients and leave to rise, covered, for 1 hour.

Sprinkle the salt over the dough. Stretch and fold the dough over itself, turning it two full rounds so the salt combines with the dough. Bulk ferment for 1 hour in a bowl or container with a lid.

Stretch and fold the dough over itself a few times while turning until it forms a ball shape. Alternatively, you can lift the dough in the middle and fold it under itself (the coil fold). Do this four times over the next 2 hours.

Leave to rise for one more hour at room temperature. If the dough has visibly increased in size and feels light and fluffy you can move on to the next step. If not, leave it for another couple of hours.

Tip the dough onto a clean surface, shape it into a loaf, and place in the proofing basket. Cover in a tea towel and leave it to rise for another 1–2 hours. Meanwhile, heat the oven with a baking steel, to 480°F (250°C). Place the bread on a steel or a baking tray and reduce the temperature to 445°F (230°C). Bake for around 40 minutes until you have an inner temperature of 203°F (95°C).

Rye Bread with Milk & Honey

Nothing beats a stodgy bit of rye bread; more rye=more stodge. Unhomogenized milk gives it a porous and soft texture and the honey balances out any acidity. We often add dried fruit or berries, making it even more popular. If you add fruit, you can reduce the amount of honey so it doesn't turn into a sweet fruit cake (although that's not a bad thing).

<u>Makes 2 loaves</u>
1.6 cups (400 g) water
1.6 cups (400 g) unhomogenized milk
1.1 (500 g) rye flour
1.1 lb (500 g) all-purpose flour
1.7 fl oz (½ dl) honey, pref. raw
10½ oz (300 g) sponge, see page 41
¾ oz (20 g) sea salt

Mix water, milk, rye, and all-purpose flour and leave to autolyze for 1 hour. Add the honey and sponge and mix well with a wooden spoon or dough hook for a few minutes until well combined. The dough should be sticky but you can add more plain flour if needed. Cover and leave to rise for 1 hour.

Sprinkle the salt over the dough. Stretch and fold the dough over itself, turning it two full rounds so the salt combines with the dough. Bulk ferment for 1 hour in a bowl or container with a lid.

Stretch and fold the dough over itself a few times while turning until it forms a ball shape. Alternatively, you can lift the dough in the middle and fold it under itself (the coil fold). Do this four times over the next 2 hours.

Leave to rise for 1 more hour at room temperature. If the dough has visibly increased in size and feels light and fluffy you can move on to the next step. If not, leave it for another couple of hours.

Tip the dough onto a clean surface, shape it into a loaf, and place in the proofing basket. Cover in a tea towel and leave it to rise for another 1–2 hours. Meanwhile, heat the oven with a baking steel to 480°F (250°C). Place the bread on a steel or a baking tray and reduce the temperature to 445°F (230°C). Sieve some flour over the top and score the loaves. Bake for around 40 minutes until you have an inner temperature of 205°F (96°C).

Buttery Tear & Share Bread

A luxurious butter bread that is baked in a cake tin and is perfect for the weekend. Fluffy and white like Japanese milk bread and sweet and succulent like American dinner rolls, brush with honey and butter for added luxury.

<u>7 pieces</u>
10½ oz (300 g) sponge, see page 41
10 oz (290 g) all-purpose flour
½ cup (130 g) milk
1 oz (25 g) muscovado sugar
1 egg
1.4 oz (40 g) butter at room temperature
1 tsp sea salt
Honey and butter for brushing (optional)

Mix all ingredients except butter and salt. Mix well with a wooden spoon or with a dough hook for a few minutes until well combined. Add the butter a bit at a time until it is blended into the dough. Cover and leave to rise for 1 hour.

Sprinkle the salt over the dough. Stretch and fold the dough over itself, turning it two full rounds so the salt combines with the dough. Leave to rise for 1 hour in a bowl or container with a lid.

Stretch and fold the dough over itself a few times while turning until it forms a ball shape. Alternatively, you can lift the dough in the middle and fold it under itself (the coil fold). Do this four times over the next 2 hours.

Leave to rise for 1 more hour at room temperature. If the dough has visibly increased in size and feels light and fluffy you can move on to the next step. If not, leave it for another couple of hours.

Tip the dough onto a clean surface and divide into 3½ oz (100g) pieces. Shape the balls by pulling the dough a few times from underneath into the middle and pinch to make a fold. Turn the balls fold down and place them on a greased baking tray, leaving a bit of space between them. Cover with a damp tea towel and leave to rise for 1–2 hours at room temperature. Turn the oven to 380ºF (195ºC).

Bake the bread in the middle of the oven, for 25–30 minutes. Five minutes before the end, brush the breads with honey and butter (optional). Turn on the broiler or place at the top of the oven to give them a golden color.

Rustic Bread Made from "Skräd" Flour & Raw Honey

"Skräd" flour is flour made from roasted oats, a preserving method where the oats were roasted in wood burning stoves, hulled, and then ground into flour. Experiment with using spelt or oat flour instead. Amounts may vary.

<u>Makes 2 loaves</u>
10½ oz (300 g) sponge, see page 41
½ lb (250 g) skräd flour
0.9 lb (400 g) all-purpose flour
1.6 cups (400 g) water
2 tbsp honey (preferably raw)
¾ oz (20 g) sea salt
Oats to garnish

Day 1
Mix all the ingredients except the salt. Mix well with a wooden spoon or with a dough hook for a few minutes until well combined. Cover and leave to rise for 1 hour.

Sprinkle the salt over the dough. Stretch and fold the dough over itself, turning it two full rounds so the salt combines with the dough. Bulk ferment for 1 hour in a bowl or container with a lid.

Stretch and fold the dough over itself a few times while turning until it forms a ball shape. Alternatively, you can lift the dough in the middle and fold it under itself (the coil fold). Do this four times over the next 2 hours.

Leave to rise for one more hour at room temperature.

If the dough has visibly increased in size and feels light and fluffy you can move on to the next step. If not, leave it for another couple of hours.

Tip the dough onto a clean surface and shape into two loaves and place in a proofing basket. Leave to rise in the fridge overnight.

Day 2
Preheat a baking steel, a baking tray, or a Dutch oven at the highest temperature for at least half an hour. Tip the bread onto a floured surface, brush with water, and sprinkle some oats on top. Score the loaves with deep, long cuts and reduce the temperature to 445ºF (230ºC). Bake for around 40 minutes until you have an inner temperature of 205ºF (96ºC).

Buttery Tear & Share Bread, page 49

Simple Herby Biscuits

When we make biscuits, crisp bread, or flat bread we usually plan ahead and feed our starter to make a larger sponge than we need. The extra sponge can be left at room temperature for a day or so, so that it gets more fermented and sour. When you make flat breads you don't need the dough to rise, so if we have planned to bake but forgotten the starter, or just run out of time (which often happens) this is the perfect solution.

<u>Makes 80 biscuits</u>
10 oz (300 g) leftover sponge, see page 41
4½ oz (125 g) rye flour
2 fl oz (60 g) olive oil
Dried herbs such as rosemary or thyme
Sea salt

Mix the sponge, flour, olive oil, and half the herbs to form a dough. Leave it to rest in a bowl with a lid in the fridge for 1 hour.

Heat the oven to 350°F (175°C). Roll out the dough on baking paper and move onto a baking tray. Sprinkle the rest of the herbs and salt on top of the dough and use a cookie cutter or knife to make the shapes. Alternatively, you can break them apart by hand once baked.

Bake in the middle of the oven for 30 minutes and leave to cool on a cooling rack.

Crisp Bread with Bran

When we sift flour, we end up with a lot of bran (the hard outer layer of the grain) which we use in different ways. One of our favorites is making a quick and simple crisp bread. We make holes in them and hang them up on a pole in the traditional way. Mainly because it looks good, but it's also a practical way of storing the bread.

<u>Makes 20 crisps</u>
7 oz (200 g) leftover sponge, see page 41
Around 1 lb (400 g) bran
3.4 fl oz (100 g) water
¼ oz (5 g) sea salt

Heat the oven to 480°F (250°C).

Mix the sponge, bran, water, and salt, adding more water if you need to until the dough is smooth. Knead the dough and divide into 20 pieces, rolling each one into a round ball.

On parchment paper, roll each ball into a thin, round shape, measuring 6 inches (15 cm) across. Make a pattern using a knobbly rolling pin and make a hole in the middle if you wish. Bake in the middle of the oven for 5 minutes until they have caught some color and the edges darken. Leave to cool on a cooling rack.

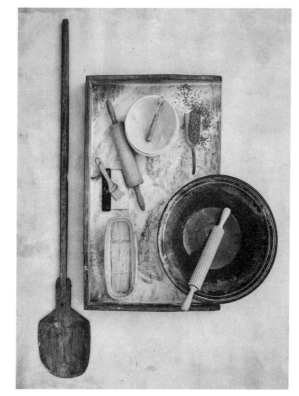

SOURDOUGH & BAKING

Keeping Chickens

Slowly, slowly I remove the lid to the nest and place my hand inside, gently stroking the hay. The coarse, uneven texture under my fingertips suddenly becomes smooth and oval shaped as I discover a newly laid egg, still warm in my hand. Despite repeating this process every morning, I still have the same childlike joy over my discovery. It's a feeling of joy rooted deeply in our genes from our hunter-gatherer days.

There are so many reasons to own chickens but none more important than the egg. In other words, to answer the question as old as time, the egg came first.

To have fresh eggs on a daily basis is a real luxury. Depending on the breed, how you care for them, and their diet, you will notice that these eggs taste very different than the eggs you buy in the grocery store.

Why not break an egg from a chicken who has been free to roam around, pecking at worms and grass, and compare it to an egg from a chicken who has lived their life in a factory and never seen sunlight?

Eggs are a complete source of nutrition and probably the world's most precious raw ingredient. We don't just use eggs for their taste but because they have an unbeatable way of adding texture and consistency to things. Without eggs we would have no mayonnaise, no meringue, and no whiskey sour. Of course, hens give a lot more than just eggs as they also give us sustenance through meat. Finally, they are also one of the loveliest pets you can have, so welcome to a life as chicken keeper.

Chickens Are a Sustainable Choice

The chicken coop is one of the more important, if not the most important, pillars of modern homesteading. If you want to create a sustainable food cycle in your home, chickens are your friend. Not only do they contribute eggs and meat, but they also convert leftover food and weeds into the most potent fertilizer you can find.

Free-range chickens work the soil and loosen it and add natural nutrients while at the same time removing pests, and we enjoy watching our chickens peck killer slugs into tiny pieces.

You can make chickens a real asset to your homesteading way of life; for example, you can use chickens to prepare an overgrown plot of land for planting or to loosen up some compost. In this way you benefit from them in more ways than one as they eat food waste and weeds and in return give eggs, meat, and fertilizer.

Buying Your Chickens

Once you've decided to take the plunge and keep chickens, there are three things you need to think about. Firstly, like all animals, chickens need tending to daily, so make sure you have the time to do this. It's good if you have friends or neighbors who can look after the chickens when you go away, and receiving fresh eggs is usually a reward in itself.

Secondly, you need to decide where the chickens should live. There are almost as many solutions to housing chickens as there are chicken owners. However, some basic needs need to be met. You need a large enough, and preferably completely insulated, chicken coop with access to an enclosed roaming area outside. Often the easiest thing to do is to fix up an existing structure such as an old playhouse or part of an old barn or similar structure. You can also buy ready-made chicken coops, as well as build one yourself from scratch. There is the investment and you also need enough space in your yard, plus you need to consider that free-range chickens don't only benefit your garden—they can make a mess of your flower beds and help themselves to your lettuce, so you need to think about where you are going to place your coop.

The final thing you need to consider is where to get your chickens from and the type of breed. There are countless different breeds to choose from, so it really depends on your personal preference. There's traditional Swedish breeds, heritage breeds, and existing breeds from all over the world. Apart from the aesthetics, different breeds have different characteristics, sizes, and levels of endurance. Even the color of the egg and the taste of the meat can differ. Finally, do you want a rooster?

Can You Keep Chickens?

Firstly, you need to make sure you are allowed to keep chickens where you live and if you need a license. For example, you can't keep chickens on a balcony in an apartment block! If you live in a residential area, you may also need to check the local regulations for keeping poultry as they may vary by state, county, and even town; you may be allowed to keep a limited number of chickens but no rooster.

Local & Heritage Breeds

Chickens (Gallus gallus domesticus) originate from the red junglefowl, a type of pheasant that lives in dense forests in India and Southeast Asia. Throughout the history of man, chickens have had a strong connection to rituals, magic, and sacrifices. During Roman times, chickens were often used as oracles to answer important questions; special cakes were baked and if the chicken ate willingly from the cake it was a good omen.

Today there are hundreds of different breeds around the world, and many have adapted to their specific environment. Even though chickens are all the same species, they can vary in size, from a bantam chicken weighing a pound to heavy brahma chickens weighing over 10 lbs.

The white eggs we consider normal today are not actually that natural. They are genetically coded through breeding to reduce the chickens' natural pigments. Most older breeds lay eggs with different pigmentations.

Most chickens on industrialized farms are hybrids, bred to gain weight quickly for meat or to produce lots of eggs. But the heritage breeds are often hardier.

In North America, heritage meat breeds include brahmas, Australorps, Chanteclers, Plymouth Rocks, and Dominiques. Heritage breeds best suited for eggs include Rhode Island reds, Australorps, Orpingtons, Chanteclers, and barred rocks.

We're keen to ensure that local breeds and heritage breeds live on, although this is not the only reason we choose these breeds. In many ways they are better adapted to our climate. For example, local breeds are often hardier, healthier, and live longer. They have also adapted to needing less food than in the past, since access to grain was not always possible. They are therefore great at foraging for their own food such as worms, beetles, plants, berries, and seeds.

Even the color of their feathers serves a purpose; to protect them from predators. A bright, white chicken that can't camouflage would not survive for long outside the chicken coop. Make sure you choose a breed that suits your needs and local climate.

Heritage Breeds

Brahma

Brahmas are large chickens—reaching 8–10 pounds at maturity—that are sometimes referred to as "gentle giants" or the "king of all poultry." They were very popular among farmers until industrial farming took over, but they're still an excellent bird for small-scale homesteaders. They're a good choice both for laying and for meat. Hens produce 3–4 brown eggs per week and often prefer laying from October through May. They're well-suited to cool climates. Be aware that you'll need enough space to accommodate the large birds and that they eat a lot, so it's best if they can roam freely and forage. They're typically quiet and docile birds, making them a good option for families with young children.

Brahmas were first introduced to the United States in the 1840s, probably from China via Shanghai.

Chantecler

This breed was developed in Canada and was first introduced to the public in 1918. Chanteclers are known for thriving in colder climates (they don't do well in the South) and are good both for meat and for eggs, laying over 200 brown eggs a year. They're not a common breed now, but if you can find them, the breed is worth trying to preserve. Hens get to 6.5–7.5 pounds and roosters weigh around 9 pounds at maturity. They're typically docile, friendly, and intelligent. Chanteclers do best with plenty of room to roam.

Plymouth Rock

Plymouth Rocks were first present in Massachusetts in 1849 and became one of the most popular chickens through the first half of the twentieth century. The barred Plymouth Rock is probably the best known of the seven color varieties: barred, blue, buff, Columbian, partridge, silver-penciled, and white. A good dual-purpose bird, the hens lay about 200 brown eggs a year and the hens reach about 7.5 pounds, while the roosters reach up to 9.5 pounds. Hens lay for up to ten years. They're a hardy bird and do best with room to roam and forage. They typically have calm temperaments.

A barred Plymouth Rock chicken

Building a Chicken Coop

A good chicken coop is the basis of keeping chickens. Chickens need a home that protects them from predators, keeps them warm in the winter, and prevents attacks from pests and disease. A chicken coop also needs to be easy to look after. When we decided to keep chickens, we built our coop from scratch so we could adapt it to our needs. It did require more work initially, but as it is easier for us to look after, we consider it a worthwhile long-term investment.

Positioning the Coop

The positioning of the chicken coop is fairly important, but it depends of course on the space you have and your needs. It's good if you can keep an eye on your chickens from the house. Being close to humans gives some protection from predators and you can keep an eye on your chickens. At the same time, you might want to avoid having a rooster crowing outside your bedroom window!

The area needs to give protection while allowing for both sun and shade. Chickens tend to be more prone to overheating, so anywhere in direct sunlight should be avoided. It needs good drainage to avoid flooding that may damage the coop and cause disease.

Another alternative is to build a mobile coop with wheels that you can move around according to the seasons.

Size

The size of the coop really depends on how many chickens you plan to keep. Usually, 20 chickens per square meter is acceptable. Chickens of average size (5 lb or under) need at least 2 square feet (0.2 square meter) per hen, preferably nearer to 5½ (0.5). You don't need to make it too big though as chickens like to huddle together to keep warm. Each chicken gives off around 10 watts of energy so a flock of chickens should be able to warm up a well-insulated coop during the winter. Subsequently it is not a good idea if the coop is too big in relation to the size of the flock.

Check the department of agriculture for rules on keeping chickens and space requirements. It may not be relevant if you are only keeping a few chickens as a hobby, as hopefully you will provide your chickens the best environment you can. Happy chickens are easier to care for!

As you plan the size of your coop, you also need to plan for the chickens' different needs; for example, they need food and water, nesting boxes, and perches that all need to be kept separately as you don't want them to sit on top of their water fountain!

Apart from the coop you also need an enclosed chicken run attached to the coop. If your chickens are free-range you don't need it to be too large, maybe slightly larger than the coop. If you are planning on keeping your chickens enclosed, it should be as big as possible.

Insulation & Ventilation

It is not vital to insulate your coop but in climates where it gets cold it is definitely recommended. You will also recoup the costs of heating an uninsulated chicken coop in the winter. Use at least 2.8 inches (70mm) thick

Our Chicken Coop:

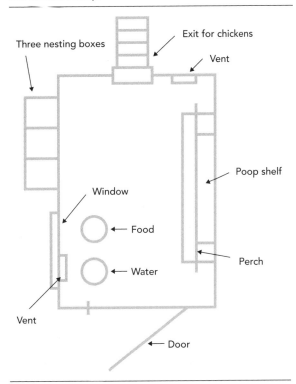

insulation. Apart from keeping the coop warm, it also reduces draft which chickens dislike. They can handle cold much more than they can handle draft and wind. Insulating the coop gives a more constant temperature indoors, even in the summer. In other words, chickens prefer an insulated coop!

Apart from blocking drafts, the coop also needs to be well-ventilated. Chickens, like all animals, give off moisture, and urine and excrement give off ammonia. If the coop is not well-ventilated it can cause rot and become a breeding ground for disease and parasites. Make sure the coop has ventilation but don't place the vents anywhere that the chickens rest such as nests or perches as it can get drafty.

Light & Openings

Chickens need light even inside the coop, especially during the darker months. Their internal clocks are regulated by sunlight so they enter the coop at sunset

The Chicken Coop

KEEPING CHICKENS

Chicken poop falls onto a removable shelf.

Being able to open the back makes the coop easier to clean.

and get up at sunrise. One or more windows are therefore a necessity. However, don't place large windows in a southern facing position as that can heat the coop up too much in the summer months and you need to keep it cool on warm summer days.

The pop hole is the door that regulates the chickens' daily routines. These days you can get automatic pop holes that can be set according to sunlight or a timer which is great if you are not an early bird or are going away for the night, plus chickens often want to get up earlier than you. A manual pop hole works just as well. We have chosen a manual one as we like the routine of opening and closing the coop—it gives us an opportunity to check on the chickens, add food and water, and remove the eggs.

It is important that the pop hole can be properly closed to protect against predators. Clever animals like martens, foxes, and badgers can coax the door open.

An airlock is also a good idea, so you have a small corridor and an inner entrance such as a strip curtain.

The pop hole is like a large vent and can create a draft when it is open, which can drastically reduce the temperature in the coop during the winter.

Nests, Perches & Dust Baths

Some areas of the coop require more detailed planning. The nests are where the chickens lay the eggs and can engage in brooding if they feel like it.

You can let the chickens share the same nests without any issues; often three to five chickens will share one nest. It's always a good idea to have an extra nesting box in case one or more chickens start to brood and take up space in the nests.

It's fairly easy to build the nesting boxes—to be honest, all you really need is a plastic box with some straw, around 12 × 12 inches and 16 inches high

(30 × 30 × 40 cm). The main thing is that the nests are cozy and a calm, sheltered space where the chicken can be left alone. They should also be easy to clean so that mites and other pests can't move in, which is why removable boxes are the simplest solution.

Something worth considering when planning your coop is how you will remove the eggs as you want to avoid disturbing the chickens when they are resting on the perches in the evenings. It's best to create a hatch that makes it possible to remove the eggs from the outside—both you and your chickens will benefit from it. Our solution was to create a nest that sticks out from the coop where we can open the roof. In this way we can simply remove the eggs without disturbing our chickens. Part of their natural behavior is to sleep on a perch, so it is important that they are the right size for the chickens to grip them. For average to large-sized chickens, 1.5–2 inches (4-5 cm) is a good size. Each chicken needs around 8–12 inches (20–30 cm) of space.

You can buy ready-made perches but you can also use a branch with the right proportions. Always use fresh wood such as birch as they can take the weight. Many chickens, such as the local breeds, have no issues flying or jumping over high perches, but heavier breeds may need a ladder to help them up.

Chickens use dust baths to keep themselves clean. If your chickens roam around they can find natural spaces in the summer months such as sandy soil where they create bathing pits. In the winter they need a bit of help, for example by placing a box of sand in the coop, but you can also use a dry layer of sand on the floor.

Cleaning & Droppings

Have a plan from the start on how you will clean the coop and make it as easy as possible for you as it will save you work in the future. It's important to be able to access the coop. If it is a large coop it's usually not an issue; in a smaller coop, you need a door or hatch. We solved it by making the back wall into a door. This way we can close the pop door with the chickens roaming outside while we clean the coop undisturbed.

The choice of materials can also make cleaning easier

and keep the coop hygienic. When you do a deep clean you need to be able to scrub the floor, meaning wooden floors aren't a great choice. Plastered floors and slabs of concrete work well as well as linoleum. The floor will then be covered with bedding that will soak up urine and droppings and the more even the floor, the easier it is to shovel up the bedding.

Making a so-called poop shelf will also aid the cleaning process as well as allow you to use this valuable resource of chicken droppings. Chickens tend to poop mostly at nighttime as they sit on their perches. By placing a shelf under the perches you can collect a large amount of the droppings and then scrape them off the shelf into a bucket on a regular basis. In this way you keep the coop cleaner longer and don't have to change the bedding as frequently. How often you change the bedding depends on the size of the coop, the number of chickens, and the season (more often in the winter). If you notice a strong ammonia odor it is definitely time to change bedding. We change it around every second week.

At least twice a year the coop needs a deep clean to prevent mites and pests from taking hold. After a long winter we spring clean the coop to make it nice in time for summer.

Scrub the floors, fixtures, and walls with soapy water. Thoroughly clean or change the perches and poop shelf and check nooks and corners where mites can be found. Chicken coops can get really dusty, so try and air it out as much as possible.

Food & Water in the Coop

Chickens need access to food and water in a clean area in the coop (not under the perches). Make sure it is easy for you to reach and change the food, and the chickens also need access to fresh water. You can make your own water dispenser but they are easier to buy as they are not particularly expensive. We prefer an upside-down hanging water dispenser with a nipple as the chickens can't get it dirty and it keeps fresh for longer.

Make a space for a good food dispenser too. Choose a larger one so you don't need to fill it up as often. Keep the dry food separate from any food scraps.

Fertilizer

It stinks, but it's worth its weight in gold. Excrement is the most important product you can get from your chickens. For a gardener, chicken fertilizer is a foul-smelling prized product that can be used all over the garden.

The reason it is such a potent fertilizer is due to the high levels of nitrogen, which are much higher than cow or horse fertilizer which also contain bedding and straw. Chicken fertilizer gets broken down fast, releasing a lot of nutrients. You need to add fertilizer from chickens more often, but the benefit is that it's fast acting. Chicken fertilizer works well during spring and early summer to stimulate growth of fast-growing vegetables.

Because it is so potent, it can be easy to use too much, so you need to be careful with the amounts. Some plants don't require as much nitrogen such as root vegetables and potatoes. A better and gentler way to fertilize is to make fertilizer water.

Use a poop shelf to collect the manure. In one year one chicken can yield around 22 lbs (10 kg) of manure.

First of all, you need to "hot compost" the manure for a period of time; this usually takes around a year if you just leave it alone. If you mix fertilizer with dry leaves in a compost bin it will be quicker.

During the year you will also get lots of bedding from the coop; depending on what you use on the floor, the time it takes to break down will vary. You can either mix it into your compost or use as a base for raised flower beds.

The Chicken Run

Apart from the chicken coop, you need an enclosed chicken run. Even if you plan to let the chickens run free outdoors most of the time, which is the best thing for them, you still need a run where they can be contained when needed. You may need to go away, or there might be a fox nearby, or maybe there is disease in the area.

The chicken run should be built based on the number of chickens you plan to keep and whether you are going to let them roam outdoors or not. Chickens need to be able to peck at greenery and if the space is too small, the ground will soon turn bare. So if you plan to keep your chicken in the chicken run, it needs to be big enough, around 7–10 square feet per chicken. If the chickens will also be roaming freely, the run can be slightly smaller.

The chicken run needs to protect against predators and birds that may spread disease. Usually, chicken wire will suffice, but it is better if you can find a thicker type with smaller holes, for example plastering mesh which can be bought in the hardware store.

Make sure you cover the roof with net to stop hawks or small birds from getting in. Ensure predators can't get in by digging net into the ground facing out at an angle around the chicken run and cover with soil and stones. This stops foxes and badgers from getting in.

Chickens need variety so make sure you provide for their needs by making sure they have protection from bad weather, and by adding some trees, branches, and perches. You can add a small compost heap in the coop as it keeps the chickens busy and they get to eat greens and look for worms.

Feed

Just like humans, chickens need a good and varied diet to stay healthy. You can buy growing feed or layer feed that contains everything your chickens need but just like us humans, chickens don't just view food as nourishment but enjoy the color and texture of food, as well as foraging for it.

A layer feed can be used as a base which can be complemented with other sources of nutrients, and free-range chickens tend to find their own extras during the summer.

Seed

Throughout the ages, chickens have been fed seeds and you should continue this. Sprinkle corn, wheat, or other varieties over their floor daily and let them forage for their own food. Do not give more than they will consume straight away as you may attract other animals.

Food Scraps

There is no better food composter than chickens. It's great to see breadcrusts, pasta, and bits of cabbage transform into eggs. View leftovers as an addition to their basic diet, and make sure you don't give chickens meat, animal products, or eggs, and make sure to boil potatoes, carrots, etc., first.

Greenery

Chickens love feeding on grass and leaves; if your chickens are free range, they will find food in the garden; however, in the winter they need a bit of help. Chickens love kale, which can be grown all year round. You can also dry grass cuttings and nettles to be used during winter. If your chickens stay in their run, you must also feed them greenery in the summer; they love grass cuttings, dandelion leaves, and chopped nettle.

Foraging

Free-range chickens tend to forage for their own food but some breeds are better at this than others. Many local breeds had to survive without being fed for large parts of the year and became experts in foraging. Chickens tend to eat anything and will forage for worms, beetles, snails, eggs, seeds, roots, and leaves. When chickens are allowed to forage, their diet tends to be more varied; it is also more stimulating for them than eating from a bowl, so if you are able to, the best and most economical way is to allow chickens to follow their natural behaviors.

Calcium

Chickens that lay hundreds of eggs a year need a large dose of extra calcium or there's a risk that the eggshells become brittle and the chicken's skeleton becomes weak. You should therefore add snail shells to their diet. Some people give eggshells, but this is not recommended as they could start to peck at their own eggs.

Predators & Disease

Suddenly and when you least expect it, a predator turns your precious chickens into a pile of feathers. Nearly all chicken owners will experience this at some point, especially if your chickens roam free. Even worse is making the same discovery inside the coop. In a flash, your entire flock can disappear if a fox or marten breaks in. Predators like chickens as they can't really fly or defend themselves and so become attractive prey. One thing is for sure, the smell of chickens will attract the local predators, so make sure to prevent this and give your chickens as much protection as you can, although of course there are some smaller pests that can wreak havoc in the coop as well.

Foxes, Martens & Badgers

Most predators would add chickens to their menu if they could. Foxes, martens, and badgers are those that most frequently roam around the chicken coop looking for a way in, especially while you're asleep. The best way to protect your coop at night is to make it as secure as possible from prying predators.

The first barrier is if you have a flap that opens out into a closed chicken run. Both foxes and badgers like to dig and can easily dig their way under a fence, so putting some metal netting below ground at an outward angle around the run is a good idea. You can also dig down and insert a metal plate or anything else claw resistant.

A roof is a good idea as both martens and foxes can climb over 6-foot fences, and the hatch should be lockable as foxes have been known to lift a latch.

Make sure the chicken coop is well-insulated as martens, and also minks and rats, can squeeze through small cracks, so don't give them the chance.

Remember that foxes can be very cheeky. If you have a fox, or even a den, nearby they can visit you during the day too so offer the chickens somewhere to hide such as thick bushes, or you can even get a dog. Remember that cats can attack chickens too, especially chicks and young chickens.

Birds of Prey

As a chicken owner you will soon get the so-called "hawk eye" and keep your eyes pointing up. The most effective chicken killer is the fearsome goshawk. This powerful hawk can take birds as large as a wood grouse so can easily attack most chickens. The goshawk will often stake their prey out before launching a surprise attack.

Above our house, which lies in open, fertile land rich in pheasants, we are regularly visited by goshawks, harriers, sparrow hawk, and white-tailed eagles. If they get the chance, they will gladly take a chicken, which is easier to catch than the pheasants. They make so many visits that we often feel like we are under constant bombardment from above.

The best protection against birds of prey is offering your chicken lots of places to hide; for example, build your coop near low bushes and trees.

KEEPING CHICKENS

Tall trees can easily become lookout spots for birds of prey. Our chickens quickly found their second home under an elderflower bush that offered both food and protection, as on a large open surface the chickens are more vulnerable.

Remember to cover the roof of the chicken coop with netting as when a bird of prey is close buy, chickens will often head there. If you have a lot of birds of prey, one solution is only letting the chickens roam free when you are in the garden yourself.

You don't need to worry that the chickens will go on any big adventures; once established in the chicken coop, they tend to stay close by.

Parasites

Even if the fox or hawk don't get at your chickens, smaller pests can certainly cause damage. Chickens can be afflicted by a host of different parasites such as poultry red mites, scaly leg mites, chicken lice and fleas, coccidiosis, worms, and other pests.

Check your chickens regularly and assess their general health: do they look well, does their comb have a nice color, are they laying eggs normally? Also check their feet, legs, and beaks regularly for signs of disease.

Just like with predators, prevention is the best protection. Firstly, keep the coop hygienic by cleaning regularly both inside the coop and in the chicken run. You can also remove risks through building properly. Poultry red mites suck blood from the chickens during the night and then hide in nooks and crannies. By blocking gaps with silicon and making the coop easy to clean, you can keep the mites from taking hold.

Mites and other pests often spread from other chickens or bird species, so be very careful when you add new adult chickens to your flock. They should be held separately from the other chickens for at least three weeks until you can confirm their health. Also, don't visit other chicken farms and your own in the same day and don't use second hand equipment without disinfecting it first.

Mites are very difficult to get rid of once they have settled in. With rigorous scrubbing with soap, vacuuming, and treatments with steam and kieselgur (diatomaceous earth) you can keep the mite levels low and, if you're lucky, even get rid of them.

Mite Traps

You can make a simple trap for mites from corrugated cardboard; it's also a good way to see if you have any unwanted visitors if you are unsure. Place the cardboard in a corner where the chickens can't access them and leave for around a week. Mites like to creep into the flutes between the liner boards and reproduce. When you remove the trap, you can burn the cardboard or freeze in a bag to kill the mites. If freezing, you can tap the cardboard against white paper to get an idea of the amount.

Disease

Chickens can get diseases such as salmonella and bird flu. Bird flu rarely infects humans, but salmonella can be transferred by eating infected eggs or badly prepared meat.

The spread of disease is generally from other chickens or wild animals. Again, you can implement preventative measures. Covering the coop and run with a roof to stop other birds from visiting and feeding the chickens inside the coop are both good options. You are obliged to report some diseases, and you can read more about this on local government websites. You will also find information about current infections that chicken owners need to be aware of.

Getting Your Chickens

Once your chicken coop is ready and you have feed and tools, it's time to welcome your brood. There are many ways to buy chickens. Often, there are local breeders, but you can also use social media to find local hobby farmers who buy and sell chickens, chicks, and eggs.

Hens (Adult Chickens)

If you are very keen, buy hens, even if they are harder to come by. You might be able to buy them from someone who has decided to stop keeping chickens or is moving. You should try and get them all from the same owner to avoid disease and parasites.

Chicks & Eggs

We think the best way to become a chicken owner is to breed a flock from scratch, either through buying chicks or even better, buying hatching eggs.

Not only will you get a healthy flock, but you will also have the opportunity to follow, understand, and influence your chickens that you will be spending so much time with for years to come. Don't underestimate the attachment you have for something you have reared from an egg. The most natural way is for a chicken to hatch under a hen but this won't work if you are building a whole flock so you will need an incubator. It is fairly cheap and easy to buy hatching eggs and they can even be sent by post. However, if you don't want to or can't hatch your own chicks, just buy them from a breeder.

Calculate Your Flock

The first thing you need to do is calculate the size of your flock. How many chickens do you want? You can't sex an egg and often you don't know until much later on what you have, so be prepared that at least half, or even more, may be roosters. In addition, some eggs don't develop as they may not even have been fertilized.

It's also not uncommon for an egg to hatch with an injured chick or for the chick to get injured in the first few weeks. A chick that looks healthy can be found dead the next day without really knowing why. Therefore, you need at least double the number of eggs for the amount of chickens you want, and preferably a few more. It is also easier to raise a flock all around the same age.

Example:

If you want 10 hens, you should hatch 25 eggs. Calculate the hatching percentage at 80 percent plus some later attrition. Divide by half to account for the roosters.

Eggs

It takes 20–21 days from you placing an egg in the incubator to hatching. There are lots of different incubators to choose from and most of them have the same basic functions. Make sure you borrow or buy one that is big enough for the number of eggs you need. The incubator copies the hen's natural behavior and part of this is regularly turning the eggs. You can get machines with both manual and automatic egg turning.

The machines also have the ability to keep the temperature and humidity stable and at the right level which is important. Don't lift the lid too often, and store in a draft-free room that has an even, warm temperature.

After about 1 week, you can shine a light on your eggs (candling) for the first time to see if they have been fertilized. Do this in a dark room. There are special lights for this purpose, but a small, strong torch also works depending on how dark the eggshells are. The darker they are, the stronger the light you need. Hold up the eggs and place the light to the larger end of the egg. Try to work quickly and methodically so you don't disturb the eggs. If the egg is fertilized and alive you should see a spidery form of the embryo and veins. These eggs can be returned to the incubator. If the egg has not been fertilized, remove them, although if you are not sure you can wait a few more days and then check again. During the first candling, also make sure that there is an air bubble. This should grow in pace with the embryo.

At 18 days you can do a second candling. At this point you are checking to see if the embryo and air bubble are continuing to grow. A fertilized egg that has stopped developing and died can be recognized by a so-called death ring around the embryo and needs to be discarded.

Hatching

A few days before the eggs hatch you should stop turning them and increase the humidity levels. Check the instructions for your type of machine. Usually, the automatic turner gets removed and more water is added. Around day 19, you can hear chirping from the machine as the chicks have broken through the membrane and are breathing the air inside the air bubble, and in time, one of the stronger little guys will peck a hole or make a crack in the egg.

In order for the chick to make a hole in the shell it needs to be hard, but the membrane inside needs to be porous and moist, which is why the moisture levels are so important during this time. Without moisture, there is a risk the chicks can get caught in the membrane and get stuck, so you must never lift the lid while the eggs are hatching.

When all the chicks have hatched, they need to stay in the machine and dry for 12–24 hours before they are moved. The chicks can survive 48 hours on nutrients from the yolk sac which they absorb, so don't worry about them going hungry at this time. Don't lift the lid until it is time to move the chicks.

Chicks

Keep your little balls of fluff in an appropriately sized box. We use a pallet collar that can be doubled or tripled in size as the chicks grow and need space. The ground needs to be stable but absorbent as chicks have special feed and drink water from a special shallow container and you want to avoid any drowning accidents.

It's common that one or two chickens inexplicably die in the first 24 hours. Another common occurrence is that one or both legs stick out to the sides. You can fix this by splinting the legs with small sticks taped on. Keep the chick separate for a few days to see if it gets stronger and can move properly.

Chicks can't keep warm to start with so they need a heat lamp to help them. It needs a temperature of around 95°F (35°C) in the first week and then you can gradually reduce the temperature each week until they are 4 weeks old and are getting their first feathers. Regulate the temperature by raising and lowering the lamp. If the chickens huddle together under the lights you need to lower it for more heat. If they lay in a circle outside the light beam you need to raise it. From 4–6 weeks a temperature of around 68°F (20°C) is enough.

Depending on the temperature outside, the chicks can now move in (with their lamp) to a separate part of the coop, and once they are 8 weeks old they can retain their heat. If you have adult chickens in the coop, separate the chicks in a smaller cage or use chicken wire to partition them. By allowing the chicks to live next to the older chickens for a few weeks, they get used to each other before living together. There will be some pecking to establish the hierarchy in the coop but keep an eye on it in case it gets too violent.

Young Chickens

Chickens become sexually mature at around 20 weeks. This is also when they start laying eggs, although this can vary between breeds. Young chickens usually keep to themselves and don't become an integrated part of the flock until they mature.

Hens

A hen lays around 5–6 eggs a week and usually only during the light seasons. In the darkest months of the year, they usually take a break from laying. Within the chicken industry, lighting is used to simulate daylight to encourage constant egg production throughout the year. This means that the hens don't get their natural break during the winter, which wears immensely on them. A laying hen is used up and disposed of after a year, whereas a hen that is free to roam with natural seasons can live for ten years or more.

During really cold winters, it may be a good idea to have a heat source in the coop, even if it is insulated. Just make sure it is fire retardant. Keep a thermometer that can be read from the outside in the coop so you can check that the temperature doesn't sink below freezing.

A brooding Silverudd's Blue has made herself at home. When a hen is feeling broody, it is a good idea to have some spare nests for the other hens.

Brooding

A hen only feels broody if she feels safe and happy with her flock and environment. If she has access to a dark, cozy nest somewhere quiet and private with a few eggs, her broodiness will be even higher. On the other hand, if you don't want the hens to brood, you need to do the opposite and provide light, airy nests and remove the eggs regularly.

If you want to encourage the hens to brood, you can place some fake eggs (you can buy these) in the nest to see if anyone takes on the task of lying on top of them. If the hen stays a few days without getting bored and losing interest, you can swap the eggs for your fertilized eggs or hatching eggs if you've bought these. You need to pick eggs that feel smooth and are a regular shape and size. Remember that broodiness can vary between breeds and individual hens.

When a hen sees a nest filled with beautiful eggs, her broodiness will peak. How many will fit under her depends on breed but usually around 7–11 eggs. If you want to support your hen and pick some perfect eggs for her, you need to collect these over several days.

Store the eggs in a cool and damp place in an eggbox but don't wash them. The temperature needs to be under 68ºF (20ºC). Use a pen to mark the eggs and put them pointy end down at a 45-degree angle. Lean them in the other direction four times per day; the mark will help you keep track.

When the hen is brooding, she doesn't leave the nest for long, just to eat and drink. In the beginning she might take longer breaks but the closer they get to hatching the less she will leave the eggs. She will get up several times a day, however, to move the eggs around and turn them and sometimes she'll remove feathers from her breast so that the eggs lie against her skin.

It's not just the attitude to brooding that varies but the quality of parenting can quite frankly vary a lot between hens. If one is a particularly inappropriate parent, another hen can step in as an adoptive mum. A hen that has chicks needs to keep them warm and protect them, and she also needs to teach them how and where to find food by taking them out on small pecking expeditions.

Roosters

Before your chickens have reached sexual maturity, you need to get rid of your roosters. You can do this as soon as you know the sex of your chickens and have picked out a good rooster (if you intend to keep one). Although if you want to eat the roosters for dinner you need them to grow a bit more; after around six months the meat has matured and tastes good. It is also easier to pluck the feathers when they've grown out a bit.

You can usually tell when it's time to remove the roosters as they start to fight with each other. It is important to act as otherwise the roosters will solve the problems themselves, usually resulting in a blood bath.

It's not always easy to tell roosters and hens apart and it also varies from breed to breed as they grow at different rates and the feathers may look different. Remember that roosters crow!

Separating Hens from Roosters:

A rooster's comb tends to grow faster and longer and they usually have thicker and larger legs.
Hens have a more rounded bottom whereas roosters are pointier with clear plumage.

In Defense of the Rooster

A common question for chicken owners is whether you need a rooster. Roosters can be seen as a bit difficult, crow a lot, and can be aggressive. You don't need a rooster and if you don't have one, one of the hens will lead the flock instead.

However, chickens are pack animals where the rooster's role is more than just about fertilization. A good rooster leads the flock and keeps them organized, reducing the risk of infighting and bullying between the hens. The rooster also forages for food and calls the hens once he's found some.

The rooster is also one of the best protectors against predators as it is his role to unite and protect his flock. A good rooster will keep watch and raise the alarm when a predator approaches. You'll quickly get to know these sounds and when to run to assistance.

A rooster is no equal for a fox or goshawk, but best-case scenario he can distract them while the rest of the flock run to safety. If a hen has succumbed to a predator, the rooster leads the other hens to safety, but it is not uncommon for the rooster to be the unlucky one.

Which Rooster to Pick?

Choosing the right rooster is important as the characteristics of that rooster will be passed on. It is normal to want to keep the best-looking rooster with the most colorful feathers, but these are not the most important qualities of a rooster. You need to choose a natural leader that is not too aggressive to either chickens or humans.

It's a fine balance between a rooster that protects his flock and one that attacks anything that moves. It is also important that the rooster knows their place in the hierarchy (below you) and does not try and challenge you and your family. An angry, aggressive rooster is no fun for you or the hens and may have to be put down.

Remove the roosters that are aggressive or easily scared. Usually the flock will naturally choose a rooster themselves to lead, which is usually the best choice. Keep in mind that all roosters can be a bit "cocky," but they usually calm down after a while. A good rooster should take care of both hens and chicks, protect, woo the hens, and find food.

If you are unsure, you can always keep a spare rooster for a bit to see if you made the right choice and then swap if needed. If you have a larger flock, you can have several roosters. The roosters will arrange an inner hierarchy with a top rooster above the other roosters. Be prepared though, because they will keep challenging each other.

KEEPING CHICKENS

Slaughtering Your Rooster

It is up to you how you dispose of your roosters. If you struggle to do it yourself, ask a friend or neighbor with some experience to help. It needs to be as quick and painless as possible. You will need an axe, a chopping block, and a strong rod, preferably made of metal or hard wood. Before the slaughter takes place, it is good to separate the birds—for example you can lock the hens in the coop and leave the roosters in the run. Kill one rooster at a time. Lift by the back legs and hold it upside down and hit it hard over the back of the head to knock it out. If your roosters are hard to catch without a chase you can use a fishing net. Catch the rooster, place it on the ground, and hit it a few times over the back of the head.

The final stage takes place outside the chicken run as you don't want it covered in blood and you don't want to stress the other roosters.

Lift the rooster by the back legs and place the head on the chopping block, chopping the head off using an axe that you can manage with one hand. Be prepared for the fact that a newly killed rooster can jerk and flap quite animatedly for several minutes. Place the dead rooster in a clean bucket with the neck downwards or hang it up by the back legs to allow the blood to run off.

Skinning or Plucking

There are two basic ways to remove the feathers, plucking or skinning, and both have their advantages. If you have lots of roosters to deal with, skinning can be a better option. It means pulling the skin off the rooster including all the feathers. Once you get the hang of it, it takes less than a minute to do. The problem is you lose a lot of the flavor that can be found in the skin. If you grill or broil the rooster the skin also keeps the meat moist.

This is why we prefer to pluck the roosters as we want to use as much as we can of the animal for food.

Nearly all parts of a rooster can and should be used. Both methods should be done outdoors, and you can use the same methods with hens.

Skinning

Place the rooster on its back and cut off the legs at the heel. You can use a knife, but it is easier with shears or pliers.

Score the inside of the thigh so you cut through the skin only, place your fingers in the score and loosen the skin from the meat and remove the skin from the legs.

Loosen the skin on the stomach by firmly but carefully separating it from the meat with your thumb and index finger. Once you have finished the stomach, place the rooster on their stomach and loosen the skin from the meat in the same way.

Next cut off the tail end and cut the wings at the shoulders. Now you can grab the loose skin and pull it from the body over the neck. Voila!

Plucking

Pluck the bird by warming a large pan of water, around four gallons or more (15 l) to 176°F (80°C). You can also fill a bucket with warm water, but you need to be able to submerge the whole bird. Wear some thin gloves and lift the bird by the legs and dip into the warm water so all the feathers are soaked through. Test a few feathers and when they come out easily you can start plucking. Pull the feathers straight up with firm tugs, starting with the largest feathers on the wings and rear.

The most ergonomic way is to hang the rooster by the legs on a branch or pole in line with your shoulders. Once complete you can cut the legs off at the heels.

Gutting

You can now carry on working in a more hygienic location indoors. Place the bird on its back and make a cut under the protruding breast bone.

Grab the gizzards and remove the innards. Be careful that the greeny-black gall bladder by the liver does not rupture. You can then cut the intestines by the cloaca.

You can now remove the lungs that sit by the ribs; in roosters you also need to remove the testicles.

Ensure the bird is healthy by checking that the liver is a nice, red color with no spots.

Keep the heart, liver, and gizzards which can be eaten and place the rest of the innards on the compost heap. You can also save the head, neck, feet, and legs. It is respectful and good for the environment to use all parts of the animals that you have just killed. Throwing away some of the best parts of the bird is also the height of foolishness.

Eggs

The most important, and most natural, raw ingredient you can get from your chickens is the egg. It is also wonderfully versatile.

It is impossible to list all the things you can do with an egg in one book—an egg is useful not only in food but also, for example, to make paint. We also use egg white mixed with chalk powder in the joints of our tile oven.

Eggs are a super product that contain almost everything we need such as vitamin A, D, E, K, B2, B12, selenium, iron, and iodine, and are also a good source of protein.

The number of eggs we get per year varies depending on the breed, from 150 to 350 from the modern laying hens, to around 200 per year from the local breeds, so we get a lot of eggs. Eggs keep well if stored properly and you rarely need to store them in the fridge unless you don't eat many eggs. In room temperature they last around six weeks and in the fridge around double this. Store the eggs pointy end down.

Meat & Bones

Some breeds of chicken are considered to be better for meat while others are better for laying eggs. This is mainly because meat breeds grow faster and are often heavier, meaning they have more meat on them. However, you can eat all breeds and you will soon notice a home-bred rooster that has been allowed to roam around your garden for the past six months tastes completely different from a commercial chicken that has sat indoors for 45 days. The meat is darker with a lot more flavor and depth. Free-range chickens are healthier and have more muscle, meaning the meat can be chewier, making it perfect for longer cook times, for example in stews.

A great way to extract the flavors is by making chicken stock. You can use nearly everything except the giblets such as the carcass, legs, feet, neck, and head.

Giblets

The liver, heart, and gizzard from the bird are delicacies that should not be passed by. Chicken liver has a lovely, mild taste that is less "livery" than, for example, beef liver. You can either fry it or make it into pâté.

The chicken heart is the magic blend of giblets and meat and the tastiest part of the whole chicken. It is also very nutritious with lots of vitamin B12, for example. Separate the heart, polish, and rinse. It should be cooked for a short time at a high temperature.

The gizzard, also known as the gastric mill, is an organ where birds, usually with the help of small stones and grit that has been swallowed, break down their food. As birds don't have teeth, the gizzard work in the same way. It is considered a delicacy that is eaten in different ways around the world from confit to deep fried and pickled. In east Africa it is tradition to serve gizzard to the oldest and most respected person at the table.

Separate the gizzard down the middle and clean out all the innards; grab the edge of the white membrane and remove it. The gizzard is good fried or deep-fried to make it crispy.

Gizzard, heart, and liver

Slaughtering a Rooster

KEEPING CHICKENS

Silverudd's Blue Stock

Buttermilk Marinated "Hedemora" Rooster

If you have some churned butter and a nice rooster on hand, you can create a miracle with just these two ingredients. Buttermilk has natural fermentation that marinates the meat and makes it more tender. With its mild fermenting properties, the buttermilk helps the protein in the chicken to break down, resulting in a lovely creamy texture.

<u>4 portions</u>
1 whole rooster, skin on, 3.3–4.4 lb (1 ½–2 kg)
3 cups (7 dl) buttermilk
½ cup (1 dl) rapeseed oil
4 garlic cloves, pressed
2 tbsp honey
1½ tbsp salt
1 tsp ground black pepper
2 tbsp chopped rosemary
2 tbsp chopped parsley

Mix all the ingredients except the rooster in a bowl until the salt and honey has dissolved.

Place the rooster in a bag (double up if they are thin) and pour the marinade over the rooster, pressing out as much air as you can before closing the bag.

Leave the rooster on a plate in the fridge for at least 24 hours, preferably 48. Turn it a few times to marinate the whole bird.

Turn a convection oven to 300°F (150°C).

Remove the rooster from the bag and leave to allow the marinade to run off.

Roast in the middle of the oven until the inner temperature of the thigh is 180°F (82°C). Raise the temperature to 425°F (225°C) for the last 5–10 minutes to give a nice finish.

Silverudd's Blue Stock

The best thing you can make from your roosters is a really good stock that hands-down beats any stock cube or store-bought stock. Few things are as versatile in a kitchen as a mild and tasty rooster stock, which can also be drunk. Bone stock is also rich in minerals and collagen.

<u>4¼ pints</u>
2.2–4.4 lb (1–2 kg) rooster (carcass, head, neck, legs, and carefully washed feet)
10½ pints (5 l) of water
1 tsp salt
1 tbsp apple cider vinegar
3 tbsp squeezed lemon juice
1 large carrot, chopped
3 yellow onions, chopped
1 leek, chopped
1 bay leaf

Start early and fill a large pot with all the parts of the rooster. Use your largest pot as you need space and there is no point in making a small amount. Add water so it covers the bones and add salt, vinegar, lemon juice, vegetables, and bay leaf.

Bring to a boil and skim off the white foam that appears on the surface. Leave to simmer under a lid, leaving a slight gap. It takes 8–12 hours for bone, marrow, and cartilage to dissolve; make sure it does not boil too furiously and add more water if needed.

When the stock is finished, sieve and pour into jars. It will solidify as it cools. It lasts for several weeks in the fridge and can be frozen to last even longer.

MORROCCAN CHICKEN

This is a simple version of a classic Moroccan chicken dish, offering a delightful marriage of salty, tangy pickled lemons and the bitterness of green olives. When Anders retreated to Marrakesh to write, this was his staple dish. These days it's our favorite dish when we cook rooster.

4 portions
1 rooster
4–5 small, pickled lemons or 1–2 fresh lemons
Around ¾ cup (2 dl) unpitted green olives
¾–1¼ cups (2–3 dl) olive oil
1 bunch flat leaf parsley
Salt and freshly ground black pepper
1¼ cups (3 dl) water

Heat the oven to 100°F (150°C). Clean and wash the rooster and place in a cast iron pot. Add the lemons and a few tablespoons of the brine.

Add olives to taste; just under a cup is usually enough. Add a generous amount of olive oil (don't hold back), salt and pepper. Add water.

Put the pot with a lid in the middle of the oven and cook for 2–3 hours turning it in the pot halfway through. It's ready when the meat is tender enough to fall off the bone. Serve with couscous, parsley, and stock from the pot.

Starting a Micro Dairy

How we wish we had our own cow. We would call her Selma and she would give us wonderful fresh milk every day and together with her calf she would graze the land and we would never take more milk than we needed.

It's not that long ago that almost every Swedish family owned a cow. Maybe we are heading back in that direction, although these days most people, including us, don't have space for a cow. Thankfully, we have great neighbors who give us lovely fresh milk.

When it comes to dairy products, our rule is that we buy milk and cream but everything else we try and make ourselves, with the exception of mature cheese. This art form is one we admit (at least for now) has eluded us.

It's surprisingly easy to produce most dairy products yourself with the help of cream and milk as your base, and they taste so much better than storebought products. However, it is also about having a respect for the raw products we use. Milk is not a disposable product and each drop is worth its weight in gold and needs to be used with love. Our advice is to buy the best milk you can, preferably from local cows.

In Sweden, cows have lived with humans for around 4,000 years and have, more than any other animal, shaped our countryside. Cows have an important heritage and are key to maintaining our eco system, which is why they deserve all the respect we can give. Out of respect for this amazing creature, we treat a butter we have churned and fermented ourselves much more lovingly than we do a store-bought butter.

Fermented Milk

Creating your own dairy products is mainly about animal husbandry and caring for the modern housekeeper's best friend: bacteria. The art of fermenting milk with the help of bacteria is as old as our relationship with cows. It's a completely natural process and as long as you leave the milk it will ferment; the important thing is which bacteria you want in there.

The fact that different types of fermented milk products have emerged in different parts of the world is a reflection of different environments and methods resulting in different bacteria getting the upper hand. In other words, climate plays a role in lactic acid bacteria.

In South Africa, amasi milk was created by fermenting raw milk in a bowl made from the calabash fruit; in northern Caucasus, milk was fermented in a goat skin with grains of yeast and lactic acid and acetic acid bacteria which created the sour and lightly alcoholic drink known as kefir. One of the oldest ways of fermenting milk is making yogurt, which was probably invented in Mesopotamia around 7,000 years ago. Yogurt is also a result of the local environment as the bacteria that turns milk to yogurt prefer warm weather, 100°F or more (40°C).

In our cold Scandinavian climate, soured milk was developed, so called *fil* or fermented milk. In the old days full fat milk was left straight from milking to ferment resulting in *filbunke*, milk that has been left to ferment, unstirred. Today *fil* or fermented milk is a more modern product where bacteria is added after the milk has been heated. Fermented milk is really a term that covers a whole host of thick, fermented milks, many which are no longer consumed today.

Fermented milk did not only vary in different parts of the world but also between farms. In the old days, people made their own fermented milk by saving some of the old, fermented culture and adding it to fresh milk, similar to a sourdough starter. Animals, location, and environment would add their unique bacteria, meaning each farm had their own flavors. Your own bacterial culture was precious and to be guarded and the local area would be known for their fermented milk with local bacterial cultures. One local culture that has survived in Sweden is known as *Långfil* or "Long fermented milk."

What Do Bacteria Do?

Historically, fermenting milk products was a way to make them last longer in times before fridges existed. These days we ferment for the taste and the health benefits, as lactic acid bacteria is good for our gut.

When milk ferments, the bacteria feed off the lactose which creates lactic acid resulting in the sour taste. The lactic acid starts a process whereby the milk proteins coagulate, thickening it. The different tastes and textures in fermented milk is a result of the different ways the lactic acid bacterial cultures complete this process.

YOGURT BACTERIA Yogurt is the result of two different lactic acid bacteria, Lactobacillus bulgaricus and Streptococcus thermophilus, working together. They prefer a temperature of around 107°F (42°C) and break down more lactose resulting in yogurt being sourer than for example "fil."

FIL Fil is created by lactic acid bacteria species Lactococcus and Leuconostoc, both of which prefer an inside temperature of around 68°F (20°C).

LÅNGFIL LACTOCOCCUS lactis is the bacterial species that creates *långfil* and contributes to its gooey texture. In a nutshell, the bacteria binds the milk's carbohydrates into long strands, hence the name *långfil* (*lång* meaning long in Swedish). The same bacteria are used to make cheeses such as cheddar.

KEFIR Kefir is created by mixing bacteria and yeast including Lactobacillus acidophilus and Saccharomyces kefir. The result gives a unique yeasty taste with a lightly carbonated feel.

Filbunke, page 88

Churned, Fermented & Brown Butter

This is the most luxurious butter there is, a butter that has been given a little bit of extra love. In the old days butter was fermented for the same reasons that milk, fil, and yogurt were, to make it last longer.

In our opinion, fermented butter tastes better. In this recipe we also add a little brown butter as the contrast between the sour and the lightly golden brown tones creates something very special.

Homemade butter is one of the easiest and tastiest things you can make and buying similar butter costs more than the cream itself. If you just want normal butter, follow the same instructions but skip fermenting and browning the butter.

In Sweden, churned milk is sadly a long-forgotten product, once part of our cultural heritage that could be found in most homes. On the other side of the Atlantic, however, it is often used for baking and is known as buttermilk. If you make your own butter, buttermilk is the liquid that remains after you have churned milk to butter. Buttermilk is thin and is a good emulsifier, meaning it gives a good consistency when used in sauces or baking.

Around 17 fl. Oz (500 g)
2 pints (1 l) organic whipping cream
2 tbsp fresh *fil* (or kefir)
1 tsp salt flakes
1 tbsp organic rapeseed oil
1 oz (25 g) butter

The easiest way to ferment cream is in its packaging. Remove the lid on two 1-pint cartons of cream and add 1 tbsp *fil* (or kefir) in each one. Put the lid back on and shake thoroughly, then loosen the lid and leave at room temperature for 12–24 hours.

The cream should have a tart taste with a crème fraiche type texture, which is basically what you have just made. The temperature in your house affects the time it takes to ferment. In our old house it varies with the seasons. If you want a really tart taste you need to wait longer, up to four days.

Once fermented, cut the bottom of the carton and pour into a bowl. Place in the fridge until it reaches around 60ºF (15ºC).

Meanwhile, brown the butter in a small pan, whisking constantly so that the butter doesn't burn. When it is done it should be golden with a nutty smell. If you want to be completely sure you have done it right, check the temperature and stop at 260ºF (125ºC). Chill the browned butter.

Add the brown butter to the fermented cream and whisk with an electric whisk or food processor. After a while you will notice the cream expanding and the whisking starts to get harder; the cream will suddenly reach a plateau and start to sink, but keep whisking until it gets watery and lumpy and you start to see small grains of butter. Note that fermented cream will take longer to churn, so don't give up.

Place the butter in a fine sieve over a bowl and leave it to drain. The churned milk should be kept as it is just as precious as the butter. After a while, use a spoon to stir and press as much of the milk out of the butter as you can so it's not wasted when you wash the butter. Once you are done move on to the next step.

To wash the butter, fill a bowl with cold water and knead the butter as if it were dough. Do this at least three times using new water each time, until the water is clear.

Place the butter in a bowl and add salt and oil. Mix with a spoon or fork so the butter doesn't melt. If you think it feels too hard then add some more oil. The butter will last for around 4 weeks in an airtight jar in the fridge.

Our Soothing *Filbunke*

Some evenings when we don't have the energy to
cook we eat a bowl of *filbunke* and some homemade
sourdough rye bread. *Filbunke* should have a lovely
yellow layer of fat on the surface and be lumpy.

Filbunke is not the same as regular *fil*. Traditionally,
filbunke is made from unpasteurized milk straight from
the cow that has been left to ferment with the help of
naturally occurring lactic acid bacteria in both the milk
and surrounding environment.

This process makes the milk last longer which was
important in the old days when milk had to be stored
while the cows were out on pasture. These days it's
almost impossible to get hold of unpasteurized milk but
there is a shortcut to making your own.

<u>2½ pints (1.2 l)</u>
2 pints (1 l) unhomogenized or full fat milk (try and buy
good quality local milk)
½ cup (1 dl) organic whipping cream
½ cup (1 dl) organic *fil* (as fresh as possible; use kefir as
an alternative)

Mix milk and cream in a pan and heat up while stirring.

Remove the pan just below boiling point, around
205°F (95°C); use a thermometer to check. Heating the
milk stops it from curdling when you add the bacterial
culture from the *fil* or kefir.

To cool the mixture down, place it in a water bath.
Remove the *fil* from the fridge to get it to room temperature.

When the milk has reached around 70°F (22°C) you
can mix in the *fil* or kefir. Pour into serving bowls and
cover and leave at room temperature.

For the next 24 hours the lactic acid bacteria in the
fil or kefir needs to do its work. After about 12 hours
check the *filbunke*; depending on the temperature in
your house and how active the bacteria are, the time
may vary. A finished *filbunke* should be loose, a bit like
a chocolate pudding, with a yellow layer of fat on top.
You should be able to use a spoon to scoop it up and it
should have a fresh, tart taste to it.

When the taste and texture is to your liking, store in
the fridge until you are ready to eat. It will keep for 3–4
days. Serve with fresh seasonal berries and fresh honey.

Honey Butter

We think blending honey and butter works so well
because they have the same inherent background: a field
full of flowers. Honey butter is not only amazing on
toast or with oatmeal, but you can also use it as filling or
frosting for cakes and other baked goods.

<u>7 oz (200 g)</u>
3½ oz (100 g) butter
3½ oz (100 g) runny honey
Pinch of salt
A few drops freshly squeezed lemon

Leave the butter and honey to reach room temperature.

Mix the honey into the butter with a hand whisk or
blender. Add salt and lemon to taste. Store in the fridge
in an airtight glass jar with a lid. Keeps for at least 4
weeks.

Kefir

We love the magic grains that transform milk into this super healthy yogurt-style drink. Just like with sourdough or kombucha SCOBY, you can easily share this bacterial culture, which in this case are grains. If you buy the grains they arrive dried and need to be activated in fresh milk. The first batch takes around a week to finish and the fermentation takes place at room temperature with the grains being reusable over several years.

Kefir can be made from all sorts of milk by placing active kefir grains in a bottle or jar and pouring the right amount of milk on top. The grains expand with age as well as become more potent so it's a matter of trial and error. We use around 2 pints of milk (1 l) per 5 grains (2 tbsp). If you use too little milk for the grains, the milk will quickly thicken and spill over and if nothing happens, or the process is slow, you probably have too much milk in ratio to your grains.

Place the kefir in a spot with an even temperature of at least 68°F (20°C) (our old kitchen is way too cold for kefir in the winter). The kefir should be ready after about 24 hours and should have a tart taste with a lightly carbonated feel and should have thickened slightly (similar texture to *fil*). Never leave kefir for more than 48 hours as the grains will swell and the kefir has a laxative effect. Remove the grains, which have usually risen to the surface, with a fork or spoon, and place in a tub with some milk so they don't starve. Place in the fridge or start a new batch of kefir straight away. The kefir is now ready to drink, make kefir cheese from, or use in cooking.

Kefir Cheese

Since we started making kefir we nearly always make kefir cheese rather than cream cheese. In its natural state it tastes like quark or cottage cheese, but we add herbs or garlic and use as a dip or a sandwich spread. If you want a creamier texture and flavor, you can make the kefir with a higher fat milk or add cream. Adding fermented cream before straining it will result in a creamier kefir cheese. This cheese will keep for around a week in the fridge.

Kefir
Flavoring such as herbs or garlic (optional)
Cheesecloth

Pour the kefir into a cheesecloth over a bowl and place in the fridge. Wait for around 24 hours until the whey has stopped dripping.

Add flavor and store in glass jars.

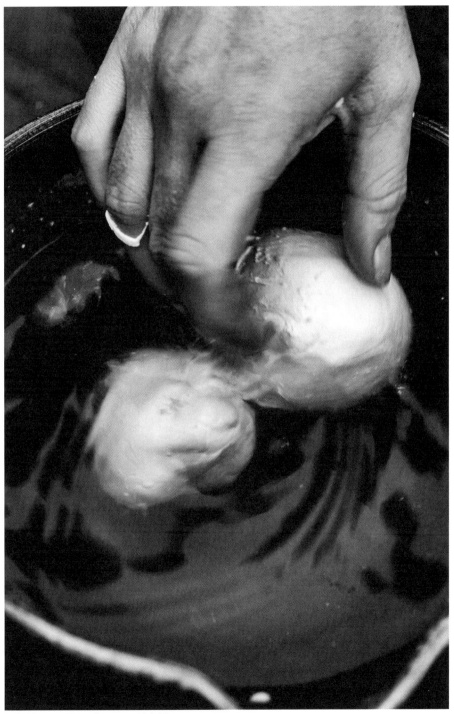

Kefir Cheese & Mozarella, pages 89 & 92

STARTING A MICRO DAIRY

Mozzarella

Italians won't flinch at sticking their hands into 185 degree (85ºC) water to make mozzarella! Their view is that it is impossible to create this work of art without feeling the hot mozzarella against their skin. So we scald our hands and curse the Italians but the result is heavenly. This recipe yields 4 balls and they taste the best if eaten within an hour of making them. If not, you can store them in the fridge in brine for 2 days.

When you make mozzarella, acidifying the milk is vital to create curds and get the right consistency. You could use vinegar or buttermilk if you don't have lemon or citric acid on hand. It is also important not to overwork the cheese to avoid it getting too hard. Try lifting it and allowing gravity to do its job rather than stretching it too much. We don't usually salt the curds as we often use it for other purposes such as making messmör (traditional whey butter) which will end up too salty.

4 balls

8½ pints (4 l) full fat milk
½ cup (1 dl) whipping cream
2½ tsp lemon juice or 1 tsp citric acid diluted in ¼ cup (½ dl) cold water
2 tsp rennet diluted in ¼ cup (½ dl) cold water

Mix the milk and cream in a large pan, squeeze the lemon over, and stir thoroughly.

Warm the mixture slowly while stirring on a low heat until it reaches 90ºF (32ºC). If you accidentally overheat it, let it cool down until it reaches the right temperature. Dissolve the rennet in the water and add to the milk while stirring for around 30 seconds. Add a lid to the pan and leave for around 20 minutes until you see a firm cheesy lump start to form.

Cut the cheese into cubes as per the diagrams. First cut the whole lump vertically with around ¾ inch (2cm) spacing. Turn the pan ninety degrees and cut the same again, giving you a square pattern with ¾ × ¾ inch squares.

Cut again in the same scores but this time tilt the knife forty-five degrees. Turn the pan ninety degrees and cut again in the same way.

Cutting the cheese into cubes:

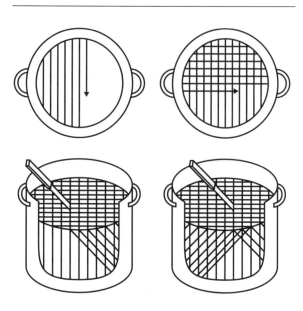

Leave for around 5 minutes until the cubes have separated from each other.

Slowly heat over a low temperature until the curds reach 104ºF (40ºC). Using a slotted spoon, move the lump of cheese into a sieve and leave it until there is no more curd coming out. Sieve the curd and heat it to around 185ºF (85ºC).

Take ¼ of the cheese and dip in the hot curds; you can place it in a sieve or slotted spoon to start with. Dip and lightly knead until you get a solid mass that can be held without falling apart.

Dip and lift the mass and leave it to hang, forming a long snake. Fold and repeat until it is shiny and smooth to touch. Fold one last time, then fold in the sides underneath to give it an even tight surface and pinch the end.

Leave the balls to rest for around 10 minutes in a bowl of warm brine. Keep the curds to make ricotta, for example.

Ricotta from Whey

The Italian word ricotta means to recook and it is made from heated up whey that is left over from making cheese. Note that there is both sweet and sour whey.

If you've added acidity to the cheese or the whey was left over from making yogurt, your whey may be too sour to make ricotta from (you need a pH level of around 6). If you do make ricotta from sour whey, do not add more acidity and make sure it is as fresh as possible.

Sweet whey is usually leftover from making hard cheese. In order for it to coagulate and create a mass of cheese it needs acidity, either through fermentation or by adding, for example, lemon juice, vinegar, or buttermilk. You can leave it for 24 hours in the fridge or use it right away by adding a dash of apple cider vinegar.

As the proteins have coagulated into cheese once already, we recommend adding some milk to give a larger volume. The recipe won't yield a large portion of ricotta but it's enough for a few sandwiches or a pasta dish. If you want more you can add more milk; full fat milk will give a creamier ricotta. It will last up to a week in an airtight glass container.

Around 3½ oz
2 pints (1 l) whey from cheesemaking
2 cups (5 dl) whole milk
2 tsp salt
1½ tsp apple cider vinegar (optional)

Heat the whey on a medium heat until it reaches 167°F (75°C) and add the milk, slowly heating to 194°F (75°C) while stirring until the cheese starts to form a mass (around 20–30 minutes).

Remove from the heat and add apple cider vinegar if needed, then leave to rest for 10 minutes, stirring now and again to stop a skin from forming.

Pour the grainy mass into a cheesecloth and leave to drain until it stops dripping. Squeeze out the last liquid, add salt, and place in the fridge.

Oat Milk

It's not a dairy product, but oat milk is a great substitute if you've run out of milk or are intolerant to dairy products, and it's great for making things like pancakes. Buying oat milk is the same thing as buying tap water in our opinion as you can make oat milk in only a few minutes. Make a few pints at a time and store in the fridge in glass bottles.

Leftover steel cut oats can be kept to make porridge, added to bread, or fed to the chickens as a snack.

2½ pints
¾ cup (2 dl) oats
2 pints (1 l) water
Pinch of salt
2 tbsp rapeseed oil

Pour all the ingredients into a blender and mix until you have a smooth milk with no lumps.

Sieve the oat milk in a jelly strainer, pressing the last drops out so you are left with a dry mass. Pour into bottles and store in the fridge, where it will last for around 1 week. Mix before you use it; unlike regular milk, it will separate.

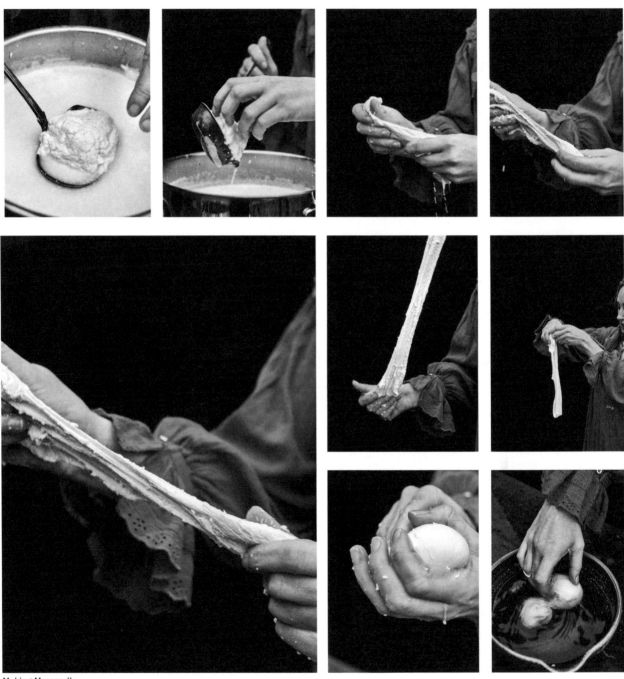

Making Mozzarella

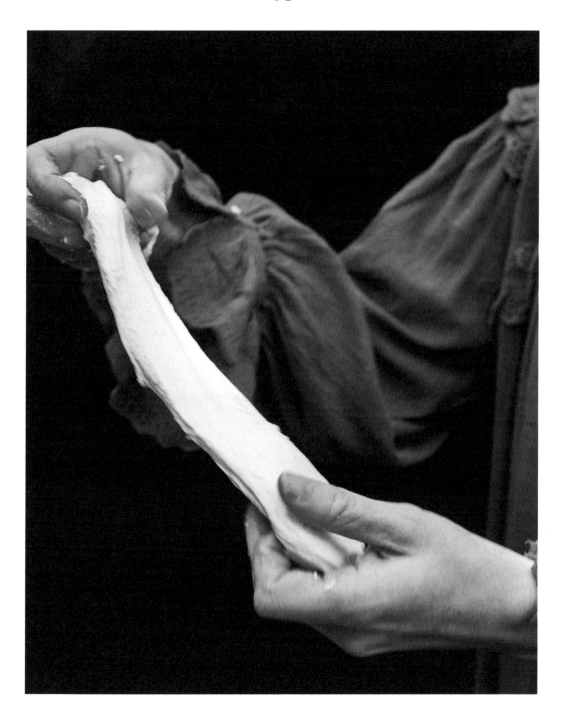

WHEY BUTTER & WHEY CHEESE

What can you make from all that leftover whey when you make cheese? Whey butter is fantastic with a salty and umami taste that makes a wonderful base for sauces and stews, and it's simply made from whey reduction and caramelized milk. Whey cheese comes from cooked, hardened whey butter. The whey from 10½ pints of milk gives 5–7 ounces of whey butter.

Around ¾ cup (2 dl)
10½ pints (5 l) unsalted whey

Heat the whey in a thick-bottomed pan while stirring (it burns easily).

Reduce the whey over a low heat stirring now and again, more frequently towards the end, until it reaches a thick consistency. Be patient as it can take a while.

Remove the pan from the heat and place in a cold water bath, whisking while it cools down. Pour into glass jars and store in the fridge. We put dollops of whey butter on a tray (ice cube molds work too) and freeze so they can be used quickly and easily in sauces.

To make whey cheese, pour the whey butter in a baking tin lined with parchment paper and bake at 160°F (70°C) for a few hours until firm. Remember it will get firmer as it cools down. Store in the fridge or freezer; in the fridge it will last a few weeks.

Compost & Fertilizer

What do you think of when you see a garden? Maybe you think of flowers, fields of grain growing, vegetables patches, and trees laden with fruits. However, the most important thing we grow is not green but brown, and by that we mean soil. To grow your own soil is the basis of a sustainable and ecologically sound garden, and it's a way you can make a difference to the environment. An example of short-term thinking is to clear the garden during the spring, removing leaves and branches, and take it all to the recycling center, only to stop off at the garden center on your way home to buy bags of soil for your new flowerbeds. In your eagerness to make your garden look nice, you lost sight of the fact that what you just bought is the same thing that you just threw away—soil. In fact, the soil you got rid of had more nutrients than the soil you just bought. The soil may not be ready the day you decide to plant your new flowerbeds, but really all you need is two to three weeks of planning.

Know Your Soil

Getting to know your soil is a good step towards understanding the needs of your garden when it comes to growing. You can't change the type of soil you have but you can work with it to make it better. Clay, silt, and sand in soil bring different challenges, but you can tackle them all in the same way by increasing the level of humus in your soil. You can change the structure and make it richer in nutrients by adding organic matter such as grass cuttings, compost, or bark. One way to improve soil is mulching but you can also dig organic matter into the soil to make it easier to plant things.

Most garden soil has a mineral base. Mineral soils can be split into clay, silt, and sand with clay consisting of the smallest particles, silt medium-sized particles, and sand the larger ones. Soil that mainly contains clay or silt are rich in nutrients and lime and retain water well while sand soils are poor in nutrients and can't retain water very well. To easier identify the type of soil you have, you can compare them with different items of food, for example clay looks like margarine, silt like flour, and sand like sugar.

What Type of Soil Do You Have?

1. If you dig down into your soil a few inches you will get to the soil that has not been mixed with mulch.
2. Grab a handful of soil and drench it in water.
3. If you can't squeeze it into a firm lump and it seeps through your fingers, it is sandy soil.
4. Quicky roll the soil as thin as possible until it breaks. If it has a diameter of around 4mm before it snaps, it's silt soil, 2 mm light clay, 1.5mm medium clay, and 1mm hard clay.

If you are really interested and want to know the details of how your soil is constructed, there are geotechnic companies that specialize in advanced soil analysis and some will accept soil samples from private people for analysis.

Clay Soil

Clay soil is nutrient-rich and retains water well, and in areas built on limestone rock it is also rich in chalk. Clay soil is separated into categories depending on how fine the particles that make it up are: light clay, heavy clay, and very heavy clay.

Coarser clay soil is drier and lumpier, which creates a space where oxygen and nutrients can bind together. Hard clay can become compact, meaning it's hard for the roots to get through or get oxygen. From a gardening perspective, clay soil is hard to work with, but by adding organic matter you can make the structure more porous. However, don't mix sand into a clay soil as you will create something like cement! Clay soil warms up slowly in the spring but will retain heat longer into fall.

The lighter in color your clay is when it's dry, the lighter it is. A darker clay is heavy.

Silt Soil

In dry environments, silt soil is firm and absorbent like a sponge. Silt soil is wet rather than liquid and is for growing things as it retains water well. However, it dries fast meaning it is often too dry in the summer and too wet in the winter. Silt soil also forms a crust on the surface after a heavy downpour, meaning it can be hard for oxygen to get through.

Checking to see if you have silt soil:

1. Dig down 8–10 inches so you can access the soil under the mulch.
2. Grab a handful of soil and drench it in water.
3. Make a fist and tap it with your other hands underneath the fist.
4. If the soil seeps through and has a glossy surface, it is silt soil. If instead you squeeze out all the water, the surface will become matte.

Sandy Soil

Sandy soil does not retain water well, meaning it dries fast. Water just goes straight through it. It is, however, easy to work with and drains well which gives the roots an airy environment to grow in. Sandy soil warms up the quickest in the spring but also cools down faster in the fall.

COMPOST & FERTILIZER

COMPOST & FERTILIZER

Nutrients

Plants need a range of nutrients and a balance between them to stay healthy. Apart from hydrogen, oxygen, and carbon which the plants get via photosynthesis, Nitrogen (N), Phosphorus (P), and Potassium (K) are also vital to all plants. The pH levels are not overly important, but most plants prefer pH levels between 5 and 6.

Nitrogen is the nutrient plants need the most of. Leafy vegetables that need a lot of nutrients can also be fertilized with nitrogen during the latter part of the growing season, but for plants that need less nitrogen, such as root vegetables, it's enough to use nitrogen feed during early spring. As a rule, you should avoid using nitrogen on woody plants (bushes, trees, and climbing plants) after midsummer. If you fertilize with nitrogen too close to harvest you will not get any fruit or berries, just lots of leaves. For perennials, you need to stop fertilizing in August in good time for winter, so the plants have time to store energy to survive winter. However, phosphorus and potassium can be used as these make the plants hardier.

Fruit trees and bushes, as well as root vegetables and leeks, have the highest need for potassium, and phosphorus is best for cabbage, cucumber, and rhubarb.

Macronutrients—nutrients plants need a lot of

NITROGEN—stimulates leaf growth. Deficiencies are seen through poor growth and older leaves turning yellow.
PHOSPHORUS—good for flowers and fruit and creates carbohydrates to fuel growth. Deficiencies are seen through dark purple or green leaves. In neutral or slightly acidic pH levels, which is common in gardens, phosphorus deficiency is usually not an issue.
POTASSIUM—stimulates sugar and starch that makes the plant hardy. Deficiencies are seen by dry edges on the leaves and leaves that curl up.

Micronutrients—nutrients plants need a little of

CALCIUM—A balance of calcium is important for the plants to withstand attacks. Deficiencies are seen by wilting leaves and lack of growth.
MAGNESIUM—Important for photosynthesis and is found in chlorophyll. Deficiency is seen by patchy leaves that easily fall off.
IRON—High pH levels can lead to lack of iron and young leaves turn yellow and fall off.

The Balance between Carbon & Nitrogen

Carbon (C) and Nitrogen (N) are the most important nutrients for the microorganisms during composting. Matter rich in nitrogen breaks down faster than carbon rich matter, but the balance between them is vital and is known as the C:N ratio. A high ratio (a high number) means rich in carbon and a low ratio (a low number) means rich in nitrogen. If the ratio is too high, there is an excess of carbon and microorganisms start to fight over the available nitrogen. When no nitrogen is available, they start to break each other down instead, slowing down the process.

The organic matter becomes available to the microorganisms by being mineralized into ammonium and nitrate. If the ratio is too low, the excess leaks out in the form of ammonia, which makes the soil more acidic.

At the start of composting there should be a perfect balance of 25–30 parts of carbon per 1 part nitrogen. Once the process is complete, the ratio should be around 10:1. How long it takes depends on the moisture and size of the matter, as well as the total C:N ratio.

We simply think of it as 1 part matter rich in nitrogen for 2 parts carbon-rich material. Or to simplify it further, every third bucket is nitrogen rich.

Carbon-rich (brown) matter	C:N-ratio
Leaves	50
Twigs	500
Wood chips	500
Straw	65
Bark	100
Newspaper	175
Wood ash	25
Fruit	35

Nitrogen-rich (green) matter	
Green manure	30
Grass cuttings	20
Horse and cow fertilizer	15
Urine	1
Vegetables	25
Coffee grinds	20
Clover	23
Hay	25

A framework with compartments makes sorting and turning the compost easier.

Bare Ground

Bare ground is unnatural, as Mother Nature strives to cover the soil with vegetation. If you leave the ground bare, it won't take long until uncontrollable, and usually unwanted, plants take over.

Bare ground is also vulnerable when it has no protection because it will succumb to erosion and the earth will move. It can occur through natural forces like rain or wind, but it can also be caused by humans through conventional farming or too much artificial watering.

Bare ground becomes more compact when rain can't seep down to the roots of the plants. Instead, the rain bounces on the surface, making the soil dense and hard.

When the ground is bare, it is also poor in nutrients as it has no vegetation that can transport nutrients into the soil via the roots.

In addition, bare ground does not bind carbon but releases carbon dioxide into the atmosphere which contributes to the greenhouse effect. Soil that has

vegetation absorbs carbon dioxide from the air through photosynthesis. The carbon dioxide is broken into carbon compound and oxygen where the oxygen is released into the atmosphere and the carbon aids growth with the excess going into the roots and binding to the soil through the joint effort of roots, fungi, and microorganisms. If you allow the plants to stay in place, more carbon is added to the soil, rather than evaporating, which is positive for the environment and an important part of so-called regenerative farming.

The best way to stop soil erosion is to enhance the structure of your soil. The goal is to have a loamy soil that is porous and makes it easy for water to seep into the ground and create the best environment for the organisms that live there.

Another way is to grow plants with deep roots that keep the soil and nutrients stable. Trees and bushes can also protect against wind. With planned growth throughout the seasons, the soil is constantly covered in vegetation and you avoid leaving it bare.

The Berkley method of composting:

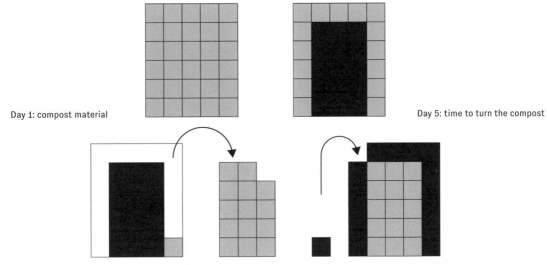

Day 1: compost material

Day 5: time to turn the compost

Day 5–18: Method for turning the compost

Berkeley Composting

The quickest composting method is the 18-day method, also known as hot composting or the Berkeley method. A normal cold compost takes 6–12 months for the organic matters to break down, but in a hot compost the same process takes 18–21 days. In other words, you will get ready to use soil in around 3 weeks as long as you can get it hot enough and turn it regularly. A few days after you have "baked" your compost the heat will start to rise as the breakdown of microorganisms creates heat. A big advantage of hot composting is that disease, bacteria, and weeds are killed by the heat. It's a good idea to have a compost thermometer to keep an eye on it. After about a week the temperature sinks and stabilizes, but if it rises to 172°F (78°C) the process stops.

Hot Composting

A hot compost should consist of around ⅔ brown matter and ⅓ green, and it mustn't be too wet or too dry. If it's too wet there is not enough oxygen for the microbial activity, and if it's too dry the microbes are unable to break down the matter and the process stops.

Once the correct levels of moisture are reached it will start again.

1. Collect your composting materials, sorting them by levels of carbon or nitrogen. As you need more carbon matter you may need to pile up fresh matter to allow it to wilt and become carbon rich. Larger items such as branches and twigs need to be made into wood chipping, so for this type of work a wood chipper comes in handy.
2. Layer green and brown items in thin layers making a total area of at least 35 cubic feet (1 cubic meter).
3. Do not turn the compost the first 4 days.
4. Once stabilized, the ultimate temperature is around 130–150°F (55–65°C).
5. From day 5 and onwards, turn the compost every second day from the outside and in and vice versa.
6. On day 18 the compost should be done!

ERROR CHECK: If the process is too slow, you have too much carbon or it's too dry—add nitrogen and/or water. If the temperature is too high, you have too much nitrogen—add carbon. If it smells sour, it's too wet /doesn't have enough oxygen—add more carbon.

Bokashi

Most of our food waste is handled by our animals. The chickens eat anything from bread crusts to old pasta while our dog will happily eat potatoes, carrots, and remnants from any slaughter. However, there is still a lot of food waste that we need to deal with.

Previously we had an isolated hot compost just for kitchen waste, but it does come with problems. For a start it attracts pests like flies and mice, and even worse, a lot of the energy in the food waste disappears when nitrogen and carbon dioxide is created through the decomposition of food.

Instead, we use bokashi which is a much more effective way to transform food waste to something good. One advantage is that bokashi doesn't smell so can be done indoors. It is a Japanese method of fermenting food waste and is not unlike the process of lactic acid fermenting vegetables, meaning it's not strictly composting, rather a process of rotting. By adding a mix of lactic acid bacteria, phototrophic bacteria, and yeast, you allow the waste to ferment in an oxygen-poor space. Once the process is complete, you dig it straight into your soil where it quickly transforms into a soil rich in microflora as well as getting carbon dioxide into your plants.

Tools

BUCKET You can get special bokashi-buckets but a regular fermentation pail with a lid works too. The important thing is that there is a tap at the bottom of the bucket (you can add this yourself); for the process to work you need to drain off the water now and again. Don't throw it away as this is perfect fertilizer for your vegetables. Depending on the food waste, bokashi water can contain a lot of salt so be careful if you are watering house plants. It can be worth having a few buckets as during the winter it can be difficult to get the bokashi into the ground.

BOKASHI-BRAN To get going with the right mix of bacteria, you can get bokashi bran, but it works just as well without. Once your bokashi is established, you can use the drained water to prepare new bokashi composts with bacteria, although the water has a shelf life. You can also make your own bokashi bran with EM (effective microorganisms)—wheat bran, molasses, and water.

Fertilizing

By adding a good balance of nutrients, you don't only get a better harvest but also plants that are more resistant. However, if you over fertilize, plants may become vulnerable again to fungi. Do a basic fertilization during the spring, a few weeks before you start sowing seeds and planting out. We use our compost from chicken manure as much as we can but also add aged horse manure since we are lucky to live next to a horse farm. During the entire summer we water our vegetables that are a year old and our summer plants around every second week with fertilizer. We stop fertilizing our perennials with nitrogen around midsummer so as not to add pressure to the plants as they grow and store their energy for the winter.

Yard Fertilizer

Yard fertilizer contains nitrogen, phosphorus, and potassium that contributes to the plants' healthy growth. Most common is to use manure from horse, cow, or pig. To create a basic fertilizer with yard fertilizer, use ¾ gallon per 35 cubic feet (3 l per cubic meter).

Chicken Fertilizer

Our chickens give us potent manure which we compost in a bucket behind the chicken coop. It is rich in nitrogen and works well for plants that need a lot of nitrogen or for a basic fertilizer as you only need just under a cup per 35 square feet (2 dl per cubic meter). Fresh fertilizer is so strong it can harm the roots of the plants.

Curing Manure

As manure from animals decomposes it is known as curing. Fresh manure is rich in nitrogen and the process by which this breaks down is so intense it generates heat, which is why you often see steam coming from piles of manure in the winter. As a fuel, manure uses nitrogen. Fresh manure can be used to improve soil; by spreading it and turning it into a clay soil it uses nitrogen from the atmosphere rather than from itself, meaning it

decomposes slower and does not give off any heat. However, you can't use fresh manure as fertilizer on your plants as it is so strong you risk literally burning what you've grown.

Compost Tea

A great way to help the plants absorb the nutrients is to dissolve it in water. By dissolving fertilizer in water, you can create your own compost tea, i.e. your own solution of nutrients. Different compost teas can be used in different ways to support growth throughout the season. Liquid nourishment can be absorbed directly by the roots and so has a faster effect on growth than fast fertilizer. Water with fertilizer every second week, stopping two weeks before harvest. It is better to do this little and often than too much too infrequently.

GOLDEN WATER Urine contains nitrogen, phosphorus, potassium, and different micronutrients. Golden water can be made using 1 part urine and 10 parts water.

NETTLE WATER Nettles are rich in nitrogen and all sorts of minerals. Place the nettles in water under a lid and leave them to ferment for a week. Mix one part nettle water with 10 parts nettles.

COMFREY & HORSETAIL Comfrey and horsetail contain lots of micro and macro nutrients. Make compost tea using the same method as nettle water.

MANURE WATER Manure water is rich in nitrogen, phosphorus, and potassium. Mix one part farm animal manure with two parts water in a bucket. Mix one part strained concentrate with ten parts water.

Compost Tea

COMPOST & FERTILIZER

Bath & Beauty

Nothing feels as good as sinking into a hot bath after some intensive work out on the land. Whether it be the backbreaking prepping and planting in the spring, outdoor living during the summer, or harvesting in the fall, our muscles are tired, our backs ache, and our hands and feet are stiff and dry. We bathe all year round; in the bathtub, in the lake, and in our outdoor wood-fired hot tub.

On hot summer days we fill it with cold water for the kids and their friends to cool down in. And on a warm summer evening, once the kids are in bed we bathe while listening to crickets and bats flying overhead. For the modern homesteader, water means time to relax and recuperate and time to use our bath and beauty products—a bit of summer conserved in a jar. We turn the bathroom into a hammam with music and scents and the kids creep in wearing their bathrobes to join us. They love a homemade spa as it's the ultimate combination of bathing, getting messy, and eating fruit.

SKINCARE FROM HERBAL OIL

Infusing oil is a good way to extract scents or skin friendly and healing properties from herbs, flowers, and seeds. The oil can be used directly on the skin or as a base for lotions, masks, or soap. Our favorites are marigold and rosehip. Marigold contains calendula, a bitter substance with healing properties for dry and sensitive skin. It also contains salicylic acid which helps to clean pores. Rosehip and rosehip seeds contain high levels of active antioxidants which is a common ingredient in anti-wrinkle creams. Apart from marigold and rosehip we also use rose, lavender, ladies mantle, raspberry seed, and mint.

3½ fl oz (100 ml) dried or partially dried herbs, flower petals, or seeds
17 fl oz (500 ml) vegetable oil

Method:
1. Place the herbs, flower petals, or seeds in a glass jar.
2. Pour the oil over making sure it completely covers the content to avoid mold. Leave at room temperature avoiding sunlight for 4 weeks. Turn the jar upside down or stir the contents daily, making sure the plants keep submerged.
3. Strain the oil through a fine cloth and pour into labelled bottles.

MULTIPURPOSE CREAM

We can't live without this cream. We use it everywhere—face, lips, feet, hands, cheeks, elbows, and knees, on chapped winter skin, dry summer heels, sore cuticles, and our children's eczema. It's also become an obligatory and much-loved Christmas present among friends and family due to its versatility. We vary the cream by using different infused oils (our favorite is marigold) and sometimes add essential oils (we like frankincense).

2½ oz (70 g) beeswax
1¼ cup (3 dl) herbal oil
A few drops essential oil (optional)

Method:
1. Strain the oil if you are using your own herbal oil.
2. Pour the oil in a heatproof bowl with the beeswax. Place the bowl in a pan of water and bring to the boil.
3. Melt the oil and beeswax while stirring.
4. Leave the mixture to cool down and add essential oil.
5. Pour and scrape into glass jars. Leave to cool down completely before adding the lids, screwing them on tightly.

Cold Process Soap

We love soaps and before we started making our own, we used to buy handmade soaps from local shops and those selling eco products. Soap bars last a lot longer than liquid soap and a rustic looking soap placed in the bathroom or kitchen makes a fine addition to your décor, looking almost sculpture-like.

Making your own soap can feel like dabbling with chemistry but it really isn't much harder than baking a cake. There are three main ingredients: fat, liquid, and lye. Then you can add color, essential oils, mud, herbs, flower petals, fruit, seeds, and almost anything else you fancy.

Fat

You can make soap from almost any type of fat, both liquid and solid and both animal or vegetable. We often use organic vegetable oils that are known to be good for skin such as coconut, rapeseed, olive, and almond oil. We rarely use more than 1lb (500 g) of fat at a time due to practicalities of working with such large amounts. The amount of fat in soap recipes is often given as a percentage or fraction.

Example:

30% olive oil
30% lanolin
40% coconut oil

If you plan to use several different fats, like the example given above, you need to start by calculating the different amount of each fat:

0.30 × 500 g = 150 g olive oil
0.30 × 500 g = 150 g lanolin
0.40 × 1.1 lb = 200 g coconut oil

Liquid:

For each 1 gram of fat use 0.35 gram liquid
500 g fat × 0.35 g liquid = 175g liquid

Lye

Sodium hydroxide, also known as lye or caustic soda, is used to harden soap (saponification). The amount of lye required is determined by the saponification value. To calculate the amount of lye needed for a certain type of fat, you multiply the amount of fat with the saponification value. As the value differs depending on which oil you use, you need to calculate the amount of lye for each oil and then add them together.

Example:

150 g olive oil × 0.135 = 20.25 g lye
150 g lanolin × 0.076 = 114 g lye
200 g coconut oil × 0.183 = 36.6 g lye

Total: 20.25 + 11.4 + 36.6 = 68.25 rounded down to 68 g of lye

If you want to make life easy for yourself there are lots of saponification value calculators online where all you need to do is add the amount of fat and it does the rest for you. We tend to use a manual saponification chart.

Fat	Saponification value
Olive oil	0.135
Sunflower oil	0.135
Rapeseed oil	0.124
Coconut oil	0.183
Lanolin	0.076
Beeswax	0.067
Almond oil	0.139
Shea butter	0.128
Jojoba oil	0.066
Macadamia oil	0.139
Borage oil	0.136
Castor oil	0.129
Cocoa butter	0.137

Cold Process Soap

Herbal Infusion with Marigold

MAKING COLD PROCESS SOAP

Lye is a strong alkali as well as caustic so use glasses and gloves for protection and stand under a kitchen fan while handling it. As a rule, always pour the lye into the liquid and fat, never the other way around. Have something acidic close at hand such as a lemon or vinegar to neutralize any lye that splashed on you. Use a glass jug or bowl if possible as aluminum turns black when exposed to an alkali.

Ingredients:

oil/fat	soap mold
jug	thermometer rubber gloves
lye	bowl
blender	protective glasses
liquid	

Method:
1. Weigh the fat in a heatproof bowl.
2. Melt the fat in a water bath on a low heat while stirring; set aside to cool.
3. Weigh the liquid in a glass jar; if you are using an herbal infusion make sure it has cooled down.
4. Pour the lye into the liquid a little at a time, stirring carefully. The lye turns the liquid murky and warm but not boiling. Keep stirring until dissolved and leave to cool.
5. When the fat and liquid have both cooled to around 104°F (40°C), pour the water over the fat.
6. Mix by hand or with a blender until it starts to thicken. Lift the spoon or the blender and dribble some soap mixture on the surface; if it leaves a trail without sinking the mixture is done.
7. Add color or essential oils (optional).
8. Pour the mixture into soap molds and leave for 24 hours.
9. Turn the soap onto a surface and cut into pieces.
10. Let it rest and mature for a month before using.

COLD PROCESS SOAP FROM MARIGOLD

7 oz (200 g) coconut oil
5.3 oz (150 g) shea butter
14 oz (400 g) olive oil
1.75 oz (50 g) castor oil
3.8 oz (109 g) lye
6.9 oz (196 g) marigold herbal infusion
2 tsp dried petals from marigold

Follow instructions on making cold process soap.

BATH SALT WITH FLOWERS

Bathing in salts is relaxing for sore muscles and it also softens your skin. We use Epsom salts as it only contains naturally occurring minerals, magnesium, and sulphate. We mix our bath salts with different flowers and herbs. Dried herbs and flowers lose a lot of their scent so you can add essential oils if you like.

1 cup (2½ dl) Epsom salts
¼ cup (½ dl) dried rose petals
¼ cup (½ dl) dried lavender
A few drops essential oils (optional)

Method:
1. Mix the ingredients and store in glass jars with lids.
2. When it's time for a bath, fill the tub with hot water and pour ½ cup (1 dl) of bath salts under running water.

YOGURT FACE MASK

Yogurt contains lactic acid, which is a type of alpha hydroxy acid, a group of acids commonly known as AHAs. AHAs dissolve dead skin cells and this gentle peeling helps create a natural glow. The combination of yogurt and honey makes the skin feel smooth and hydrated.

½ cup (1 dl) yogurt
2 tsp honey

Method:
1. Mix the honey into the yogurt, mixing thoroughly.
2. Smooth a thin layer over your face and neck, avoiding the eyes and mouth.
3. Leave the mask to dry for 25 minutes, then rinse with cold water.

HONEY HAND MASK

The hands are the one part of the body that probably get the worst deal from gardening and frequent handwashing. This mask both exfoliates as well as moisturizes. Make a dry mix that can be kept in a jar and whipped into a quick mask when needed.

Dry mixture
Just under 1 cup (2 dl) dried flower petals
¼ cup (½ dl) oats
¼ cup (½ dl) raw sugar

Mask
2 tbsp olive oil
1 tbsp honey
1 egg yolk
1 tbsp dry mix, see above

Method:
1. Mix the ingredients for the dry mixture and store in a jar.
2. When you are ready to use the mask, mix olive oil, honey, and the egg yolk thoroughly. Add the dry mixture, making a grainy batter.
3. Rub into the hands and wrists and leave for 15 minutes. Rinse with lukewarm water.

ROSEHIP SCRUB

This scrub is perfect to polish and exfoliate very dry skin on the feet, knees, or elbows.

½ cup (1 dl) raw sugar
½ cup (1 dl) rosehip powder
2 tsp honey
¼ cup (½ dl) herb oil such as rosehip oil
A few drops of essential oil (optional)

Method:
1. Mix all the ingredients.
2. Massage into damp skin with small circular motions and rinse in lukewarm water.

Bath Salts with Flowers

BATH & BEAUTY

Home Spa & Honey Hand Mask, page 118

Gardening

Everything starts with a seed, some water, and a handful of soil. From these three simple ingredients, life appears. The magic of cultivating plants is about creating the right conditions for new life to grow. To care for and harvest something that we have grown ourselves satisfies something deep inside us. Maybe it is because for thousands of years, until only a few generations ago, this was the main source of work for humans and what gave us meaning.

If you want to start your journey to be more self-sufficient, growing and cultivating is the first step and it's how we started off. We began with a few raised beds on the deck and ended up with a 10,000-square-foot kitchen garden.

Growing stuff for us isn't just about putting vegetables on the table, it goes deeper than that. Maybe we are trying to connect to an experience that has previously eluded us? We both grew up in homes where fruit and vegetables were purchased from a store and consideration was rarely given to how or where they grew. Some small amounts of crops were planted but it was mainly just a bit of fun.

We wanted our children to have a better understanding of how to grow food and how it all connects, to make a valuable contribution to the process and also appreciate the opportunity. Many children grow up these days not even knowing what real vegetables look like, or they think they're made in a factory.

We are more aware these days. Who doesn't want tasty vegetables rich in nutrients and free from toxins and that have been sustainably grown? It's not always easy to make sustainable choices though, and we were spending more and more time trying to make the right choices in the store instead of spending the time growing our own veggies.

We didn't believe we could be completely self-sufficient in providing vegetables for the family, but it was more about connecting to something more basic. Being able to touch the soil and feel something growing out of it, to understand the process and to avoid having to think about our choices all the time. It is also about being thankful and humble for the hard work that growing vegetables involves.

And maybe the most important thing is realizing that that carrot or potato covered in soil and lying in the palm of your hand is the best tasting vegetable in the world—because you grew it.

Everyone Can Grow

You can pretty much grow stuff anywhere you want, from a tiny gap in your window or a box on your balcony to a vast garden paradise. Gardening can always be adapted according to your own skills. For example, if you have never grown anything, the best choice is probably not to dig up a thousand square feet of land. Start small and allow your plants to grown in tandem with your knowledge, passions, and energy levels. Taking care of a large area of plants takes lots of planning as well as knowledge and hard work. It is also worth seeing what grows well where you live before you go too big.

As a first step you can start with a few pallet collars and vegetables that are easy to grow and give a good harvest such as carrots, squash, spinach, lettuce, onions and potatoes, and herbs such as basil, mint, chives, and thyme.

Once you feel comfortable with these you can grow vegetables that need a bit more preparation and care such as cabbage, artichokes, garlic, and leeks. You will be surprised how much a couple of pallet collars can hold.

It is better to hold back a bit in the beginning so you can reap the rewards rather than taking on too much and losing interest if it fails.

The basics of growing vegetables is relatively easy, but at the same time can be very hard. Even those who have been at it for years, even decades, can at times feel like a novice. A lot of the work is about creating a controlled environment that works for specific plants. At the same time being a gardener also means allowing yourself to be guided by Mother Nature and her cycles. One year in the garden is never the same as the next and plants that were successful one year can be afflicted by cold, snails, bugs, or drought the next, but this is all part of the challenges of being a gardener.

Finally, a word of warning: gardening won't just bring life to your balcony or garden, it will also change you. As a gardener you develop another level of consciousness and presence in relation to your environment. You`ll start to follow the changes in the weather and the movement of animals. You will want to understand the structure of the soil, the scents of the garden and all its colors. And you will start to love rain. You have been warned!

Climate

What sort of climate do you have where you live? If you have never grown plants before you have probably never thought about it. Knowing which gardening zone you live in is important knowledge for a gardener. Different plants prefer, or perform best in, different zones. You are not necessarily bound to just one zone because you live in a certain part of the country—even the local weather and the microclimate are important to consider.

The United States is divided into thirteen gardening zones (or hardiness zones) with zones three through ten being on the continental United States and the others in Alaska and Hawaii. For some plants gardening zones are important, such as some fruits and berries. When you buy fruit trees and berry bushes they usually state which gardening zone they recommend. If you order from another country, the zones are different and may not give an accurate picture of your climate.

Many vegetables, fruits, and berries can be grown anywhere in country, but may have different requirements. In higher zones it is more important to pre-sprout certain vegetables and give them a more sheltered and sunny position in the garden or grow them in a greenhouse. Some plants, on the other hand, prefer a colder climate and grow better in the north.

It's important to choose varieties that are hardy in your zone; certain plants have been cultivated for colder climates, so the variety you choose can make a difference. Read the descriptions or labels and do some research before ordering seeds or buying plants.

Overall, hardiness zones can give you an idea of what you can plant, but they can be misleading. The local climate plays a just as important, if not a more important, part and this is usually divided into three parts; macro, meso, and micro climate.

MACROCLIMATE: The climate in your region, often the same as your gardening zone.
MESOCLIMATE: The local climate in your garden.
MICROCLIMATE: The climate for individual plants in your garden.

The mesoclimate is affected by topological and geological conditions such as lakes, mountains, or forests in the area. Or if you live high up or in a valley or north- or south-facing.

During late winter and early spring, you can often clearly see the differences in the local climate. Where the snow melts first usually has a better climate for planting while areas where snow remains the longest are colder zones and are also more prone to frost. However, this doesn't paint the whole picture as the wind also plays an important role.

Something else that plays a part in climate is soil, which bridges the meso and micro climate; clay soil is colder than sand soil, for example.

Next is the microclimate, which focuses on a very small area in your garden such as a singular plant. Changes in the microclimate can be extreme and make a huge difference. Understanding which plants prefer a sunny south-facing wall and which thrive in light shade or even total shade is often more important than knowing the hardiness zone.

The most sensible thing to do is to plant most of your vegetables in a spot that avoids any extremes.

You can also influence and support favorable microclimates by planting trees and bushes or setting up boards to protect areas.

Seasonal Changes

No two years are the same and the changes in your garden are affected by sunlight, rain, and wind. A dry summer can destroy a crop one year, in the same way a long cold spell can. An early or late frost can decimate a kitchen garden, but usually it's a bit more subtle and most plants will have good and bad years.

The change in climate will also affect the surrounding nature, a mild winter can cause a snail invasion; a dry summer promotes flea beetles while another year favors cabbage butterflies. It is always worth cultivating a range of crops and not just one or two types.

Where Should I Plant?

Where to plant is of course dependent on what you have to work with, but here are a few things to think about:

PRE-SPROUTING Many crops need to start their life in a warm and protected spot without any risk of frost or pests. Make sure to plan for these spaces to avoid your entire home turning into a greenhouse. Maybe you can create a room specially for pre-sprouting plants or use a greenhouse with frost protection.

CLIMATE Plant your crops in a space with a good meso and micro climate and preferably sheltered from strong winds that can lower the temperature of the land and harm certain crops.

LOCATION Your vegetable plot is a space where you will spend a lot of time, both planting and harvesting. If you have to run to the other side of the garden just to cut some chives for a sandwich, it quickly gets tiresome, so the nearer the kitchen you can plant, the more of the green stuff you'll eat.

SIZE If you just plan for a few pallet collars you can keep them outside the kitchen window, but if you want to be able to expand your garden in the future you should find a good location from the start that will allow you to indulge your ambitions.

WATER Whether you use water from a tap, a well, or from the skies, it makes life much easier if the water is within easy reach.

PESTS A kitchen garden with lots of crisp vegetables is an enticing environment for all sorts of animals like deer, hares, voles, and a variety of birds. Being close to humans gives some protection but you need to consider how you will protect your crops from the start, such as fencing them off if need be.

TOOLS The larger the garden, the more tools you will collect. Make a proper space to store your spades, forks, and hoses near your garden and they will last longer.

SPACE A kitchen garden is mostly about the crops, but don't forget to enjoy it. Make a space that is inviting so you can sit and enjoy your hard work.

GARDENING

What Should I Grow?

For the hardened gardener, planning for the next season is one of the highlights of the year. It usually starts in the depth of winter when packets of seeds are brought out to be inventoried, tubers are inspected, and new seeds, plants, and trees are ordered or exchanged. The growing season begins in your head and a large part of it is the anticipation. Maybe you want to try some new varieties, or move existing plants to a better spot? Maybe the garden needs to be extended? Here is what you need to consider when you plan for your garden.

Grow Vegetables That You'll Eat

Most importantly, grow food that you and your family will eat. Focus on several varieties of one vegetable that you like; this doesn't just give you a better chance of a good harvest but also means a variety in taste as well the possibility of harvesting throughout the season. It's ok to have a breadth and variety of vegetables but choose a few basic items that you know will be eaten and grow more of these.

Be Realistic

We know it's not easy, but the thousands of varieties that seems so fun and easy at the start of the season can turn into a jungle by the end of it. Assess the time you have to spend gardening and try and adapt your ambitions accordingly.

Grow Vegetables You Can Store

It's lovely picking some fresh lettuce but remember to grow things you can store. If you don't have a large root cellar for potatoes or root vegetables, focus on winter tomatoes, onions, and winter squashes that can be stored at room temperature.

Don't Choose Hybrids

If it says F1 on the seed packet it means it's a hybrid, i.e., a cross. The plant is first generation meaning the next generation will look very different. If you plant F1 varieties it can be hard to gather the seeds if you want the same result the following year as you can't predict the result. It's best to use tried and tested varieties first if you know you want to save some of the seeds.

Pick Heritage Varieties

If you can, choose heritage (or heirloom) varieties which can also be bought from larger seed sellers these days. Many of the general hybrids today can't be used for future generations as they only last a generation or so. Heritage varieties are usually at least 100 years old and are hardy and well adapted. Modern varieties often give a better yield but in our experience the heritage varieties have a better flavor. Research has also found that modern cultivation of plants prioritize quantity over quality meaning less nutritious vegetables, and surely you don't want to grow the same flavorless carrots or tomatoes that you can buy in the store!

Grow Throughout the Season

Plan to grow your vegetables so that they ripen throughout the season and not all at once in August. Pick both early and late varieties of carrots and potatoes and sow lettuce and peas in batches. Harvest some of the onions to use fresh in the summer but leave the rest to keep growing so that you always have something to put on your plate.

Experiment

One of the great advantages of growing your own food is variety; you can grow things that can rarely, if ever, be bought in a store. Each season try and introduce something new. Keep your favorites, but add something fresh and exciting each year.

Plan Ahead

Don't just plan for the coming season but use some time and space for more long-term projects that may not give you harvest now but in the years to come. Try perennials such as asparagus, sea kale, and tree onion.

GARDENING

Techniques

No-Dig

We're huge fans of the no-dig method, which is basically what it sounds like—you avoid digging, saving both time and your back. Digging disturbs the micro life and releases carbon dioxide, which are two things you definitely want to avoid. Long-term it is also harder to dig out unwanted plants than to outgrow or smoother them.

There are only two reasons to ever dig up the soil: if you want to create tiers or dig up a stone to use in the garden.

Mulching

Mulching is a method of enhancing the soil where you try to avoid any bare ground by covering it with organic matter. Mulching can be considered a type of direct composting on your plants where the mulch gradually decomposes and contributes to a more loamy and nutrient-rich soil. In addition, it stops water from evaporating and makes the soil better at retaining water. The layer is around 2–12 inches (5–30 cm) thick depending on how compact that mulch is. Usually straw, bark, grass cuttings, and leaves are used as well as leftovers from harvests such as greens, stems, leaves, and autumn leaves, newspaper, wood shavings, and seaweed.

The greener and richer in nitrogen the mulch, the more nutrients you are adding. During the fall it is worth reducing the amount of green mulch and instead using more brown matter, which is rich in carbon.

Lasagna Gardening

We often create raised lasagna garden beds, so called because carbon-rich (brown) and nitrogen-rich (green) organic matter is layered like a lasagna. The method is similar to direct composting that can be made on top of the ground.

Always begin by taking inventory of what materials you have to make a compost bed and use what you have rather than following exact instructions. If you don't have old cardboard for the base, then use newspapers or old clothes in natural fabrics. If you don't have horse manure, use nettle or gold water, and if you don't have any greenery or grass cuttings, use old vegetables and flower bunches. As long as you use organic material, nature will turn it into soil, and the more materials you have to add, the faster you can make your compost bed.

The balance between nitrogen and carbon and between damp and dry will determine the speed of the process. Just like in hot composting, you need around two-thirds brown and a third green. Coarser material that takes longer to break down should be at the bottom and lighter matter should be placed higher up. To plant in the compost beds, you can make a small pit with soil for the plants or place a layer of soil on top. In this way you can plant straight into the compost bed. Create your lasagna garden in the fall and leave it to decompose until the spring.

Lasagna garden basics

LAYER 7	Finish off with compost and straw. Continue to layer green and brown until you reach the top.
LAYER 6—BROWN	Fall leaves
LAYER 5—GREEN	Grass clippings
LAYER 4—BROWN	Twigs or wood chippings
LAYER 3—GREEN	Coarser fresh garden waste and garden compost
LAYER 2—BROWN	All the greenery will now be getting nutrients and start to grow but as you don't want this to happen in the bed, cover everything with carboard placed in a thick layer around the bed. With no light and no photosynthesis, the plants can't process the nutrients and will die.
LAYER 1—GREEN	Place a layer of composted horse manure or whatever you have at hand; it could be chicken manure, nettle water, urine, or even dog poo.

Hügelkultur

If you have access to some large logs, you can build hügel beds, and if you have access to really old, rotten logs you also have a gold mine of biodiversity to plant in. Hügelkultur means "mountain culture" or "raised culture" in German and is a way to make a compost bed with mainly larger and coarser material from wood such as logs, branches, and twigs. Using coarse materials slows down the decomposing process and nutrients are released into your plants for a longer time. At the base, place large logs, then branches, twigs, shavings, garden compost, and leaves. Finally, cover the whole bed with a thin layer of soil to create a mound. To stop the bed from moving in heavy rain, you can also make a frame from logs.

The advantage of using logs in this way is that you make good use of decaying trees. Rotten trees, so-called dead wood, are extremely rich in a variety of life. Insects, fungi, moss, and larva all contribute to the decomposition of the wood and make it easier for the microorganisms to do their job. The process uses nitrogen, so you need to add nitrogen by adding mulch such as grass cuttings, and you should also water with nettle water during growing season.

The logs store lots of moisture that does not evaporate due to being covered, meaning hügel beds are a great solution for a very dry spot in your garden. Traditionally hügel beds are 6½ feet long, 3¼ feet wide, and 3¼ feet high ($2 \times 1 \times 1$ meters). You can obviously make it smaller if you want.

Planting in a Bucket or Pot

Most things can be planted in a bucket or a pot. You will need to be aware of the size of the vessel to make sure that the crops have enough space to grow and develop. You can make a more effective use of space by growing some things upwards, such as beans, tomatoes, and cucumbers, and you can actually become quite self-sufficient by just growing things in pots on your balcony or window sill. Some plants, such as potatoes, are better grown separately to avoid disease that is spread through the ground.

Pallet Collars

Using pallet collars is popular in cities but also in more suburban gardens. The collar is flexible and simple in its design, and you can add them together, both lengthways and on top of each other. You can fill your pallet collars in many different ways and it is also easy to fill them with leaves in the fall. Come spring, once the microorganisms have done their job, you have a lovely loam soil to plant in. Mulching also works well in pallet collars, and adding a slug barrier is a good idea. You can buy ready-made ones that fit pallet collars but you can also make your own from chicken wire or bug screens for windows, and staple them onto the pallet.

Hügel bed basics

10. Straw
9. Soil
8. Compost
7. Fall leaves
6. Wood chips
5. Grass cuttings
4. Twigs
3. Garden compost
2. Branches
1. Logs

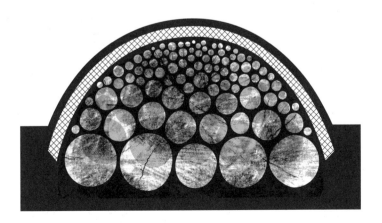

Hügel Bed

GARDENING

Crop Rotation

Something you should plan for from the start is crop rotation as planting the same crops year after year in the same soil is not good for many reasons and you need to let the crops rotate.

The two most important reasons are to retain a nutrient-rich soil and to avoid disease. Many plants can be afflicted by earth bound disease—for example, cabbage can be affected by clubroot while potato can be affected by brown rot and blight. By rotating the crops, you can prevent these diseases from taking hold in the soil. Some pests also prefer certain plants to spend the winter in, so crop rotation can also help prevent pests.

Another just as important reason to rotate your crops is that you automatically make the soil better as different crops absorb different types of nutrients. If you grow the same crops in the same spot you risk draining the soil, making it impoverished, and some minerals and nutrients will become completely depleted.

By adding fertilizer, mulching and intercropping different plants you reduce these problems, but if you rotate the crops the plants can actually help each other instead. Crops should rotate in cycles of four or more years, so if you have four plant containers or raised beds, you let the crops rotate between these over four years.

An Example of a Four-Year Rotation:

YEAR 1. LEGUMES Peas and beans are perfect as a crop starter, not just because they grow fast and give a good harvest but also because they enrich the soil by retaining nitrogen. Leave the plant parts in the soil for the following season to get extra green fertilizer.

YEAR 2. HEAVY FEEDING PLANTS The following year you can plant crops in the same spot that require a lot of nitrogen such as cabbage, leeks, pumpkins, and squash.

YEAR 3. MEDIUM FEEDING PLANTS The third year you can plant crops that have a medium requirement of nutrients in the same spot, such as beetroot, radish, onion, and marigold.

YEAR 4. NUTRIENT DEPLETED SOIL The fourth year you can plant crops that don't need many nutrients. Two prime examples that yield a good harvest in nutrient-poor soil are Jerusalem artichoke and potatoes. The following year you can start a new cycle in the same place and plant legumes that add nitrogen again.

Indicator Plants

A thriving plant hasn't just ended up in its location by chance but grows there because that place fulfills that plant's individual needs. When we stop fighting against different types of greenery and instead try to understand what nature is telling us, a whole new world of knowledge opens up to us. A plant's choice of space can tell us something about the conditions of that location, hence the name "indicator plants." The thistle, for example, with its long taproots, chooses a soil that is dry and compact, so if lots of thistles are growing in one spot, it is an indicator that the soil needs loosening and cultivating for you to grow anything in it. The opposite is nettles, which choose to grow in nitrogen-rich soil, meaning that this soil is rich in nutrients and good to plant in. Nettles are amazing in their skill to absorb and retain nitrogen in their leaves, which is why we make nettle water to fertilize with.

Companion Planting

Companion planting is an old and very beneficial farming practice; letting different types of crops grow in the same space is an effective use of space. Our goal is to try to grow things at different levels both above and below ground. The "three sisters" method is where you plant some at a low level, like pumpkin or lettuce, with something that climbs, such as beans or cucumbers, with something tall and stable, such as sunflowers or corn. Even root systems can be divided into vertical and horizontal roots.

Grow crops throughout the season. We grow low, quick-growing plants at the start of the season so that they quickly cover the ground and stop unwanted seeds from taking hold before the slower plants get going. We often sow marigold, which flowers early on, around larger vegetables like squash and cabbage.

Companion planting means you can avoid the vulnerability of monocultures. If you get disease or pests on a specific plant, you won't lose everything in one go. In addition, some pests prefer a specific scent and get confused if you plant mint next to your cabbage or lemon balm next to the roses. It is always good to check which family a plant belongs to so you can rotate the families when you change crops to avoid soil-bound diseases.

Some plants also act to deter pests from other plants. A common example is to plant carrots with plants that deter the carrot fly, such as onions. African marigold combats roundworms and marigold deters the larva of the great white. Borage is good for all sorts of pests.

Some flowers can also be used to attract pests so that the vegetables growing behind them escape any greater damage. Nasturtium attracts aphids, marigold attracts hoverflies whose larva eat the aphids, and aromatic flowers attract the Spanish slug.

There are even more complex advantages when it comes to the interplay between the plants. Planting crops that retain nitrogen with leafy vegetables that need a lot of nitrogen is a classic example. Or planting something with taproots which will loosen the soil and draw oxygen and water into the soil can help plants with weaker root systems.

Annuals, Biennials & Perennials

Plants with different life cycles can be divided into three types: yearly plants (annuals), two-year plants (biennials), and multi-year plants (perennials). If you plan to start growing things it is important to learn these categories as it's a deciding factor in where you place your plants and plan crop rotation within your garden.

A yearly plant means it grows, blooms, and sets seeds all in the same year, such as herbs, watercress, and some cabbages. Biennials have a two-year cycle and they don't bloom or set seeds until the second year. These days we grow many biennials as if they are annuals, even though they have several years in them. Rutabaga, parsnips, and carrots are all biennials that gather energy for the following year through the nutrient-rich roots that we harvest. Even many cabbages are biennials although we tend to harvest these before they bloom.

Perennials are plants that live for more than two years and grow and bloom year after year. Asparagus, artichoke (in warmer areas), chives, rhubarb, and ramson are all perennials.

When you plan your garden and to rotate your crops, you need to separate the annuals and perennials; this is also the case if you want to collect seeds. You can also move biennials that you want to collect seeds from to an isolated spot at the end of the season.

Companion Planting

GARDENING

The Modern Homesteader's Favorites

How you plan your garden is really up to you; plant what you will enjoy growing and eating. Some crops don't give huge harvests depending on where you live but can still be exciting to grow, such as melons. Some crops require lots of work and care and others barely any. It's never been easier to grow exciting crops of root vegetables, legumes, herbs, and other plants—seed companies, garden societies, and even individual sellers offer thousands of different varieties.

If your main aim is to eat more homegrown produce, there are certain crops that both give a good harvest and are easy to grow. Here are some of our favorites.

Root Vegetables

When other crops fail us in our kitchen garden, the root vegetable is what we turn to. Most root vegetables are easy to grow and can be stored and thus are the backbone of our garden; they are always there but don't cause any fuss. Beetroots and carrots are obvious choices—both can be sown straight into the ground and thrive in a sunny, open spot with loose, loam soil. You can grow them in a pallet collar or straight into the ground but you can't move them once they're planted.

Carrots can be sown once the soil has thawed in early spring while beetroot should be sown slightly later in May to prevent them from blooming.

Both carrots and beetroot need potassium which can be added to the soil by fertilizing with seaweed or wood ash fertilizer.

It's important to remove weeds before the growing season starts so that the seeds will grow well. You can also protect them with a fiberglass blanket as deer love beet greens and carrots are often afflicted by the carrot fly. With carrots you should grow both summer and fall varieties and store them.

Storing beetroot and carrots depends on what space you have. The best way is in a root cellar or similar. We've had the best success with storing root vegetables in buckets of sand. Another alternative is to store them underground, but the easiest is just to leave them in the garden until you need them, unless they're likely to get buried in snow. Beetroot tends to fare better than carrots. Choose varieties that can be stored and cope with sub-freezing temperatures.

Parsnips are great for storage and can be left in the vegetable patch all winter to be harvested early spring when the larder is empty. In other words, the parsnip is the season's first primeur. The parsnip needs lots of fertilizer and needs some tending to in its early stages through weeding and watering, but once it has developed a little bump it can mainly be ignored. The parsnip can be sown straight into cold soil at the same time as the previous year's harvest is collected.

Potatoes

Potatoes are magic; pop a tuber into a nutrient poor piece of land and a few months later you have twenty tubers. They barely need any tending to and can be stored for a whole year, so it is hardly surprising that potatoes are often cited as the cause of the huge growth in population in the 1800s. From a small vegetable patch you can pretty much become self-sufficient on potatoes. You can also grow potatoes in a box or bucket.

You should grow potato varieties that mature at different times as well such as floury types for mashed and purees, and firm types for boiling and frying.

SOIL & CLIMATE Potatoes like most types of soil but grow best in airy, porous, sandy soil. You can also grow potatoes in straw. From our own experience of this, the advantage is a clean and simple harvest but the disadvantage is that the Spanish slug loves the moist straw bed and will happily munch its way through the potatoes. Potatoes are sensitive to frost and prefer a sunny, warm spot.

PLANTING Plant out when the soil is around 46°F (8°C). If you are planting straight into the ground, place them with a distance of around 10 inches (25 cm) between them and at a depth of 2–4 inches (5–10 cm). The space between the rows should be around 1½ feet (50 cm).

If you are planting in a bucket, you can fit 2–3 potatoes in a 5-gallon (20 l) bucket. In a pallet collar you can fit around 8 potatoes.

CARE Potatoes tend to look after themselves but a few times during the season you need to prune the potatoes in the ground or they will be green when they appear above the soil. Pruning also gives the potatoes more soil

Carrots

GARDENING

Jerusalem Artichoke

GARDENING

to grow in as you pour soil around the stem so that all the potatoes are covered.

Once planted, you don't usually need to water the potatoes unless it is very dry.

HARVEST You can harvest throughout the season without pulling up the whole plant—just push your hands into the soil along the stem and search for the tubers, carefully turning them loose. Don't forget to save seed potatoes for next season. Sometimes you will get lots of "green" potatoes, which have been exposed to sunlight and developed chlorophyll. Green potatoes are toxic but they can be used as seed potatoes.

STORING & PREPPING Early varieties: An early harvest to give you some sweet new potatoes in time for midsummer is a must. We usually plant fewer of these. A good early season potato is Mariana.

By pre-sprouting early season potatoes they will mature faster. Place the potatoes in an egg carton, on a tray, or in a box with sand. Pre-sprout in a light and warm environment; it takes around one month for them to wake up properly. You can also speed things up by growing the potatoes in a bucket.

Mid-season varieties: We usually grow more of the summer potatoes as these are the ones we will be eating during the summer and into early fall. Our favorite, which can also be stored, is the amandine potato. Summer potatoes can also be pre sprouted, just like the early varieties.

Late varieties: A good potato that can be stored is the one we grow the most of and this potato will last until next year. Our personal favorite is the tasty almond potato. Once harvested, they need to be cured to give them a tough skin. Store in room temperature in a dark spot for around 10 days without being exposed to sunlight. Once finished, they should be stored in a space that is between 40–45ºF (4–7ºC) with a fairly high level of humidity. The best option is a root cellar but a cold garage with a frost protector works as well. If you can't store the potato, you can leave it in the soil or create an underground storage in the ground and cover it with organic matter.

DISEASE & PESTS Potato is often afflicted by potato blight (Phytophthora infestans), which appears as dry, brown patches on the leaves. It can also attack the tubers and other plants, such as tomatoes. As soon as it appears on the leaves you need to remove and burn them. Don't grow potatoes and tomatoes in the same soil the following seasons. Unfortunately, the Spanish slug also loves potatoes, especially the blue, pink, and black varieties we've noticed.

Jerusalem Artichoke

Just like potatoes, corn, and tomatoes, Jerusalem artichoke is a treasure that was cultivated by the Native Americans.

SOIL & CLIMATE Just like the potato, most soils are fine for Jerusalem artichokes, but they prefer a sandy, loam soil.

PLANTING Plant them 4 inches (10cm) deep with 20–27 inches (50–70cm) between the plants and rows. Jerusalem artichoke take up space and some grow over 10 feet tall.

CARE it's almost impossible to fail with the Jerusalem artichoke. It gives a good harvest even in the most barren or grassy soils and barely needs to be watered or fertilized. It is also a hardy plant that can stay in the soil all winter and still be harvested the following spring.

The Jerusalem artichoke is almost too easy to grow and can become a bit like a weed that is hard to get rid of. All it takes it forgetting a small bit of root for it to take hold and nothing will stand in its way. We once planted Jerusalem artichoke in bedding invaded by the feared ground elder and the ground elder lost, so avoid planting it near other crops and instead place it in your worst bit of land or in a separate box or even an old compost heap.

HARVEST It's best to harvest as you need it; cut the stem a bit above the ground and pull up the whole root system. You can use your hand or a digging fork to get them all.

STORING & PREPPING Jerusalem artichokes are harder to store than potatoes and can shrivel up if it's too dry. You can store them in buckets of damp soil in cold storage or an open bag in the fridge.

DISEASE & PESTS They say voles like Jerusalem artichokes but we haven't noticed this.

Legumes

Some of the best things you can grow are legumes and peas due to their high nutrition content. They are not only full of vitamins and minerals but also a good source of protein, which means they are a good alternative to meat, eggs, and dairy products (or indeed can complement them). They also contain resistant starch, or prebiotics, which feeds your gut flora's healthy bacteria.

This, together with the fact that they grow fast, give a good harvest in a small space, and add nitrogen to the soil explains why legumes should have a place of honor in every kitchen garden.

Pea plants in the Fabaceae family have a great advantage as they live symbiotically with bacteria that sit on the roots of the plants. The bacteria catch and store nitrogen from the air instead of the soil, which a lot of other plants are dependent on. The nitrogen is absorbed by the plant and the bacteria get their necessary carbohydrates in exchange. This means that plants in the Fabaceae family often prosper in spots where other plants can't grow. We often witness this growing power in the summer along our roads, together with the wild lupine which belongs to the same family, which many have a love-hate relationship with.

In our garden, this special skill creates magic. Before the interplay with the bacteria gets going, you can give the legumes some help with a bit of fertilizer.

We grow as many beans as we can of different varieties and one advantage is that they grow really well alongside other vegetables.

All legumes contain different levels of lectin, a natural toxin (a group protein) that the plants produce to keep insects away. By parboiling and cooking dried and fresh legumes, the lectins are broken down.

Broad Beans

The broad bean is loved the world over and plays a part in many classic dishes from Chinese bean paste to Egyptian falafel. It is often a companion plant to potatoes and peas.

SOIL & CLIMATE Likes most soils but prefers a nutrient-rich loam soil.

SOWING In contrast to many other beans, the broad bean is not sensitive to cold soil so can be sown or potted out as soon as the frost has passed. Soak the beans for 24 hours before planting them to wake them up and plant at around 2 inches (5 cm) depth with a distance of 6 inches (15 cm) between the plants.

CARE Most broad beans don't grow very tall, around 3 feet (1 meter), and don't need support, or just a very simple one. Give them some fertilizer at the start of the season. They can cope with a few degrees below freezing.

Broad beans don't like to get too dry and need regular watering.

HARVEST In contrast to, for example, green beans, you don't eat the pods but just the large beans. Harvest them when they feel full and firm when you squeeze the pod. Harvest them as they ripen, and once a plant is harvested it can but trimmed to give a second harvest during the summer.

STORING & PREPPING You can freeze the beans or dry them to eat later. If you plan to dry them, leave the pods on the plant to shrivel and turn black.

DISEASE & PESTS Broad beans are often afflicted by aphids. You can fight these by spraying the plants with water from a hose or spraying soapy water on them. Trimming the plant after the beans have grown also seems to work as the aphids tend to sit at the top of the plant.

Green Beans

One of the summer's best early crops are the wax, dwarf, and green beans. If you haven't grown beans before you are probably still familiar with haricot verts, which are green beans that are harvested early on.

SOIL & CLIMATE They prefer a sunny and slightly protected spot to grow. Plant them in a loam soil. They do not need a lot of fertilizer.

SOWING Sow when the soil temperature has reached 54°F (12°C). They are sensitive to cold soil and run the risk of rotting if it is too cold when they are planted. You can also pre-sprout for an earlier harvest but don't do it too early if you don't want to create a jungle in your windowsill or greenhouse.

Legumes

GARDENING

GARDENING

CARE The main thing is that they have something to climb on as green beans turn away from the sun and upwards and some can reach over 10 feet tall. The easiest method is to leave them to climb up a vertical stake, but towers and other frames from longer sticks or metal frames work well too. Choose the height at the start depending on the variety as it can be hard to change afterwards.

HARVEST Just like with haricots vert, most common beans can be eaten whole if not harvested too late. Different varieties have different pods. Make sure you pick the beans regularly as it will stimulate the growth of more beans.

STORING & PREPPING Parboil common beans in lightly salted water. Freeze any extras for the winter.

DISEASE & PESTS Common beans are hardy and are rarely affected by disease or pests; however, they are very popular among deer.

Peas

A summer salad is not complete without some sweet sugar snaps. Most of us are familiar with the common green pea, or garden peas, but there is a whole range of other varieties of peas that you can grow from sugar snaps, to snow peas, to garden peas, to field peas. Field peas were a common crop in the old days and there are several exciting heritage varieties such as blue pea and grey pea.

SOIL & CLIMATE Just like beans, peas want a lot of soil and prefer loose, loam soil.

SOWING Sow straight into the soil when the temperature is around 50°F (10°C). Can also be pre-sprouted between April and May. You can soak them 24 hours before sowing.

CARE Most peas grow tall and need support. Peas, like all legumes, don't need fertilizer as they take the nitrogen they need straight from the air. Water regularly during the whole season. The peas' leaves turn yellow and the whole plant shrivels if it is too dry.

HARVEST A large advantage of peas is that they grow fast, from seed to harvest only takes a few weeks, which also means you can sow new peas during the season at the same pace that you harvest.

STORING & PREPPING Peas can usually be eaten raw. Snow peas and sugar snaps are eaten with the pod while field peas are grown to be taken out of the pod, dried, and stored.

DISEASE & PESTS Peas aren't just popular among humans but also birds. They love poking up newly sown peas, so cover the seedlings with net or a garden fabric.

Cabbage

No garden is complete without a range of cabbage. It is not only tasty and healthy, it is also an attractive plant to keep in your garden. The cabbage family has a long list of varieties such as curly kale, cavolo nero, savoy, white cabbage, and broccoli. In recent years we've introduced a few new exciting Asian varieties such as mizuna, pak choi, and tatsoi.

SOIL & CLIMATE Cabbage doesn't like heat and grows best during spring and fall. Cabbage tends to need a lot of nutrients and needs a well-fertilized soil as well as regular fertilizing during the season. Cabbage needs a lot of nitrogen so it can be worth planting it somewhere you have previously planted legumes. You may also need to fertilize with nitrogen, such as nettle water. It is a crop that needs to be rotated to avoid soil-bound diseases such as clubroot taking hold.

SOWING Some cabbage varieties can be planted straight into the soil once it has warmed up, such as curly kale and cavolo nero. Even rutabaga and turnips can be planted straight in the soil as well as most Asian varieties. However, you usually get an earlier and better harvest is you pre-sprout varieties like kale, cavolo nero, and white and savoy cabbage, and it also means you protect the cabbage during peak summer when it is particularly vulnerable.

Pre-sprout the cabbage in a container about 4–6 weeks before planting out. Repot at least once and harden off the plants before planting out by gradually getting them used to the outdoors.

GARDENING

CARE Protect with a cabbage netting that allows water and light through. Cabbage is vulnerable to attack and the best way to avoid it being eaten up is to protect it. Two of the worst culprits that can eat all your seeds are snails and the larva of the large white. You can find out more about how to fight these under the heading "Disease & Pests."

MAINTENANCE Fertilize during the season with nettle water and make sure the plants don't dry out. Water regularly during the summer—the more you water, the lusher the cabbage. An even moisture is good and you can achieve this by mulching, covering the soil with grass cuttings, weeds, and silage.

HARVEST Cabbage is an easy vegetable to grow and harvest and gives food for a long time, from summer to winter. Most varieties are harvested during the fall when the head has rooted and it feels firm. Cut or break the head from the plant. White and red cabbage can be left for longer.

Collards can be harvested during the whole season and it's often the last vegetable left standing once winter arrives. Don't forget to protect your winter crops against hungry deer and hares.

STORING & PREPPING What makes cabbage so popular is the fact that it is so healthy. It's bursting with chlorophyll, and it's hardy. Cabbage is something you can basically grow all year round and it remains, green and proud, in your garden long after most other vegetables have died. The cabbage head can be stored for several months in a root cellar or any other cool space.

DISEASE & PESTS Just like a child, cabbage is well loved but can be difficult to care for. Few crops attract as many unwanted guests as the shimmery green cabbage, and it has almost an unnatural power over deer, hares, birds, larva, flea beetles, and snails. Despite all these problems, we grow cabbage year after year and maybe this should be seen as a sign that cabbage really is irresistible to everyone, even us.

Summer & Winter Squash

What happened! It seems only just now there were a few weak seedlings and suddenly its transformed into a magical forest that seems to weave its way along the ground. Growing squash is to see the real power of nature, so be prepared for what's to come. Summer squash and zucchini is harvested and eaten throughout the whole summer. Winter squashes and pumpkins can be stored for up to a year.

SOIL & CLIMATE Squash wants a nutrient-rich and damp soil, so you can mulch with grass cuttings. You can cover the ground as they start to mature to protect them or they can be grown in a compost heap or a hügel bed, which is perfect for this nutrient-hungry plant.

SOWING Pre-sprout in pots around a month before you plant them out but not earlier as there is a risk that they may grow too fast. Plant them out when the risk of frost has passed and harden them off. You can also protect them with garden fabric.

Winter squash is just as it is called, a squash with a tough exterior that ripens late in the season and can be stored. Both summer and winter squash are sensitive to frost and should be planted out when the risk of frost has passed.

CARE Growing fruit takes a lot of energy for squash and the plants need a lot of nitrogen-rich fertilizer throughout the season. Unimpeded, a summer or winter squash can grow out of control and take over plants in the vicinity. Control it by keeping the number of fruits per plant to two to three, which also speeds up the ripening process. They are great for covering the ground, but you can also tie them against trellises or allow the pumpkin to wrap itself around a tree.

Creating the large fruits uses up a lot of liquid, so water them regularly and keep the soil moist. Hügel beds can hold a lot of moisture, which makes them a good way to grow squash.

HARVEST The flowers can be harvested in the summer and are great to fry, but harvest them in the afternoon so the flower has had time to pollinate. Summer squash

and zucchini can be eaten newly harvested and some varieties can be stored for several months. Winter squash and pumpkins should be stored and left to ripen from late summer into fall, although harvest it before the frost. Make sure the fruits don't lie directly on wet soil as it can cause them to rot. Place straw or other dry materials underneath. A sign that the fruit has ripened is when the shaft has dried. You can tap the pumpkin and if it sounds hollow it's ready to harvest. The fruit should be cut off with a little bit of the stem. Leave it to harden for a week or two in a sunny, dry spot such as a sunny window. Turn the fruit now and again so the whole fruit is exposed to sun. During this process the peel hardens and the fruit sweetens up. It also gives it a longer shelf life. After this the fruits can be stored indoors for 3–6 months, sometimes more.

STORING & PREPPING Winter squash and pumpkins are a good choice for the modern homesteader as not only do they store well but in contrast to many other vegetables, they taste better once stored. Another advantage is that they can be stored in room temperature and therefore don't need a cold, damp storage room. With many different varieties, they are decorative and can be kept on shelves, large bowls, and even the floor. We store most of ours in the root cellar, but keep some in the kitchen and dining room, and as we eat them we bring more inside.

DISEASE & PESTS The Spanish slugs love a newly planted squash seedling. Established squash plants, however, have such growing power that even a whole army of slugs wouldn't have time to eat them up. In addition, the adult plants have rough, almost thorny, leaves and stems, that the slugs dislike, so protect the plants when they are small and fragile.

Another problem that can occur is that the fruit rots for various reasons. Make sure they grow in a dry place and remove the flower from the top of the plant once it wilts.

Corn

Corn is beautiful, both as a plant where it stands majestically in the garden with its silvery whisps and once harvested, when the cobbs can be hung to dry in the kitchen. The difference in taste between bought and homegrown corn is indescribable. Both the flavor and sweetness is completely different from storebought corn. We also grow flint corn which, while it only makes enough flour for a few tacos, are so beautiful that we don't want to be without them. Last, but not least, we grow corn for popcorn. This is more for the children's sake, so they understand and respect what goes into their bag of popcorn.

SOIL & CLIMATE Corn prefers a nutrient-rich loam soil. They like a lot of water and nitrogen, so they grow well in a hügel bed and mulched with fresh green matter, or companion planted with legumes that bind nitrogen. Legumes that grow upwards can also support the corn plants.

SEEDS & PLANTING Corn should be pre-sprouted indoors in May under plant lights or in a sunny window. Plant in soilblockers, pots, or troughs 2 inches (5 cm) apart and at ⅓ inch (1 cm) depth. Cover the pot in plastic and keep the soil moist but not wet. Repot when they are around 4–6 inches (10–15 cm) tall. Harden off the plants and plant them out when the soil temperature is around 59°F (15°C) and the risk of frost is over.

CARE Corn needs a lot of nutrients. Use fertilizer water 1–2 times a week during the season. Remove any side shoots at the bottom of the stem as they steal energy from the plant and will not develop any cobs. The male flower is the whisp that is at the top of the plant. The female flower, which will turn into the cob, sits further down against the stem and consists of a bunch of silky threads. Each thread on the female flower will develop into a corn cob once it's pollinated, which the plant might need some help with. Some years we've tapped and shaken the plants and hoped that the pollen flying around will attach to the threads. The result of this is cobs with gaps between the corn. We have a better

method now whereby we simply cut off the male flower and smack it against the female flower.

HARVEST When the silky threads at the top of the cob have wilted, it is time to harvest. They should feel firm to the touch and the corncobs should be obvious. If you open the husk and look inside, the corn cobs should have some color, and if you stick a pin in a kernel, a milky white liquid appears.

STORING & PREPPING Sweetcorn tastes best when it is fresh. You can boil it in salted water and chuck it on the grill. The corn kernels can also be removed and frozen. Corn for popcorn and flint corn should be dried before they are used. Hang them up at room temperature.

DISEASE & PESTS Corn can be afflicted by aphids in the fall and small birds also love to eat corn once it is ready to harvest, so it's important to get there first!

Corn

GARDENING

Tomatoes

In our family the love of tomatoes knows no bounds and we grow them in all sorts of colors, flavors, and sizes and it is impossible for us to pick a favorite.

SOIL & CLIMATE Tomatoes need a light, nutrient-rich soil with enough moisture. They need at least 3 months of sun and heat in order to ripen outdoors. In our northern climate the hardy varieties can be grown directly in the ground in a warm place, but first they need to be pre-sprouted indoors so they can get a head start once they are planted out in the beginning of June. Be careful not to move the plants outdoors if the night temperature is too low as tomatoes don't like temperature under 46ºF (8ºC). During cold summers you may need to harvest them despite being green in September if they don't have enough time to ripen before it gets cold again. In a greenhouse, tomatoes have no problems ripening in time.

SOWING Sow the seeds indoors in a mini greenhouse or under see-through plastic with airholes at the end of February/beginning of March if you have a short growing season. Do a little research to see what timing makes sense for your hardiness zone. Cover with a thin layer of soil and place under a lamp to avoid gangly plants.

Replant them once they grow to 2–4 inches (5–10 cm). Tomatoes need a distance of 12–22 inches (35–55 cm) between the plants and 20–28 inches (50–70 cm) between the rows. Fill with soil just below the first set of leaves. If they start to grow sideways you can push them down deeper into the soil; you want to end up with a stable and strong plant.

CARE Tomatoes do need a lot of tending to, but you get just as much back. If you want, you can prune any really tall plants once, just above the second set of leaves, so that the plant will divide into two. In this way you get three times the harvest as the newly cut shoot generates a new plant. Place the shoot straight into a pot with damp seedling starter, but remember you will now have three times as many plants to tie up and take care of.

Any tall plants need to be tied up. We use tomato hooks in metal that keep year after year. Tall plants usually need their side shoots removed while bushy tomatoes

don't. Removing the side shoots means pinching off the small shoots that appear between the main stem and leaf branch. In this way the plant's energy is diverted into the fruit rather than growing new branches.

If you grow tomatoes in a greenhouse or indoors by a sunny window, you first need to pollinate your plants. The best way to do this is with a brush, but we often just lightly shake the flowering branches now and again.

Water your plants with fertilizer regularly every second week until the plants bear fruit. Tomatoes need to be watered evenly or they risk cracking.

HARVEST Cut your tomatoes off to avoid breaking any branches. Harvest beefsteak tomatoes just as they change color and leave them to ripen in a bowl indoors to reduce the risk of cracked fruit. Smaller tomatoes and cherry tomatoes are best harvested once they have reached their final size and color. Harvest winter tomatoes on the vine as late as possible to make them last longer. These can be hung up inside and last all winter.

STORING & PREPPING Our top five ways to store and prep tomatoes are:

1. Tomato sauce
2. Tomato ketchup
3. Sundried tomatoes
4. Sweet and sour sauce
5. Freezing them whole

DISEASE & PESTS Tomatoes can be afflicted by several types of fungi such as mildew or potato blight, grey or leaf mold, which appears as patches on the leaves or fruit. If they are growing in a greenhouse there is also a risk of spider mites.

Tomatoes

GARDENING

TOMATO SAUCE AROUND 2 PINTS (1 L)

Once winter is over we have a whole freezer full of tomato sauce and it's one of the backbones of our kitchen. We change the seasoning depending on what we plan to use it in such as a stew, pizza, or pasta, or even a strong shakshuka.

10–15 large tomatoes (adjust the amount depending on the variety you have at hand and the size of your baking tray)
3 shallots or 1 large yellow onion
2 cloves garlic
1 bunch fresh herbs (basil, oregano, thyme, parsley) (optional) or 2 tbsp herb salt
1 pinch chilli salt, depending on the strength
Olive oil
Salt and freshly ground black pepper
1 tbsp honey
2 tbsp apple cider vinegar

Heat a convection oven to 400°F (200°C).

Halve the tomatoes and place them on a baking tray cutside up so they fill the whole tray. Chop onion and garlic and place over the tomatoes.

Add some salt and pepper and, if you like, fresh herbs or herb salt. Drizzle some olive oil on top. Cook for 40 minutes until the tomatoes have completely softened and release liquid.

Pour everything, including the liquid, from the pan into a blender. Blend until you have a smooth puree and then pour it into a pan. Add salt, honey, and apple cider vinegar to balance the taste and simmer on a low heat until you have the desired consistency.

Onions

A kitchen isn't complete without onions and it's one of the oldest crops we have. There are even paintings in 5,000-year-old Egyptian tombs depicting onions, and they were just as much of a staple in Rome around the time of Jesus's birth as they are today. In other words, growing onions is very much an heirloom skill.

One reason for the popularity of onions, apart from their lovely taste and their ability to enhance dishes, is that they are easy to grow and store.

SOIL & CLIMATE Onions prefer a nutrient-rich and well-drained soil with lots of sun. Because of this, they work well planted at edges such as by a border or rockery for extra warmth.

SOWING The easiest way to grow onions is to buy heat-treated onion sets, and you can find organic ones. Plant out when the soil temperature is around 50°F (10°C). Onions can be planted in rows or in containers where you fill a box with onions. Throughout the season you can remove the seedlings to allow the remaining onions to grow big.

If you want to grow onions from seeds you need to start early as they can take a while to grow. The benefit with growing onions from seeds is that you have many more varieties to choose from than when you buy onion sets such as yellow and red onions or shallots.

Broadcast sow in containers in February or March and cover with a plastic sheet with small airholes. Keep it moist and place under a grow light. At the start you need a bit of heat but once the seeds start to grow this is less important.

Leave them to grow in the container until the roots are strong, as it is easier to replant them without damaging them. Replant them in soil blockers or rootrainers in nutrient-rich soil and water now and again with fertilizer, for example with gold water. When the risk of frost has passed you can harden them off and plant outside.

CARE Heat treated onion sets don't flower as easily, which is a good thing. Early flowering can also be a problem if the onions are exposed to drought or frost and get stressed, so it is important to water the onions evenly throughout the season.

HARVEST Onions can be harvested at any time during the season, either as the whole onion set or by cutting off the greenery and leave the rest of the onion to grow.

If the onion starts to flower it will stop developing. You can see this through a stiff stem that grows out of the greenery which will develop into a flower. If this happens you need to harvest and eat it straight away as you won't be able to store it.

The onion is ready to harvest and store once the leaves bend and turn yellow. Harvest on a dry day and hang it up or place it somewhere to dry, preferably in a dry airy spot outdoors. If it's raining you can also dry onions inside, but make sure you spread them out properly on a table or tray.

STORING & PREPPING After 3–4 days, the onion has dried and can be stored. Onions should be stored at room temperature in a dry place. If it is too cold, the onion can start to sprout, so never store it in the fridge.

A wooden box or basket works well. Another traditional way, which is both attractive and practical, is to braid the onions, which can then be hung in the larder or by the stove.

DISEASE & PESTS Onion sets can be infected with black mold, which is a fungi that has come with the seed. It thrives in a damp summer and turn the leaves yellow and in severe cases the whole plant can wilt. Onions sown from seeds can be affected by the onion fly which can be seen by the leaves turning yellow where the onions soften and stop growing. The small yellowy white larva can be seen where the leaves meet the onion.

Leeks

The leek is a bit of a prima donna when it comes to onions and likes a bit of extra care and attention in order to for her to proudly grow during fall, but she is worth the extra work as she will then shine her green glow across the snow even into the winter.

SOIL & CLIMATE The leek has a huge need of nitrogen and potassium and prefers deep loam soil due to its long roots. They need a warm and sunny spot.

Onions

SOWING Sow as early as you can, preferably in February. Sow sparsely in a container and place under a grow light. By soaking the seeds for 24 hours before you plant them you can get them to grow even faster.

Once the leeks have become gangly, around 4 inches (5 cm) tall, you can cut them down by half, which will give you a stronger plant. Fertilize once or twice during pre-cultivation.

Around 2–3 months after sowing, when the plants are strong and 4–6 inches (10–15cm) tall, they can be planted out. Place them at 6 inches (15 cm) depth by digging a trench and give them at least 4 inches (10cm) between the plants.

CARE As the leeks grow, trim them to get long, white stems. Water your leeks regularly until the plants are established; after this you only need to water them in extreme dry weather.

HARVEST Leeks don't need to be harvested for storage as they can cope with cold weather. If you leave them in the ground over the winter they can freeze to the spot if you don't add some bedding like straw or leaves. You should harvest them before they start to bloom the following spring.

STORING & PREPPING If you choose a hardy winter variety, you can leave them out all winter and even go and dig them out of the snow when you are ready to cook with them.

DISEASE & PESTS Just like with other types of onions, the leek can be afflicted by the onion fly.

Garlic

Garlic has been revered for thousands of years as an herb and for its healing properties, and it was thought it could scare away everything from nasty colds to witches. For a homesteader, growing garlic is an obvious choice that doesn't take much work. It reproduces via its cloves, meaning you don't need to get any extra seeds. Use cloves from an organic garlic from a certified source. Garlic bought in grocery stores often contain soil bound diseases.

Garlic can be split into two main groups depending on if they have hard stalks (hard necks) or soft stalks (soft necks). If you want to be able to braid it, you need to pick the latter. In the culinary world, however, hard necks are considered the better option, and they are easier to peel. In other words, the choice is completely up to you.

SOIL & CLIMATE Garlic needs a sunny spot with nutrient-rich soil, just like other types of onions.

PLANTING Garlic should be planted during fall, as late as possible before the cold comes and the soil freezes. Garlic needs to have time to set roots before winter, but it doesn't need to grow shoots. Place the cloves around 4 inches (5 cm) deep with around 6 inches (10 cm) between them.

CARE Garlic does not like any competition so be careful to get rid of weeds over the summer. During spring and early summer you should give the garlic a bit of extra fertilizer; we usually poke down some chicken pellets. Garlic can survive without water but if it gets really dry you may need to add some.

HARVEST The garlic is ready to harvest early summer once the leaves turn yellow and the ends are dry. If you wait too long, they lose shelf life as the protective casing cracks. Make sure the garlic is white and not green. During spring and summer you can harvest the greenery, called scapes. To harvest the garlic, carefully tease up the entire bulb including the stalk.

STORING & PREPPING Leave the garlic to dry properly in an airy spot outside or in. Garlic should dry for a few weeks until it is dry through. After this they can keep for at least 6 months at room temperature. The soft necks can be saved on their stalk and braided or you can remove the stalk and store them dry in a basket.

DISEASE & PESTS Garlic is seldom affected by disease or pests, but one irritation can be the onion fly. It winters in soil, so if you are afflicted you should move your crop to a new site.

BRAIDING   ONIONS

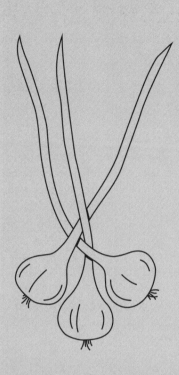 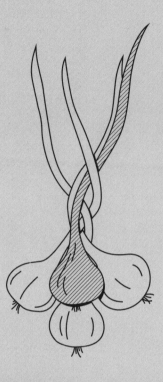 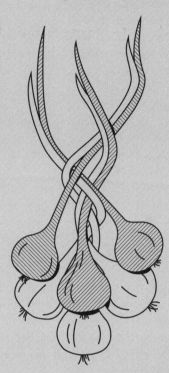

1. Start by sorting the onions into three different sizes: large, medium, and small. You need at least 9 onions for a short braid, but we prefer them longer. If you make a really long braid, it is lovely to attach the ends and make a wreath. Start the braid using your biggest onions and move to the medium-sized ones after a few twists, depending on how many you have, and make the final twists with the small ones.

2. Place a large onion with the strands facing towards you and the end facing away. This onion will be at the end of the braid.

3. Place two large onions with the ends facing away and the strands crossed. The cross where the strands meet should be as close to the base of the onions as possible.

4. To make the braid more stable you can tie some jute around the cross where the strands of the three onions meet. The jute will now be handled as a strand and be braided into the rest of the onions.

5. Make one turn with the strands (so three braids, right, left, right).

6. Place a large onion on top the of cross in line with the first onion.

7. Place two medium-sized onions crossed with the strands on each side of the large middle onion. The cross where the strands meet should be as close to the base of the onions as possible.

8. Braid one turn.

9. Repeat with new onions for as long as you want the braid to be. Then braid the strands to the end and secure with some jute string. Tie a loop so you can hang it up.

Braiding Garlic

GARDENING

Perennial Favorites

Even if most kitchen gardens are dominated by annual or biannual vegetables, perennials also have an obvious place. They are loved by gardeners as they often give a big harvest for not much work. For obvious reasons perennials need a space outside your crop rotation to grow.

Asparagus

One of the spring's first primeurs hardly needs any introduction, but it does need a lot of planning. If you don't already have asparagus when you get a new garden, it is one of the first things you should plant as it can take a few years before it gives any real harvest.

Growing asparagus is mainly about preparation and it is worth finding a good spot for it as once established, an asparagus plant can grow for decades.

SOIL & CLIMATE Asparagus has sensitive roots and doesn't like to be moved. It wants sun and deep, sandy, lime-rich and well-drained soil. You can plant it in a raised bed that can be added to with more greenery.

SOWING & PLANTING For the quickest results, buy plants that already have a developed root system. You can grow them from seeds, but it will take up to 6 years before you get any asparagus. If you decide to sow from seeds you will get both male and female plants. Female plants yield less harvest and have a shorter life span but both types will give you berries in late summer that can be sown in the fall.

CARE Keep weeds and other plants away, especially during the first few years. Asparagus can cope with dry conditions and doesn't need watering during a normal summer with a bit of rain, although in extreme heat it can be needed.

HARVEST You should wait at least a year before you harvest. The first year you have to be careful not to affect any future harvests, so in your very first year of harvesting you can take one or two shoots per plant and leave the rest so you don't weaken the plants. Harvest when the asparagus is around 8 inches (20 cm) tall, before the tip has bloomed.

STORING & PREPPING Asparagus is best eaten fresh, but it can be kept a week or two in the fridge. You can eat it raw or cooked and we prefer it fried or grilled with a blob of butter and some herb salt.

DISEASE & PESTS Older plants can often be afflicted by fungi such as rusts and different molds that live in the leaves over winter. Prune the leaves often on the older plants during fall; the newer plants are resistant. We have not had any issues with disease on our asparagus, but they have proved very popular with voles.

Rhubarb

Rhubarb is popular in northern climates. In those old days, the rhubarb root was acknowledged for its medicinal properties, especially for its laxative effect, and was both expensive and sought after. Today it's primarily the tart stalks which are enjoyed in pies and other baked goods.

SOIL & CLIMATE Rhubarb is easy to grow and will often survive in the most forgotten gardens. Rhubarb plants are not fussy and can grow in most soil and weather conditions. We keep our rhubarb both in the sun and under trees. Most of all they like well-drained soil with some manure.

SOWING & PLANTING Rhubarb spreads most easily by dividing them in the fall. You can also sow them directly into the ground or pre-sprout them indoors. Seeds are sown at about 1 inch (2 cm) depth with 6 inches (10 cm) between them.

PLANT Plant outside with around 3 feet (1 meter) between the plants. The first winter you can protect them against ground frost with some straw, grass, or leaves.

CARE Add compost to your rhubarb in the spring using chicken manure and maintain it with nettle water, which it likes. Only water it if it looks like its wilting.

HARVEST Be careful if you harvest your rhubarb plants in the first two years after planting them. After this they can be harvested throughout the season from spring to late summer. When you remove a stalk, take a firm grip at the bottom by the root and snap it off. You might need to wobble it a bit, but you shouldn't need a knife.

If you have a large rhubarb, you can divide it, which helps to regenerate the plant. Dig it up and divide it into smaller plants with a shovel. This is best done in spring.

STORING & PREPPING Harvested rhubarb can easily be stored in the fridge for about a week or you can cut it into chunks and freeze it. We make pie, compotes, marmalade, and chutney from ours, but the kids love just eating the sour and chewy stalks.

DISEASE & PESTS Rhubarb plants can suffer from several infestations such as the black bean aphid, but it is fairly resistant to most things.

Rhubarb Strips

These rhubarb strips taste so good we barely ever make them anymore as we are sick of hearing the kids nagging for them. The recipe came about by chance after we made rhubarb wine (see page 294) and had lots of sugared rhubarb strips left over. Of course, you don't have to make wine every time you make these strips. The leftover syrup is wonderful on desserts or to make cordial from.

<u>13–15 strips</u>
13–15 large rhubarb stalks
2.2 lb (1 kg) white sugar

Rinse and trim the stalks and crush them with a rolling pin or meat tenderizer, but make sure they still stick together.

Place the crushed stalks in a large bowl and pour over the sugar. Mix thoroughly and cover with a kitchen towel

Leave for 1–2 days, stirring a few times with a ladle to make the strips soft.

Sieve the rhubarb strips and leave them to drain for a few hours. Once they start to dry, place them in a fruit dehydrator. If they are large, it can take a few hours. They are finished once they are stiff and have turned dark but still have a bit of softness about them. Store them in a jar in your larder. They should last a long time, but in our experience they generally don't.

Ramps

Some are lucky and have a whole forest of ramps outside their window while others never find anything. This delicacy of the onion family has a garlicy but still unique taste. We grow a small crop of ramps in the shade of a large rock that attracts rainwater. The tufts peek out year after year but don't really spread.

SOIL & CLIMATE In nature, ramps prefers a shady place with a moist loam soil, preferably in a leafy forest or in a grove. Find a damp place in shade or partial shade, for example a grove or behind a building. Avoid anywhere that pine trees grow as ramps needs a chalky and nutrient-rich soil. You can raise the pH levels by scattering some wood ash.

SOWING & PLANTING Ramps can be sown from seeds but it's easier to order developed plants. You can plant them in the fall when there is a high level of moisture in the soil, which gives the plants a chance to establish. If you are not sure about the location, you can test a few plants in different spots and see which they prefer. Add some compost when you plant them and place the bulbs three times as deep as their own height. Plant them sparsely with 4 inches (10 cm) between them.

CARE Ramps needs constant moisture to survive. Plant them in a dip or near a river if you can. A good idea is to lead rainwater to your crop; if not you will need to water them daily. Once established in a place where they can thrive, you don't need to look after them.

HARVEST Allow the ramps to establish for at least a year before you harvest.

STORING & PREPPING Ramps are a spring primeur that should be eaten freshly as the taste and texture can't be preserved. We often use it to make pesto or chop it over an omelette or frittata.

DISEASE & PESTS Nothing seems to afflict this onion plant; in fact, its strong scent keeps animals at bay.

Rhubarb Strips

GARDENING

Orpine

Many people consider this to be a flower but the beautiful orpine is also a delicate, perennial primeur that can be used for all sorts of things—including, in the old days, love divination.

There are several varieties such as the regular wild Orpine with yellow flowers as well as the purple emperor with white, purple, or pink tones that is most common in domestic crops. The plant has a long history as a medicinal plant but was used as early as the Middle Ages for food.

SOIL & CLIMATE The orpine is a perennial that can make do with some of the lesser spots in the garden where it might be both rocky and arid; however, they do want sunshine.

PLANTING Place a plant or cutting into a flower bed, a rock garden, or a pot; the Orpine will easily set roots.

CARE Like many other perennials, Orpine can be divided with a sharp spade during fall to propagate more plants. Taking cuttings is also easy—just cut off a shoot during late summer and plant directly into the soil.

Orpine is easy to grow and doesn't need much once established. Due to their thick leaves, they can store water, meaning they can survive in dry conditions. Give them some water and fertilizer as you plant them, but apart from this they will look after themselves.

DISEASE & PESTS Just like other succulents, Orpine can be infested by both spider mite and mildew during warm and dry summers and even deer like the taste of the juicy leaves.

HARVEST The whole plant is edible for large parts of the season. The root contains a lot of carbohydrates but should, just like the stem, be boiled to remove the bitter taste. It's mainly the meaty, green, and crispy leaves we enjoy. They taste a bit like sugar snaps and can be eaten raw. During late summer and fall the Orpine flowers also attract the honeybee and bumblebees.

STORING & PREPPING As Orpine stores water, we use the leaves in the same way as we do cucumber, in a salad or gazpacho.

Tzatziki with Orpine

Around 1½ cups (4 dl)
½ cup (1½ dl) finely chopped Orpine leaves
1¼ cup (3 dl) yogurt
1 tbsp squeezed lemon juice
2 cloves garlic
1 tsp apple cider vinegar
1 tsp chopped mint
1 tbsp olive oil
Salt and freshly ground pepper

Place the chopped Orpine leaves in a kitchen towel and squeeze out the liquid. Pour the yogurt in a medium-sized bowl and add all the ingredients except the olive oil. Season to taste and drizzle some olive oil on top.

Dried Herbs

GARDENING

Herbs

During the summer we enjoy herbs in cold sauces and thirst-quenching drinks, and during winter we use them dried when cooking but also to make herb bags and smudge sticks. We grow quite a wide variety of herbs from the Mediterranean and Asia with a mix of local herbs that traditionally were used to make up ladies herb bouquets, as well as the classic herbs used in schnapps.

In our herb garden:

anise	lovage
anise hyssop	marjoram
basil	mint
borage	Norwegian angelica
chervil (Danish and Spanish)	oregano
	parsley (flat leaf)
chives	rosemary
cumin	sage (common sage)
dill	Siberian chives
fennel	southernwood
garlic chives	summer savory
hyssop (blue)	tarragon
lavender	thyme
lemon verbena	wormwood

An herb garden or even just a few herbs is a necessity for a modern homesteader. The benefits of herbs are more than just their obvious place in the kitchen as they attract pollinators and are at times so hardy that they can be harvested throughout winter. Most herbs, although not all, are perennials.

You can plant herbs in your kitchen garden, but it's usually better to create a separate herb garden near your house if the kitchen garden is slightly farther away.

SOIL & CLIMATE Most herbs are easy to grow and don't need much water or nutrients once established. They do want sun though and don't like a heavy or wet clay soil.

SOWING & PLANTING Most herbs are perennials, meaning they return every year, so choose a space where you won't need to move them. Plant new herbs in August so they have time to establish before the winter. In the Spring, fragile shoots can be affected by the frost.

Dig a medium-sized hole for the plant and water it but don't add compost. Instead add compost around the area with a mild compost manure as you plant them out. If the soil is acidic you may need to add some lime as herbs like a lime soil.

Some herbs like basil, dill, cress, and coriander are annuals at our latitude and need to be grown each season. Basil should be pre-sprouted indoors as it is very sensitive to frost whereas dill can be sown straight outdoors.

CARE Perennial herbs don't often need much care apart from water during dry periods in the summer and a bit of fertilizer now and again. Use nettle water or dry compost on the surrounding area. Some herbs need more water, not least those in the onion family as well as annuals such as basil and dill.

Herbs that get new shoots each year can be completely cut down such as mint, tarragon, and lovage. Woody herbs need to be polished and trimmed such as hyssop and lavender.

HARVEST Herbs can be harvested continuously as you need them throughout the season.

STORING & PREPPING Now and again throughout the season it is worth harvesting a bit extra to freeze or store to make herb salt. Herbs are easy to dry. Hang them up in small bunches in an airy spot or place them on an herb dryer. Don't forget to flavor alcohol and vinegar with herbs.

DISEASE & PESTS Most herbs can withstand both disease and pests due to their often overbearing smells. Some herbs, such as basil, however, are liked by slugs.

SMUDGE STICKS

Smudge sticks originate from Native Americans who dry sage to use in ceremonies to cleanse and bless people and places. We think they spread both a lovely smell and feeling and we make them in lots of different combinations of dried herbs and flowers, such as mint, lavender, rosemary, and thyme.

Around 20 sprigs of fresh herbs
cotton thread such as butcher's string

Method:

1. Trim the sprigs to make them the same length, around 4–6 inches (10–15 cm).
2. Place the sprigs in a bunch and tie at the bottom of the stalks. Twine the thread around and upwards several times so it winds at an angle towards the top. Turn it over and do the same thing downwards so the string makes a criss-cross shape. Tie the string off at the point where you started.
3. Leave to dry for at least 2 weeks on a plate.
4. Light the end and blow out the flame once it has caught, leaving it to smolder and smoke. Use water to extinguish it when you are finished.

Disease & Pests in Crops

Gardening is not easy. Not only do you have storms, frost, and cold weather that can kill your plants, but you also have a whole host of fungal spores, diseases, insects, and other animals that wish to harm your crops. This is an unavoidable aspect of gardening that you really just need to accept.

It's really a natural part of life. Growing crops is an infringement on nature when you try to grow a certain crop over another. For example, you want carrots, but nature wants a jungle of diversity instead. It's not that strange that many of the crops we love are also loved by others as they are rich in nutrients and free from poisons, and the work to retain as much as you can of the harvest is a natural part of being a gardener.

Postwar, this work has mainly been done using chemicals in large-scale farming with catastrophic results to animals, biological diversity, and in some cases even humans. Instead, the answer lies in nature itself with old, tried-and-true tricks.

By creating more diversity in your garden, you prevent many attacks without even realizing it and it could be the pile of old, rotting logs behind your house that end up saving your artichokes. A garden that has a wide variety of both plants and animals results in a biodiverse garden that is more able to withstand attacks.

Deer & Rabbits

The most frequent visitors to your kitchen garden are usually deer and rabbits, especially what we call "urban deer," who live near humans and can be considered tame, meaning they become a real pain. As soon as you plant something, they eat it, and they often strike in the early hours of the morning.

Deer cause a lot of problems to gardeners, which is evident by the number of methods there are to stave them off. The situation transforms gardeners into witches, brewing concoctions of bloodmeal, urine, sheep's wool, garlic, and cayenne pepper to name a few. You can also buy more advanced items designed to scare off deer and rabbits with light, sound, and water but in our experience, the only way to keep deer away is through physical barriers.

The visits are more frequent during spring and fall when nature doesn't offer as much. Cabbage and beetroot tend to be at the top of the menu for deer, so protect sought after plants with garden fleece in the spring and chicken wire in the fall. If you have big problems, consider protecting the crops with fencing or net. The net should be six feet tall to give proper protection against deer. For rabbits, the height is not as important, but the net needs to be securely attached to the ground.

Voles

Another visitor who can cause a lot of issues in the garden is the vole. The vole looks like a slightly rounder, larger mouse. You can identify it by holes in the ground. Whereas the mole places soil over the hole, the vole places it adjacent to the hole. The mole's hole is also taller and pointier and they don't eat plants but do like slugs and insect larva.

Voles mainly cause issues by attacking the roots and crops from underneath and they can also damage fruit trees and berries. They are harder to fight as it can be difficult to stop them from digging under. If it becomes a big problem, the only really effective solution is to dig a net around 3 feet (1 meter) into the soil around the crops. There are also vole traps you can buy although we find the best antidote is the cat.

Birds

In our garden we are constantly visited by pheasants, magpie, thrush, and sometimes even our own chickens, who can cause damage if they are allowed to continue unimpeded. Birds cause the most issues during sowing and harvest and there have been many times that we have had to start again after hungry birds have poked our freshly sown broad beans and seeds out of the soil. At harvest it's mainly legumes that are top of the menu, although larger birds are also fond of lettuce and can pull up potatoes and weaker carrots. During late fall the pheasants have even started eating our leeks.

Keeping birds away from your crops is the same as with larger animals: best done with a physical barrier. Protect your crops with garden fleece in the spring and chicken wire in the autumn when the fruit starts to appear. Using a more durable wire in metal is better to avoid birds getting stuck in it.

Slugs

Slugs, especially the infamous Spanish killer slug, can

bring even the most harmonious gardener to the brink. It is almost impossible to get rid of and with a seemingly endless appetite, slugs can easily destroy entire crops. They cause the most damage during the early part of the season when they attack fragile shoots at their most vulnerable and you should have several forms of attack against them. Our advice is to do this in three steps:

Firstly, you need to remove anything in the environment in the vicinity of the crops that the slugs are attracted to. Slugs need a moist environment where they can hide and come out in the rain or during the evenings and at night when the humidity levels in the air is higher. If you have big problems, you should remove rocks, piles of greenery and leaves, old logs, and any areas of tall grass and weeds. Keep the surrounding area as dry and exposed as possible. Also remove anything that slugs enjoy eating outside of the crops—even fallen fruit is a popular target.

The next step is to protect against attack with the help of some kind of barrier. The most effective in our experience is a plank with a slug edge. You can buy slug edges in the store but you can also make your own using a stiff mosquito net that can be stapled onto the top edge of the plank with an overhang of around 1–2 inches (3–5 cm).

Finally, the actual physical action against the slugs is important, especially during spring and early summer as the snails that have overwintered start to increase in numbers. Have a routine whereby you regularly go out and pick up any killer slugs you can see. Do your round in the evening after the rain. Cut them in half or pour them into boiling water. Place slug traps in strategic places around the garden. You can make a simple trap from an empty milk carton which you fill up with some beer. The snail is attracted to the smell of malt and will drown in the beer.

The most effective way to fight against snails is to turn them into food. We were delighted when we saw the way our young roosters swallowed killer slugs whole. Not all chickens will eat slugs though, so this may be an exception. However, chickens do eat slug eggs if they are allowed to roam free, so why not set the chickens loose on a compost heap full of snails? They'll clear out the snails as well as loosen up the soil.

The best defence against the slug is the duck. It is usually the Muscovy duck that is known for its love of slugs, but all ducks eat them, although of course each duck has their own personal tastes. While some slug connoisseurs can eat hundreds of slugs, others turn their noses (or beaks) up at them. You can read more in the chapter on ducks.

Flea Beetles
Maybe not the worst marauder in your garden, but these little beetles are aesthetically irritating when they perforate the vegetables like a hail storm. The sound of thousands of flea beetles jumping between the cabbage leaves is not something you want to hear. These are small, black beetles and are part of the leaf beetle family and cause most damage on delicate radishes, turnips, cabbage, and arugula.

Covering small plants with cabbage netting or garden fleece can give good protection. Flea beetles prefer a dry environment so by watering often and with abundance you can get rid of them. Mulching can also help to some extent against attacks.

Flea beetles winter in the soil so crop rotation is a good way to prevent larger infestations. If you need to deal with flea beetles in a certain area or in one of your garden beds, you can plant something they dislike the following season such as onion, garlic, or Jerusalem artichoke.

Aphids
The aphid is a well-known garden plunderer and can attack anything from ornamental flowers in a pot to large crops. There are many varieties of aphids that gather in large colonies, preferably underneath leaves or on fresh shoots. They suck liquid and life from the plant and spread disease and other attacks. Severely affected plants may stop growing, which can be devastating to your crops, so it is important to act quickly. Apart from regularly checking your plants for aphids, you can also look for small white scales on the leaves as discarded aphid skin is a clear sign that your plants are under attack.

Certain crops are affected more than others, such as the broad bean, which is often afflicted by the black bean aphid. The good thing about aphids is that they are relatively easy to get rid of.

You can squish them or wash them away with a strong jet of water without damaging the plant. You can also spray the aphids with a solution of soap and water: Mix one part yellow soap (soap made from liquid rosin) with 5 parts water

Motheaten Cabbage

GARDENING

in a spray bottle. Don't use it when it's bright sunshine out as it can damage the plant. Repeat after a week or so.

Large White & Cabbage Moth

At some point during the summer the cabbages suddenly appear. Their strong leaves flex and glisten in the sunshine but in the blink of an eye your cabbage crop has suddenly turned into a sad graveyard where chewed off stems point towards the sky like bare ribs. It's no surprise then that the large white and the cabbage moth, or in actual fact their larva, are so feared among gardeners and their appetite seems insatiable. If you decide to grow cabbages, you can be sure that at some point your crop will be attacked.

It's best to prevent the attacks if you can. A good start is to pre-sprout the cabbage and put them out once they are strong and healthy as they will more easily resist the attacks. Another way, which is often sadly necessary, is during large parts of the summer to cover the cabbage with a net. Occasionally a moth or butterfly will get through, but it does prevent larger infestations that might ruin an entire crop. The cabbage will get their revenge during the fall, when the cold reduces the appearance of insects and you can take great pleasure in unveiling them.

As with all pests, some years are better than others. The large white can stay over winter and reappear around May, but most of the attacks come from second generation bugs from July onwards. The cabbage moths often appear with southern winds and like the large white, they are usually at their worst in July and August.

You can predict when the attacks are about to happen when you see small white butterflies flapping around the cabbage. From laying their eggs, it takes around 14 days for the large white's larva and 7 days for the cabbage moth's larva to hatch. You can find the eggs in bunches underneath the leaves and squash them but it is quite hard work. Apart from using a net to protect the crop you can use biological protective measures.

Bacillus thuringiensis is a soil-dwelling bacteria that is harmless to birds, mammals, and humans but produces proteins that are poisonous to certain insects including cabbage larva.

You can buy the bacteria in powder form and mix it with some water and dish soap. Spray during dry weather as soon as the pupa have hatched and repeat a couple of times a week. The larva will die within a few days and the bacteria will decompose naturally.

Soil-Bound Diseases

The worst thing that can happen to you as a gardener is that your soil gets sick. It goes against the nature of gardening and can be difficult to get rid of as some diseases can stick for several years.

It is important to retain healthy soil and take preventative measures by, for example, rotating the most afflicted crops such as potatoes and cabbage. It's also important to use seeds and bulbs from reliable sellers. For example, don't plant garlic you've bought in a grocery store as it may carry disease.

Cabbage that is planted in the same place year after year can be affected by the notorious clubroot that attacks and warps the plants' root system. It means the plants can't absorb nutrients and water, and so they wither and die. Clubroot is caused by the protist Plasmodiophora brassicae that also attacks bok choi, grass, radishes, rapeseed, and daikon. Once the disease has got hold in the soil it can stay for up to 20 years, which means during this time you can't grow these vegetables in this area.

Another soil-bound disease is potato blight, which mainly affects potatoes and can cause brown rot. It is a fungi whose spores winter inside the earth. These are then spread by the wind and you can recognize them by the fact that the leaves turn yellow and then brown.

If the disease is allowed to take hold it will spread down to the tubers that can also be affected by brown rot. Potato blight can also spread to tomato plants and can quickly decimate an entire harvest, which is why potatoes and tomatoes should not be grown together or even near each other.

If the greenery has been infested, you need to remove and destroy it as soon as possible, for example by placing it in the garbage or burning it. If the tomato plants are affected there is not really much you can do but pick any green tomatoes and then destroy the plant. The spores from potato blight can remain in the soil for at least three years. In large scale farming the disease is usually taken care of with chemicals but it is still hard to get rid of. It is therefore important to buy good quality potato tubers as this is one way through which the fungi can spread.

Beneficial Garden Animals

An area that lacks diversity with few crops, plants, bushes, flowers, and environments is also less resilient against infestations and pests. The key to a strong garden is diversity, from birds and insects all the way to bacteria and microbes in the soil. We know that the use of chemicals during the twentieth century to fight against pests and disease had great short-term effects, giving us bigger crops. In the same way monoculture farming, where one type of crop is planted over a vast area, made farming more effective by giving larger harvests. However, the rewards are short-term and the price we pay is impoverished soil and the mass destruction of insects and animals. We also run the risk of monoculture farming practically inviting pests, plants, and disease in as eventually they become resistant to the chemicals.

According to studies, 40 percent of the global agricultural land will soon be untenable to cultivate due to lack of nutrients, toxins, and soil erosion, all because of unsustainable highly intensive farming methods. Each year around 24 million acres (10 million hectares) of land become unusable. We are losing land to grow on due to an increase in urbanization and forestry. The only sustainable solution is to develop agricultural methods that are sustainable and underpinned by biological diversity. Your garden is a microcosm of this development, and this is where you need to start.

As we have already noted, gardening is an encroachment on nature, but you can work to create diversity and balance to strengthen your garden's resilience.

In the same way that there are animals, insects, bacteria, and viruses that can harm your garden, there are animals that can be seen as beneficial and these often balance out the aggressors. A classic example that we have already mentioned are ducks and slugs, but you don't need to build a duck house and breed ducklings to achieve this effect as many of these beneficial animals already live in your garden.

Create a Beneficial Environment

To attract more beneficial animals into your garden and keep them healthy and happy, you need to create a good habitat for them. Poisons don't belong in a garden whether they are intended for insects or weeds. Even ecological products or those that claim to be kind to the environment can contain substances that are harmful to some organisms.

In recent years we have seen how organic fertilizer has poisoned plants as it contains remnants of the herbicide clopyralid. The poison can kill off the insects that fight pests naturally and reduce your garden's natural "immune system." These poisons don't only affect the diversity in your garden but they risk ending up in your food as well.

Apart from a poison-free environment, beneficial animals also need to be housed and fed. The fact that many varieties have recently been under threat is not only because of environmental toxins but also due to the fact that we are too rigorous in cleaning up in forests, farms, and gardens. Modern forestry and farming have led to fewer fields and dying forests, which means that many of the environments that have been biodiverse are just as threatened by extinction as some animals. The same problem can be seen in our gardens that are often cleared to an inch of their lives as old trees, logs, and piles of leaves are removed, which affects everything from hedgehogs to wild bees.

The same thing happens when it comes to food, as the same threatened environments can offer food to lots of animals. You can grow lots of plants to attract these beneficial animals to give them food, especially by growing local heritage varieties.

Generally, its best to lay the foundation for different ecologies in your garden and give the best footing for different animals, from growing crops and maintaining meadows to offering sandy spots and shady areas.

If you can, it's a great idea to have a pond in your garden as this offers ecologies to lots of beneficial animals such as frogs, salamanders, insects, and birds.

Pollinators

Without these we would barely have any fruits or berries. We usually say that a third of our food is the result of pollination. Pollinators obviously include the honeybee but also the wild bee, bumblebee, hover flies, and butterflies that play just as an important, if not a more important, role in pollination. In the United States there are more than 4,000 varieties of solitary bees and over 40 varieties of honey bees.

To attract pollinators to your garden you need to feed them throughout the season, from early spring to late fall. A productive kitchen garden should therefore not only be green but also contain some flowers. The best plants that offer both you and your pollinators food are sage, lavender, thyme, dill, and cranesbill. Another way to attract honeybees, bumblebees, and other pollinators is to sow green compost flowers such as Lady phacelia.

If you can though, the best way is to leave part of your garden to become meadowland. A well cared for meadow can create a huge diversity of plants and flowers and might even attract the otherwise shy solitary bee.

Ladybugs
Another important and beneficial species is the ladybug as they are one of the biggest enemies to aphids. The most common one is the red one with seven spots but there are about 150 different varieties in the United States. A ladybug can consume 50 aphids a day and even their larva are huge consumers of aphids. In fact, the ladybug is so effective that these days you can buy them to tackle your pest problems.

However, by creating the right environment you can attract them the natural way. Apart from eating insects, they also like pollen, so a way to attract them is to plant things that will attract them. Ladybugs like chives (flowering ones), cosmos, dill, Norwegian angelica, and ornamental onion. Early flowering plants are also important such as crocus, willow, pussy willow, and hazel. Ladybugs overwinter in sheltered areas, often in wood, so make sure you have an old pile of firewood or some old logs nearby.

Earwigs
Earwigs can be considered the insect version of the wolf. Maybe it's due to their appearance, as the earwig is certainly the garden's most talked about predator.

During their lifespan, a single earwig can consume thousands of aphids. However, earwigs eat more than just aphids and some years, especially if there are many of them, they can also eat plants and flowers, and dahlia buds seem to be particularly popular.

Sadly, we tend to focus on the damage they do, which is mainly aesthetic, rather than the good work they do, which is by far more important than the damage.

Earwigs chase and eat aphids, mites, and plant lice that can cause a lot of damage to vegetables, fruit, and berries, so to remove earwigs from your garden is to do it a disservice as you risk disturbing the balance between beneficial animals and pests.

If you have an infestation of aphids you should try to attract earwigs by offering them a place to stay. An upturned clay pot filled with dry grass is usually irresistible to earwigs.

Other Lice Hunters
Apart from ladybugs and earwigs, there are a host of other animals that love lice and can be beneficial to your plants, for example true bugs, soldier beetles, mites, parasitoid wasps, spiders, and green lacewing. In some cases, they provide double the benefit such as the hover fly, as while the insect is an important pollinator, the larva is a predator that can consume 100 aphids a day.

Often these insects appear naturally in your garden if it is free from poison, is diverse, and offers shelter nearby such as old logs and piles of leaves. If you have a lot of infestations, for example spider mites, you can buy beneficial bugs such as the spider mite killer (Phytoseiulus) which is a better alternative to chemicals that will also kill any beneficial animals.

Bats & Birds
During its childhood, a blue tit is served up to 15,000 insects by its parents. Small birds and bats are central in keeping the diversity balanced and making sure that certain insects don't take over. Apart from flying insects they also like larva, and tits are also fond of rose grain aphids. Some of the most important consumers of insects are the old-world flycatchers, blue tits, and great tits. These birds are important as they start to chase insects early in spring when most predatory insects aren't yet active, and at sunset the bats take over.

We should add that great tits can cause a whole load of trouble with beehives in spring. They knock on the hives and pick on stiffened bees. An easy way to protect the bees is to hang a bit of spruce over the entrance or temporarily put up some chicken wire around the entrance.

The best way to attract birds and bats to your garden is by offering them a home. Small birds like small

birdhouses with an entrance of around 12–14 inches (30–35 cm) in width. You can also leave bird feeders out over the winter.

Batboxes are slightly different as the entrance is underneath. Use rough and untreated wood on the inside as it helps the bat to grip. Place the box at least 6 ft (2 meters) above the ground in a western or southerly facing direction, although it should not be placed in full sun.

Harvest Your Own Seeds

Our happiness is complete when we close the crop circle by not only harvesting our own crops but also the seeds for the following year. Taking seeds from flowers is easy and can be done in steps to save time. Mark your favorite plant with a string or something similar to make sure you can identify it once it starts to wilt. It is important to allow enough time for this process—the petals should have fallen off and the seed case or pod should be completely dry. Some seed cases need to drop their seeds or discard them when they are ready, and you can harvest these by placing a linen towel or sheet around them, or tie a bag around them. Harvest seeds during late summer and fall in dry, sunny weather. We remove the whole seed stalk and case and place them, according to their type, in paper

bags or coffee filters. In this way they can be dried and stored to be removed or shaken off at a later date. Mark the bags so you don't mix them up come spring. The bags are folded and stored in a dry, cool spot out of sunlight.

We harvest seeds from both vegetables and flowers as well as from perennials, biennials, and annuals (but not the F1 varieties). To harvest seeds from biennials such as carrots and kale, you need to leave them in the soil so they bloom for a second season. Not all seeds from all plants are true to type so the seeds can result in a plant that looks nothing like the original one. This is because the pollinators have gone from flower to flower and cross-pollinated. If you want to avoid this, you can isolate your favorite flowers with bags around them and pollinate by hand using a brush.

Taking seeds from vegetables that have borne fruit is also simple. When we harvest beans and peas, we always place some aside that we leave to dry and shrivel before we remove them and pop into bags to be used in spring. Tomatoes, squash, and cucumbers should preferably be overripe (although not rotten) before they are harvested if you want to take seeds from them. Scoop the seeds out with the jelly or stringy flesh and place on paper to dry. Once dry you can fold the paper and place in a seed bag or envelope.

GARDENING

Drink Cabinet Classics

Just as every season has its flavors, every season has its drink. When you're chilling on the deck on a summer's evening, dirt under your fingernails, nothing tastes as good as a traditional British fruit cup. Cold winter nights in front of the fire, on the other hand, call for an Old Fashioned to warm us up. A gin & tonic, though, can be drunk any time of the year!

A well-stocked drinks cabinet is a must if you like a tipple, but it takes time and money. Thankfully, there are many classic drinks you can make yourself from ingredients that grow in your own backyard. Not only do they taste better, but you can also add your own twists to your drinks.

A Garden of Flavors

All you really need to mix up some classic drinks are a few glass jars, some spirits, and a bunch of herbs. A collection of herbs and spices is the mixologist's main tool, and the more you have the more you can experiment. Once you've learned the basics you can easily adapt the drinks according to your taste.

Depending on where you live, it may be too cold to grow all the spices you might need, such as cardamom, cinchona bark, cinnamon, and vanilla. You can get most of these in the grocery store, but even better is to order from specialist spice stores where the selection of whole spices is usually better.

The range of flavors you can grow on your balcony or in your garden is almost endless. In addition, lots of great flavors can be found growing wild, such as St. John's Wort, polypody, spruce shoots, and juniper berries to name a few.

You can read more on how to create a varied spice collection on page 166.

Infusions

When you add spices, berries, or other items to a spirit you create an infusion. This can be done with oil, water, or in this case, spirits that have the ability to absorb flavors. A stronger, more concentrated infusion is called a tincture. In simple terms, stronger alcohol dissolves fat soluble substances and weaker alcohol dissolves water soluble substances. The advantage of alcohol is that from around 20 percent strength it conserves flavors so they can be stored for longer, although the flavors may change or reduce over time.

How much flavor your infusion will absorb depends on the amount of spices and their strength, as well as the time you leave it to infuse. With gin, for example, you only need a day or two, whereas bitters need a lot longer to mature.

KRUSENBERGS   HOUSE GIN

Mixing a gin & tonic has become a Friday tradition in our house. Just like our Friday bath under the apple tree, it is a ritual that marks the end of the working week.

Lately some great local gin makers have arrived on the scene, but it's not hard to make your own as the most important ingredient—the Juniper Berry—can be found in many forests and fields. Gin was invented in the Netherlands during the seventeenth century and the name derives from the Latin for Juniper, *Juniperus*. This recipe can be adapted according to personal taste. When making gin, up to 120 different ingredients can be used, so it will take trial and error to find your personal favorite. If you want a cleaner, less spicy note, then remove cinnamon and star anise from the recipe. If you are lucky enough to have your own quince tree, you can use this instead of lemon.

It takes three years for junipers to mature and get their dark blue hue. Normally junipers are picked in late fall, but you can find ripe junipers all year round. Pick them carefully by hand or place a cloth under the bush and carefully hit the branch with a stick to loosen the ripe berries. Dry them spread out on a plate or in a mushroom drier to make them last longer. You can also use fresh berries.

23½ fl oz (70 cl) vodka
2 tbsp fresh or dried juniper berries
Small piece of lemon rind, around 2 × 0.5 inches (5 × 1 cm)
Small piece of orange rind around 1 × 0.5 inches (3 × 1 cm)
1 tsp honey
½ star anise
6 black peppercorns
6 cardamom seeds
½ cinnamon stick
½ tbsp dried thyme
1 currant leaf (optional)

Clean and sterilize a jar or glass bottle with a wide neck. Place all the ingredients in the bottle and pour the vodka over them.

Leave the bottle in a dark, cool spot and turn or shake the mixture once or twice over the next 24 hours.

Leave for 24 hours before tasting. If you want more flavor, leave it for a bit longer but no more than 24 more hours as the spices will overwhelm the flavor. Once you are happy, sieve the gin and, if you can, leave it a few days to allow the flavors to settle. The gin will last longer if stored in a dark place.

Vermouth

This is the king of mixers and a classic ingredient in some of the world's most famous drinks, such as dry martini, negroni, and Manhattan. Vermouth is a strongly aromatic fortified wine named after its main ingredient, wormwood (after the German wermut). Your vermouth should last around a month in the fridge.

<u>Dry white vermouth</u>
1 bottle of dry white wine
1 tbsp dried wormwood
1 tsp bitter orange
2–3 pieces licorice root
2 tsp dried camomile
2 juniper berries
6¾ fl oz cognac

Lightly crush the spices with a pestle and mortar and pour into a glass jar with a clip-top lid. Add the cognac and leave in a dark cupboard for about 2 weeks, shaking it now and again. Remove the herbs and add dry white wine.

<u>Sweet red vermouth</u>
1 bottle of red wine
1 tbsp dried wormwood
1 tsp bitter orange
2–3 pieces licorice root
2 cardamom pods, crushed
2 tsp dried camomile
2 juniper berries
1 star anise
½ cup (1½ dl) caster sugar
6½ fl oz (2 dl) cognac

Heat 6½ fl oz of the wine in a pan and bring to a boil. Add the spices and simmer gently for around 10 minutes. Remove the pan from the heat.

In another pan, melt the sugar and stir until it caramelizes and turns a nice brown color.

While the sugar is melting, sieve the wine to remove the spices and almost bring to a boil. Pour the caramelized sugar over the wine and stir until dissolved. Add cognac and the rest of the wine. Taste and add more cognac and sugar if needed.

Limoncello

This southern Italian classic is childishly easy to make yourself—the only thing you need is really good lemons. Traditionally, limoncello is made from Sorrento lemons, but other varieties also work well. It is important that the lemons are organic because it is the peel that plays the main role. Limoncello is simply made by infusing lemon peel. What you are looking for are the essential oils found in lemon peel and which are dissolved in the alcohol.

23½ fl oz (70 cl) of vodka
Peels from 5 organic lemons
¾ cup (150 g) caster sugar
3⅓ fl oz (1 dl) of water

Peel the lemons. Try to only use the outermost skin as the white skin adds bitterness.

Pour the vodka over the lemon peel in a sterilized glass jar or bottle with a wide neck and leave for about 2 weeks. Stir every now and then.

Dissolve sugar in the water in a saucepan and let cool. Then pour the sugar solution over the infusion. Leave for a few more days at room temperature before tasting and straining.

You should now have a sweet and smooth limoncello. If you want a more acidic version with more flavor, mix the lemon juice into the infusion at the same time as the peel.

Summer Cup

Orange Liqueur

Making your own triple sec is just as simple as making limoncello. It's lovely on its own, but is also a vital ingredient in many drinks. Plus, it adds an exotic twist to our summer cup recipe. Use organic oranges if you want to avoid a bitter aftertaste.

17 fl oz (50 cl) vodka
Peel from 3 organic oranges
1 tsp dried bitter orange
1 vanilla pod
4 cloves
6¾ fl oz (2 dl) sugar or honey
3½ fl oz (1 dl) water
6¾ fl oz (20 cl) cognac

Peel the lemons; try to only get the top layer as the white bit (the pith) adds bitterness.

Mix the orange peel, dried bitter orange, vanilla pod, and vodka in a jar and leave for 2–3 weeks.

Add the cloves and leave for 24 hours before straining.

Dissolve the sugar or honey in water in a pan and leave to cool down.

Mix all ingredients with the cognac and leave for a few days in room temperature for the taste to mature.

Summer Cup

The most summery of all summer drinks is this thirst-quenching British classic, the Summer Cup, which combines grassy notes with exotic fruits. Grab your floppiest sun hat, deck yourself out in white linen, and enjoy this drink while playing a game of croquet.

6¾ fl oz (2 dl) water
6¾ oz (2 dl) caster sugar
1 bunch mint
1 bunch lemon verbena
½ cucumber
10 fl oz (3 dl) gin
6¾ fl oz (2 dl) red vermouth
3½ fl oz (1 dl) orange liquor
Tonic or ginger ale

Heat the water in a pan and add sugar. When the sugar has dissolved, add mint, lemon verbena, and cucumber and simmer on a low temperature for around 5 minutes.

Leave to steep for a few hours.

Sieve and mix the syrup with gin, vermouth, and orange liquor in a bottle. Leave your summer cup to mature for a few days in the fridge.

Mix the drink by adding one part summer cup and two parts tonic or ginger ale. Pour into a glass and fill with ice and seasonal berries and fruit.

Limoncello, page 179

Bitters

Each drop of bitter is worth its weight in gold. That bitter splash added to a drink can change everything, finally achieving the balance of sweet and sour and adding depth and complexity to your drink. Traditionally bitters, usually mixed with bitter herbs, were seen as a miracle cure that could heal sea sickness and stomachaches. Fortunately, bitters found their way from the apothecary shelves and into the drinks cabinet.

There are basically two types of bitters, aromatic bitters and citrus bitters. We like both and they use many plants and herbs that you can grow yourself or pick in the wild. The king among bitter plants is the renowned wormwood, which is a must-have in any mixologist's herb garden. Even fennel, camomile, and cumin can add a bitter flavor. Another great bitter is so common you can't avoid stepping on it and that is the dandelion, or rather the dandelion root.

Bitters from Wormwood & Orange Peel

There are lots of ways to mix bitters, but we find the most bitter of them all is the marriage of orange peel and wormwood. This bitter works well at Christmastime when there is an abundance of orange peel and you can harvest leaves from your wormwood plant.

6¾ fl oz (2 dl) vodka
1 organic orange
1 tbsp dried or 2 tbsp fresh wormwood
¾ oz (20g) caster sugar

Peel the orange, including the pith as it adds bitterness.

Dry the orange peel in an oven set at 250°F (120 °C). Around 20 minutes in a fan-assisted oven is usually enough—just make sure they don't burn. You can also spread them on a plate to dry, but this takes a day or so.

Gently crush the peel into half-inch pieces.

Mix the peel, wormwood, and vodka in a glass jar with a tight lid and leave in a cool, dark place for 3 weeks, shaking it now and again.

Taste the bitters after 3 weeks; if you want more flavor, leave for one more week.

Use a cheese cloth to sieve the liquid. If you have tiny bits of orange, use a coffee filter. Caramelize the sugar in a frying pan and add to the bitters.

Dandelion Bitters

One of the best flavorings for bitters is almost impossible to get rid of: the dandelion. It's usually the dandelion's golden flowers that are used, for example when making wine, but even the part that grows below the earth can be used. Dandelion roots are considered so healthy that they are sold at a high price in health food shops. However, you can easily collect enough yourself by digging them up. The best way to get the root is to focus on larger plants growing in well-drained locations such as gravel or vegetables patches. You can use a dandelion weeder to help. Once the plant's removed, cut the root off and trim and wash it. Cut it into half-inch pieces and place on a kitchen towel, a sheet, or a mushroom dryer. When the pieces have completely dried, you can store them in an air tight jar until you are ready to use them.

12 fl oz (3½ dl) vodka
½ inch ginger
3½ oz (1 dl) dried pieces of dandelion root
2 × 1 inch (3cm) piece of orange peel

Slice the ginger into thin slices and mix all the ingredients in a glass jar or bottle. Leave in a dark place for 1–2 months, shaking it now and again.
Sieve the liquid and keep in a bottle with a tight lid.

Bitters

Rumtopf

Garden Rumtopf

Rumtopf originates from central Europe but is also very popular in Denmark. It is childishly simple to make. Pick the best summer berries you have in your garden, pour into a glass jar together with sugar and alcohol (rum is traditionally used but vodka works as well) and forget about it for a few months. Once matured you end up with delicately conserved fruit that can be used in desserts as well as a decent liqueur for cold winter days. We tend to use our liqueur as a base for other drinks.

During the early summer, find a large glass jar with a lid and find a cool, dark place to store it in. Throughout the summer, fill it with ripe fruit and berries such as strawberries, wild strawberries, red and black currant, raspberries, blueberries, cherries, plums, and peaches.

1 part granulated sugar
2 parts berries
Alcohol to cover

Place the berries and sugar in a glass jar and fill with alcohol until it covers the berries and sugar. Repeat each time you add fruit or berries during the season.

Leave the rumtopf to rest until Christmas when you can open it and enjoy a ripe taste of summer.

Schnapps — Wormwood & St. John's Wort

Flavoring your own schnapps is a craft that has survived in today's society of ready-made products due to its simplicity. In the past it was a way to disguise the bad taste of fusel in alcohol, but these days it is more to do with the fact that it tastes good. You can add almost any flavor you like to alcohol and new flavor trends are constantly emerging. We prefer to keep it simple. The kings of flavor when it comes to alcohol are wormwood and St. John's Wort. We grow the bitter tasting wormwood ourselves while the St. John's Wort grows wild behind the shed.

25.4 oz (75 cl) alcohol (neutral vodka)
1 tsp honey
Wormwood or St. John's Wort

Wormwood

The best time to pick wormwood is at the end of the summer when they have small yellow flowers which will give your schnapps a yellow tinge. If you don't want to wait, you can also use the green leaves for flavor. Place some twigs in a bottle and leave for a week or until you have the right level of bitterness. Strain and add honey to taste.

St. John's Wort

St. John's wort is harvested late summer when yellow buds appear. Try to pick them before the petals have opened up. Pick partway down the stem and cut the buds off with scissors. The buds contain a substance called hypericin that gives the schnapps the yellowish-red color it's known for. Leave for 3–5 days, strain, and add honey to taste.

Beekeeping

We have placed a large wooden block under an old apple tree, and in the early summer mornings, to sit down with a cup of coffee feels like a little piece of heaven because this is where our beehives are located.

As soon as the first ray of sun lays its warm hand across the hive, the first bees awaken. They will rest a while before they open up their wings and take off into the sunshine. More follow and soon the sky is transformed into a motorway with tens of thousands of bees in movement. You try and follow a singular bee to see where it's heading. Is it the small white blackthorn flowers that are of interest, or the field of dandelions next to the horse field? Or maybe the newly bloomed tulips?

On return they are laden down with nectar and their back legs are crammed with pollen, small balls in shades of gold, lemon, and orange depending on which flowers have been visited, and the air becomes heady and sweet.

Much of the work that happens in the garden is either invisible or very, very slow—the bacteria that decompose our compost, the life cycle of fungi and plants, the constant movement of earth by the worms. But the great thing about bees is that you can feel, hear, and see what's going on.

You can follow the bee from a larva as small as a grain of sand, to pupa, to worker bee. You can see them make beeswax, protect the hive against predators, and finally reach the top of their career ladder, collecting nectar as a worker bee. The beehive makes tangible the circle of life.

Bees have also been the corner stone of a modern homesteader, which is hardly surprising. Not only do they pollinate flowers, vegetables, berries, and fruit trees, but they contribute with a vast amount of important raw ingredients such as honey, beeswax, and propolis. These products can in turn enhance thousands of other products. So if you get the chance to keep bees, you have taken a huge step closer to being self-sufficient.

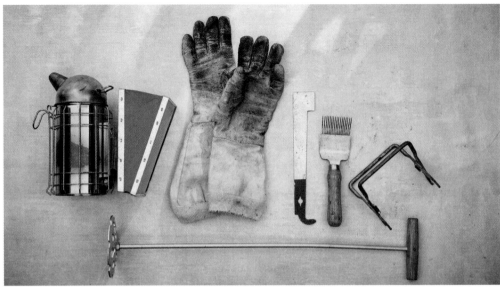

From left to right: Smoker, gloves, hive tool, uncapping fork, honeycomb tongs, honey stirrer

Get Started

If you are a newbie, beekeeping can seem daunting, mysterious, and quite complicated, but don't let this put you off. With knowledge and practice anyone can become an apiarist (beekeeper), but just as with all other animals, you need certain routines to ensure the bees are happy, and it takes responsibility.

It was mostly by chance that we took on a role as beekeepers, even though we had been considering it for a while. When a neighbor advertised that he wanted to move away from beekeeping, we decided to take a chance. He wanted someone in the local village to take over so the bees would keep visiting his garden, and a few months later we nervously lifted two boxes of 40,000 bees into the trunk of our car and drove home. With the help of our neighbor and a whole load of reading we went from happy amateurs to passionate apiarists.

Beekeeping is a craft that you never stop learning about, and as a beekeeper you are constantly surprised and amazed by the bees' abilities.

Attending a course can be a great way of learning the trade and apart from knowledge it is also a good way to network—or of course you can also just start and learn as you go along.

The number of tools and machinery can be a turn off, and beekeeping can become a bit of a materialistic endeavor, but if you just want a few hives for your own use, you don't really need much and can start with quite simple tools. The main thing is that you start. It's easiest to buy a readymade colony (a box of 5–10 frames) with bees that have a queen. However, if you don't want to take the step and keep your own bees, there is an alternative which is a hive share where you contribute to a colony and get a share of the produce. You can also support your own local beekeepers by buying honey directly from them.

How Does the Colony Work?

There are several subspecies of the honeybee (Apis mellifera). The different subspecies have slightly different properties, so do some research and talk to other local beekeepers to determine which is right for your area and needs.

The colony is one large organization that is controlled by a singular queen. The whole society revolves around her and she is the only one who lays eggs.

Bees feed, clean, build, stand guard, and collect food in the form of nectar and pollen. The drones are male bees whose only function is to mate with the queen.

Just like everything in nature, the colony follows the rhythm of the seasons. In the winter the bees are dormant and live on the nourishment collected during the summer. The so-called winter bees keep the queen alive by creating a globe in the hive where the inner temperature is always 68ºF (20ºC), which they achieve by constantly changing places with each other and eating.

When it warms up in March or April, the colony comes to life again and the first bees venture out to collect nectar and the queen starts to lay eggs to increase the size of the colony. The winter bees that have been alive since the fall die and are replaced by new drones.

The colony varies in size during the year from up to 80,000 bees during the summer to a lot less during the winter dormancy. During the summer the bees collect as much pollen and nectar as they can to last over winter. Depending on where you live in the country, this continues into the fall when it gets too cold and the bees become dormant again.

The rhythm of the colony also means the beekeeper's work is seasonal with most of the work taking place from May to August.

What Is the Beekeeper's Role?

The honeybee was one of the first animals domesticated by man, and honey and beeswax are products that are just as useful today as they were hundreds, even thousands, of years ago.

These days a colony would not survive for very long without help from humans due to disease and mites, so the relation between man and bee is an important symbiosis. As a beekeeper it is your responsibility to make sure the colony is healthy and has everything they need. In return we get honey, beeswax, and other products, and everyone is a winner from the vital process of pollination that bees contribute to.

We think it is important to view our relationship with the bees as a collaboration, where we take but also give.

The hive is not a factory where we try to get as much honey as we can; we take what we need and let the bees keep the rest.

The Beehive

Honeybees' natural environment has always been nooks found in nature, mainly in trees. Beekeeping developed when man tried to help bees find homes, for example, by chopping into tree trunks to make spaces for them.

Later on, different hives developed that assisted in beekeeping and today the most common hive is the stackable hive, which consists of a square box usually containing 10 frames where the bees build their colony on honeycombs that have been added by the beekeeper. The advantage of the stackable hives is that it makes them easy to look after and also increases the colony with new frames and boxes.

There are different types of stackable hives with different size frames. It is easiest if you use the same type of hive for the whole colony.

Lately it has become popular to use hives that are meant to mirror a bee's natural environment. One of these is the top bar hive where the bees extend their own frames by building the honeycombs from bars.

Good plants for bees:

Spring	Summer	Fall
Wood squill	Blackberry	Borage
Crocus	Viper's bugloss	New York aster
Dandelion	Raspberry Clover	Lacy phacelia
Winter aconite	(all types)	Orpine
	Oregano	
	Lavender	

Fight the Lawn, Not the Weeds

One reason that bees and other insects that live off nectar and pollen have greatly reduced in numbers over the last few decades is the increase in industrial farming. Fields full of diverse species have disappeared to make way for large scale growing of one type of crop. But even house owners are guilty with their trimmed lawns that are just as poor in variety as the monoculture of the big farms. If you own land, or a garden, you can easily do something about this by basically doing nothing. Don't mow your lawn, especially not during spring or early summer, or even better, turn part of your garden into a field. As a beekeeper, it is easy to change your view on weeds, as the hated dandelion is beloved by bees because it is rich in nectar and pollen. We never mow our lawn when the dandelions are in full bloom. If you have to cut your law, do it in the afternoon as the dandelion only gives nectar during the morning. Another super plant that lives on lawns with just as much pollen and nectar as the dandelion is the clover.

Instead of trimming, ripping weeds, and scattering seeds, lime, and fertilizer over your lawn, leave it to flourish instead. By increasing the biodiversity on your land you not only make your bees stronger and more resilient but contribute to the entire ecosystem.

There are also other ways to help wild bees and other insects. Rather than making an insect hotel, leave old logs and stumps to rot in a corner of the garden as they give housing and protection as well as nourishment.

Try to contribute as much diversity as possible and grow flowers that give nectar and pollen in early spring and fall when your bees need sources of nectar. Easy to grow are lacy phacelia and borage that you can grow in batches through the season. The former is perfect as green manure and the latter on a plate.

Disease & Pests

A sad but unavoidable reality of keeping animals is the need to combat and prevent disease and parasites and the bee colony is no different. Bees can be afflicted by a host of diseases from the stomach sickness nosema to an attack of American foulbrood. In wintertime the bees can also be attacked by mice, which can destroy the whole colony.

The worst threat against the colony though is from the varroa destructor which spread to the United States in the late 1980s. These days most colonies are infected with varroa and it is up to the bee keeper to keep the mites at bay as they weaken the immune system and ability to fight off other infections. If the colony is greatly infected, bees will be born with deformed wings and won't survive for long.

Fighting varroa can be done in several ways but from an ecological perspective the main way is to treat the hive with different natural acids such as formic acid, oxalic acid, and lactic acid, which the mites hate.

Rules & Hive Location

In the United States, each state has its own regulations. Some states require an inspector to oversee the treatment and handling of bees and one of their most important roles is to ensure that infectious diseases do not take hold and spread. Research your state's beekeeping regulations before you start a hive.

You can keep bees even in built-up areas, even on the roof of terraced houses, but in order to keep good neighborly relations you should check with them first and avoid your bees flying over the neighbor's yard or a road that is busy with cars or people. In built up areas bees need good access to water so they don't end up swimming in the neighbor's pool.

There are different views on where to best place your hives, but as a rule of thumb it should be a spot that you might choose to sit by yourself on a sunny spring day. It's important that there is open space in front of the hive so the bees are free to fly, at least 16 ft (5 meters). Try to protect the hives from strong side winds if you can.

BEEKEEPING

The Beekeeper's Year

Winter/Spring—January–March

When your bees awaken depends completely on the weather, and it is usually a sign of spring when the bees start buzzing around the hives. The first thing the winter bees do when they leave the hive is a so-called cleansing flight where they empty their bowels after having held it in all winter.

During the spring when the colony comes to life it is time for the beekeeper to start preparing for the season and it's a good time to take stock of your equipment and make any necessary purchases to have everything ready.

During the winter you should not disturb your bees at all as among other things you risk letting in cold air that can cool down the colony. Try to keep an eye on the colony though. Have they survived? How strong do they appear?

The most important thing is to try and gauge how much food they have left as it's not unusual for bees to starve to death in the spring, especially if there is a cold snap. There are few food sources in nature during the spring and at the same time bees need a lot of nutrients as the queen starts to lay eggs. If the colony is active and the bees have done their cleansing flight, then you can carefully lift some honey frames to see how much is left.

A better way is to weigh the hives by making a scale; in this way you can document the weight of the hive throughout the year without disturbing colony.

Spring—April–May

This is the time the bees come alive. Over a few weeks nature will explode and the bees will be in a hurry to collect pollen and nectar from pussy willows, apple blossoms, cherry blossoms, and dandelions. The beekeeper will also have his hands full now until fall.

A dry and warm day in April is the time to do a thorough review of the hive when you can take serious stock of what life is like inside the hive. There are three important tasks.

FIND THE QUEEN She is not always easy to find but you recognize her by her size. Also, there is usually a space around her. If you find the queen and make sure she is laying eggs, all is well.

If the queen has died you have two alternatives: either combine the colony with another one or get a new queen. You can either buy one from a beekeeper that raises queens or, if you have several hives, you can make a new queen.

CLEANING THE HIVE After the winter, the bees need a bit of help to remove bees that have died over the winter. And the base needs cleaning. It should, preferably, be scrubbed clean with soap but you need to work fast as the longer the hive is open the more it cools down. The temperature should be around 68°F (20°C) inside.

GIVE THE BEES SPACE A really important task during the spring and early summer is to give the bees enough space. The colony is growing fast and it needs space for larva, honey, and pollen. If the bees are finding the hive too small you risk getting a swarm.

From April to mid-July the hives need regular attention. We usually go through them every 10 days but you can do it less often if you don't have the time. It is about following the development of the colony. At some point at the end of May, depending on where you live, it is time to add the first honey super which is where your honey will end up. The honey super is separated from the rest of the hive by a grate that the worker bees can pass through but not the queen. It is also important to check for signs that the bees are about to swarm.

Summer—June–July

In June the hive is usually at its largest with upwards of 80,000 bees, and this is also when the overflow of honey is seen in the hive and honey super. It is important to keep the bees busy now, and when the first honey super is half full it is time to add another one. But early summer is also a time that bees like to swarm, although this usually subsides by mid-June.

SWARMING Most people have seen a swarm of bees at some point in life and it is a sight that people both marvel at and fear. Among beekeepers, swarming has traditionally been spoken about as something negative or even a mistake, but bees swarming is completely normal and it's the way they increase in numbers. What happens during a swarm is that the colony divides and the queen leaves the hive with half of the worker bees. The swarm stays nearby, often in a tree, while the lookout bees find a new home for the colony. To ensure the hive survives, the queen lays eggs for a new queen to take over, and when she is born the old queen leaves.

The negative view of swarming is just a myth made up by man, as beekeepers lose bees and honey. Swarming is actually a natural phenomenon which should be appreciated if you are lucky to see one.

However, there are other reasons you should curtail, or at least try and control, the swarms, as they can cause problems in a densely populated area. It is also a problem that is caused by humans, as there are more chimneys than hollow trees and the bees don't see any difference between them. Another reason is that due to parasites, a wild swarm won't survive for very long on their own.

There are two ways to handle swarming, either by catching them or preventing them. A sure way to tell if the bees are about to start swarming is to look for the queen cells, which are larger cells that are built outside the honeycomb cells.

The best way to handle a swarm is to see it as a gift and give your bees a new home on your own land, giving you two colonies instead of one. You can catch the swarm or make an offshoot, meaning you divide the colony and trick the bees into thinking they've already swarmed. Move the queen to the new colony and let the old one create a new queen, or you can purchase a new queen.

HONEY EXTRACTION At some point after midsummer it's time for one of the highlights of the season, extracting the honey. The honey is ready when cells are covered in a white wax with no honey visible. Once most of the frames in the honey super are full, it's time to start slinging the honey. The frames don't need to be completely covered—if even a third are covered, the honey is ready. If you take the frames too early the honey still contains water and there is a risk that it will ferment and become inedible. There are tools to measure the water levels in honey, but you can also do a simple splash test. If you are not sure, tap the frame against the edge of the hive. If the honey splashes, it's not yet ready.

When you harvest the honey frames you can brush or shake off the bees and place them in a safe spot as they will want their honey back. This is why it is important to sling the honey indoors with the windows shut, as otherwise you will soon have a whole host of visitors.

When the honey frames have been removed, you need to sling the honey. If you have a traditional honey extractor, cut off the white wax and leave it to drain in a sieve—it is pure wax that can be used in creams amongst other things.

When the first golden yellow, floral scented early summer honey starts to pour out of the extractor, our children will be at the ready with their spoons. It's sticky but that is just part of the fun. Honey lasts a long time, but it is never better than when it is fresh with a warm and runny texture. Fresh honey is a raw product that most people will never have the pleasure to taste, which is a shame as it should be appreciated in the same way we do with the first harvest of potatoes or asparagus. Newly extracted honey is always runny; usually it will crystalize, although when that happens depends on which flowers the bees got their nectar from.

If you are not planning to keep a lot of bees, you don't need any fancy tools to fill your first honey jars—a manual honey extractor works just fine. If you have a top bar hive you can also use a juice extractor. You can even let the honey run off the frames on their own, although this takes time, and it can be hard to get all the honey out of the cells. Don't underestimate the joy of simply cutting the honey out of the comb and eating it though.

If you have several hives, it is worth investing in a proper honey extractor, which will make the work a lot easier. The advantage of a honey extractor is that you can quickly return the clean frames to the hive. It's even faster, and more fun, if there are several of you working together as slinging honey from several hives can take time.

The number of times you harvest your honey is dependent on several things such as how much time you have, if it's a good year for honey, and how much you want to leave for the bees. If you harvest little and often you can get single flower honey, which is honey from a specific flower, for example the light dandelion honey or the minty linden honey. The final harvest usually takes place around the end of August.

THIRSTY BEES Apart from nectar and pollen, bees need water just like all other animals. If you have a pond, a river, or another source of water nearby this usually solves itself. Otherwise, it's a good idea to offer water in the vicinity of the hive, especially during hot and dry summer days, as otherwise you risk your bees looking for water where you least want them, such as the neighbor's kids' wading pool or leftover glasses of water. You can make a simple bee waterer by covering a large plate with a stone or marbles and filling it with water so

more honey than you need and leave as much as you can in the hive. We prefer having more hives and taking less from each one.

WINTERIZING Some of the honey you take from the bees has to be replaced with a sugar syrup. You can buy these, but we prefer to make our own with organic sugar. One colony needs around 33lb (15kg) of sugar to survive the winter, but how much you give them depends on how much you let them keep.

Feeding needs to happen straight after the last harvest, especially if you have taken a lot of honey. Feeding can take a few weeks but should be complete once the frost comes, which in some parts of the country can happen as soon as August/September. How you feed your bees depends on what type of hives you have, but most common is a contact feeder or a rapid feeder that you fill with the sugar syrup.

SUGAR SYRUP RECIPE

2.2 lb (1 kg) white sugar
1.5 pints (0.7 l) water

Method:
Heat water and dissolve the sugar in it, multiplying the amount to make as much as you need. Remember that each solution gives 2¾ pints of sugar syrup. The solution can be lukewarm when you give it to the bees as it is easier for them to drink it.

---

the bees can land on the stones and avoid any drowning accidents.

Autumn—August–December
In August it is time to prepare for winter and the bees becoming dormant. The risk of swarming is reduced as the bees hurry to collect as much pollen and nectar as they can. August is also a good month to do your final harvest when you collect the last honey from the hives.

The honey you take from the bees needs to somehow be replaced, which most beekeepers do by feeding them with a sugar syrup. Traditionally, many beekeepers, not least the commercial ones, try to maximize their harvest and leave very little for the bees, but recently this practice has been questioned as honey contains so many natural nutrients that are hard to replace. Don't harvest

BEE HEALTH AND FALL When the last honey has been extracted, you also need to treat the colony for the varroa mite. This has to be done now to avoid acids getting in the honey and to give the bees the best start for the new year without too many mites.

Do a final check and then treat the colony with formic acid, and then later on in the fall with lactic acid and oxalic acid. You can find instructions on treatments online.

Bee Products

For the modern housekeeper, the colony gives you lots of important products such as honey and beeswax. However, the colony gives so much more than this and you can even harvest pollen, propolis, and bee bread. There are even more unusual products such as royal jelly and bee venom.

Honey

No two honeys are the same as honey is a natural product and reflective of the environment the bees find themselves in. You may have heard the word "terroir," French for "land," in the context of wine production, and the word describes the way in which climate, soil, and geographical location affects the wine.

For honey, this process occurs naturally—honey is a product of the millions of flowers that bees collect their nectar from. A regular pot of honey contains the flavor of several million flowers.

The flowers don't only contribute with taste, but different sugars that affect the way in which the honey behaves—for example, if it stays runny or the speed at which it crystalizes.

Contrary to what some might believe, bees do not collect honey from flowers; the honey is a product that the bees create from nectar. To make honey, the bees add enzymes and a dozen different lactic acid bacteria which breaks down complex sugars. The second part of the process is drying, as bees reduce the water levels in the honey which preserves it. Honey dries by the nectar being moved between bees, but also through fanning.

It's an amazing process that you can observe on a warm summer's evening as thousands of bees synchronize their wings to create an air current to dry the honey, filling the air with the heady, sweet scent of honey.

Single Flower Honey

Single flower honey is a fairly new phenomenon that is becoming more and more popular. It means the honey tastes of a specific flower like dandelion, linden, clover, raspberry, or Calluna. Throughout the season the bees will intensively target nectar from a specific plant that is in full bloom, which gives the honey a unique character.

Dandelion honey is bright yellow and floral and mild in taste and Calluna honey is amber-colored and rich. But even single flower honey can vary depending on "terroir" as there are over 1,000 types of dandelions, for example.

If you keep your eyes open, you can harvest the single flower honey by extracting it straight away after a particular flower blooms. Another way to get different types of honey is to extract it regularly several times during the season, for example early summer, high summer, and fall, which will give you honey with completely different characteristics.

Runny or Set Honey

In northern areas, honey is usually set, or crystallized, but in more southern areas, runny honey is more common. The simple explanation is that different flowers affect how quickly the honey crystallizes. When the honey is extracted, it is runny and when it sets depends on the combination of sugars. Some honey sets almost right away, such as rapeseed honey. Honey contains several types of sugar such as glucose and fructose and it is the levels of the latter that is the deciding factor for if and when the honey sets.

Beekeepers that have fields of rapeseed nearby are often in a hurry to start extracting as soon as the flowers bloom as rapeseed honey can start setting while still in the hive. Other honeys, such as the acacia honey, stays runny. Calluna honey can stay runny for over a year.

A lot of the imported runny honey that is sold has been chemically or heat treated. If you heat honey over 185°F (85°C) it will stay runny permanently, but you will also kill any enzymes and bacteria that make the honey healthy, as these disappear at around 145°F (63°). A better way to ensure you have runny honey all year round is to freeze some of it straight after extracting it as it will stay runny and at the same time retain the health benefits.

Spreadable Honey

We prefer to use most of the honey the way it is, raw and untreated, although in time crystals will form as it sets, and it can get a bit grainy. If you want a smoother texture that can be spread on toast, there are two things you can do.

Mixing Honey

Once the honey has been extracted and sieved, you can mix it. It should be stored in a cool space, around 57°F (14°C), as the process will be faster. Mixing honey is heavy work, so it is easier to use a honey mixer or a large ladle. You can do it by hand, but with a strong drill and honey mixer the work is much easier to do.

Mixing honey smashes the crystals and gives the honey a smooth consistency. The process needs to be repeated daily until the honey becomes viscous and murky and, depending on the honey, the time can vary, but don't wait too long as you still need to be able to pour it into jars.

Creamed Honey

The method we prefer is creaming honey, meaning you increase the honey's natural process of setting, which gives a smoother honey. The benefit of this is that it is faster and you can pour the honey into jars after just a few days.

RECIPE FOR CREAMED HONEY

Raw honey, 3% of the total amount you want to cream
Crystalized honey, 10% of the above amount

Example: if the total amount you wish to cream is 220lb (100 kg), the recipe is as follows:
6½ lb (3 kg) raw honey
10½ oz (300 g) crystalized honey

If you don't have any honey from previous years, buy the smoothest local honey you can find.

Method:

1. Pour the raw honey in a bowl and mix in the crystalized honey.
2. Stir or whisk until completely mixed. Place it in the fridge with a lid or towel over it.
3. Stir twice a day but for no more than a minute at a time as it can't get too warm. After 2–3 days, it's ready and should be firm but creamy when you stir it.
4. Mix it with equal parts newly harvested runny honey. Using the example above, 116 oz (3,300g) creamed honey with 116 oz (3,300 g) raw honey. Stir until completely blended.
5. Pour the creamed honey in a thin drizzle into the bowl with the raw honey 220lb (100 kg) while stirring at the same time. Wait until the air bubbles disappear before pouring it into jars.
6. Store the honey in a cool place, 54–57°F (12–14°C). A week later the honey should have a firm and smooth consistency and is ready. Don't forget to save some crystalized honey for the following year.

BEEKEEPING

Beeswax

If you carefully lift a honeybee by its wings and turn it over, you might be lucky enough to see the beginnings of one of nature's true miracle products. From the glands on the back, clear beeswax pokes out. Beeswax is a complex combination of esters, alcohol, and scents, which gives it its unique smell. Beeswax is one of the most precious and versatile materials there is and has been acknowledged for this throughout history. In the "Odyssey," Odysseus uses beeswax as ear plugs to protect his crew from the siren's fatal songs. Daedalus created wings with the help of beeswax that he attached to his son Icarus, and even if this wasn't the best idea, a modern homesteader can use beeswax for everything from making candles and skin creams to different types of wax.

Wax is a by-product that you get when you extract the honey. It comes in different colors, from almost completely white to a deep yellow and even red. As a beekeeper you need to look after your wax and differentiate between its different qualities.

Wax Cappings

The wax that the bees use to cover the honey cells with is known as wax cappings and is distinguished by its white color. As it is usually newly produced, it is made up of pure wax, which is different from the honeycomb, which is usually yellow or dark. When you come to extract the honey, you should remove the wax cappings.

Cleaning Wax Cappings

When you remove the wax cappings, some honey will usually attach to it. Place the wax in a sieve and leave it to drain off as much honey as possible. Fill a plate or bath with water and pour in the wax. Wash the wax methodically until it crumbles and gets a gritty appearance and then place it in a sieve. You can either wash the wax again or carefully rinse it under running water in the sieve to get rid of any leftover honey. Save this honey water as it can be placed back in the hive or you can make mead from it.

Cleaning the Honeycomb

Sometimes the honeycombs break and need to be replaced. You should also check them every year and replace any old ones to ensure the bees stay healthy. If you use a top bar hive you naturally get a lot of honeycomb as you are harvesting entire sheets of honey. The honeycomb often contains by-products such as old honey, pollen, and remnants from any acid treatments, so you need to clean it thoroughly.

Melting & Sieving Wax

There are several methods to melting honeycomb and the best way is to do it straight from the frames. It is fairly easy to build a simple steam wax melt or sun wax melt and you can find blueprints on the internet. If you have a large bee farm you can use a steam juicer, but you won't be able to use it for juice afterwards.

Melting Wax in a Steam Juicer

Fill the steam juicer with water and leave it to boil. Add the beeswax in a heat-resistant nylon bag, such as the ones you use to make beer. You can even place them on top of an old piece of cloth or towel. Most of the dirt will stay in the nylon bag, which can be emptied and cleaned between melting. Leave the melted wax to run into a bowl half filled with warm water. The wax floats and will solidify on the surface and not stick to the bowl. Any by-products that are left get stuck underneath and can be easily scraped off.

Remember that all the tools you use for handling wax should not be used for anything else as wax is difficult to completely remove. It can be hard to get all the dirt off and if you have bought beeswax sheets, you can never be sure what they previously contained. For beauty products, you should only use wax cappings that you know are newly produced and clean.

Pollen

If you study the bees in flight, you will soon spot them—the pollen baskets on their legs. Heavily laden, they come in to land with little balls hanging off the back of their legs. Shades of poppy red, lemon yellow, and glimmering green can be seen, depending on which flowers they have visited. Bees collect pollen, which they make into little balls with the help of nectar.

For the bees, collecting pollen is just as important as nectar. While honey gives the colony carbohydrates, pollen is a source of protein. It is also packed with vitamins, minerals, carotenoids, and flavoids—antioxidants. Pollen has more protein than beef and is used as a health supplement these days as well as in the production of beauty products.

Pollen is a super product that has a unique taste, nutty and sweet, although this varies depending on the flower.

Extracting & Storing Pollen

To collect pollen, you need a special tool called a pollen trap. There are different types, but they generally work the same way in that a comb brushes the pollen baskets as the bees enter the hive. The pollen grains fall into a hole or a box, but don't leave the pollen trap for too long as pollen is vital in the production of new bees.

Deal with the pollen right away as it can start to turn moldy otherwise. As soon as it has been harvested, the grains should be frozen for at least 72 hours.

Fresh Pollen

Fresh pollen has a soft and creamy consistency and a strong, sweet taste that can vary depending on the flower it comes from. Store it in the freezer until you are ready to use it.

Dried Pollen

Dried pollen grains are hard and have a milder flavor, but drying them makes them easier to use, such as when you want to sprinkle them over a desert.

Spread the pollen out on a baking tray to dry in a fan-assisted oven on a low temperature, around 85°F (30°), with the oven door ajar. You can also use an electric mushroom dryer with mosquito net at the bottom. When the pollen grains are done, they should be light and airy.

Washed Wax

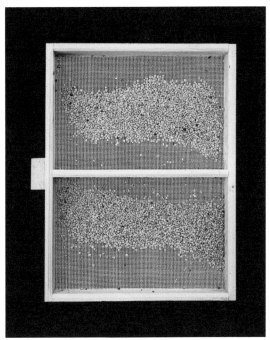

Pollen

Propolis

When you lift the lid of the frames of the hive you might notice them sticking together. This is the propolis, a dark, sap-like substance that the bees use to protect the hive (their immune system). Cracks, holes, and other gaps are filled with propolis to keep bacteria, fungi, and pests out. It is a form of sap that the bees collect from the buds of leafy trees and sap from pine trees. Just like all other products that stem from the colony, propolis varies depending on the environment. It begins with a sticky consistency that hardens over time.

Research has found that propolis has good antibacterial properties and is also effective against fungi and viruses. It can be used both as raw produce as well as in health food supplements.

Harvesting Propolis

The easiest way is to use a so-called propolis screen that can be attached at the top of the hive. The bees will fill the gaps, which usually takes a few weeks. After this you can freeze the screen, enabling you to scrape off the propolis. You can also scrape off propolis with a knife or straight from the frame if you just want a small amount. The propolis can be stored as is and lasts a long time. A common way to use it is to make a tincture.

PROPOLIS CULTURE

3½ oz (100 g) unflavored spirit (the strongest you can find, preferably over 60%)
⅓ oz (10 g) propolis

Method:
1. Mix by hand or use a pestle and mortar to get it as fine as possible.
2. Mix the propolis with alcohol in a jar with a lid and store in a dark place, shaking the jar now and again. After one or two months, the propolis should have dissolved depending on the strength of the alcohol.
3. Strain the mixture though a coffee filter and store in a bottle with a pipette. The tincture lasts several years.

Bee Bread

Just like the honey, bees store pollen in the honeycomb. Inside the hive, the pollen goes through a transformation which changes its taste and consistency. The bees mix the pollen with honey and ferment and store it in the cells, which get covered with honey. The finished product is known as bee bread and has a strong umami taste, which distinguishes it from the sweet pollen.

The bee bread sits in the honeycomb and can be harvested with a little tool called a pollen grip. You can also cut or break the bee bread out of the honeycomb.

Bee bread should be handled the same way as pollen and either frozen or dried to make it last.

Fresh Honeycomb with Ice Cream

BEEKEEPING

BEE'S KNEES   1 DRINK

Every successful harvest should be celebrated with a Bee's Knees made from raw honey. This drink was invented in Paris in 1921 at the Ritz and became a classic during prohibition. It means, "the absolute best" and the blend of gin and honey is just that!

1¾ fl oz (5 cl) homemade gin, see page 178
1 fl oz (3 cl) freshly squeezed lemon juice
1 tbsp raw honey
Lemon peel to garnish

Dissolve the honey in the gin using a cocktail shaker. Add lemon juice and ice and shake. Pour into cocktail glasses and garnish with lemon peel. Drink and then mix up another one.

Hot Drinks

We don't really need hot drinks to survive but most of us consider hot drinks a vital part of life. Some of us don't wake up until we smell the coffee beans being ground. Personally, we don't really wake up until we sit in front of the fire with something warm in our hands, and sleep is never so sweet as after we've drunk a large mug of tea. Hot drinks give us something more than just filling a basic need—they reach our soul.

It is not surprising, then, that many rituals have developed around creating drinks, such as Japanese and Chinese tea ceremonies or the modern equivalent of baristas showing off their skills.

For a modern homesteader, the garden offers a host of possibilities. In the summer we pick and dry a range of plants, herbs, flowers, and berries that we can enjoy during the winter months. To be fair, we don't grow coffee, but we do buy raw organic beans from small local sellers and roast them, which is a ritual in itself, and one every coffee lover should experience.

Tea & Herbs

Tea is actually a drink made from the tea plant, Camellia sinensis, but it has become an umbrella term for drinks made with all sorts of herbs and plants. In China, tea has been drunk for thousands of years, whereas in Europe it did not gain popularity until the eighteenth century. The climate in the more temperate parts of the United States does allow for tea to be grown, but it's a fairly niche crop. Even in the colder regions, our gardens and forests are full of tasty things to brew "local tea" from. During the summer we throw leaves and herbs such as mint, raspberry, and blackcurrant straight into our teacups. In late summer we dry berries, flowers, herbs, and leaves so they'll be ready to brew tea during the winter months. It's fun and easy making your own tea and it also tastes good.

Brewing Tea

There are lots of different ways to extract flavor from herbs and your method will depend a bit on the herbs and plants you use as well as the result you are after. In the world of coffee, macerating coffee has become popular, i.e. cold brewing coffee. For both coffee and tea this method gives a milder drink as there is less time to develop any bitter properties. Tannin is usually released through heat, which can be avoided by a gentler cold brew.

Some herbs or herb parts need to boil for longer in a decoction to draw out more flavor. This may be the case if you're using roots, for example. Brewing tea often calls for something in between, where the herbs can infuse for a short time in hot water. The traditional ways of brewing tea are quite different from what we are used to in the west—the tea is brewed for a short period of time several times over using the same tea leaf.

You can get different tastes from the same herbs by just changing your brewing method.

Drying & Storing

During the growing season, you can brew tea using freshly picked herbs, but make sure you store some for the winter too. The difference between using fresh and dried herbs is mainly about the amount you use. As a rule of thumb, use twice as many fresh tea leaves as you would dry ones.

Drying leaves is easy and often the best way to store herbs, plants, flowers, berries, and anything else you want to make tea from.

We use lots of different drying methods. The gentlest way is to air dry plants. If they are dried in heat, for example in an oven, they can lose taste.

When it comes to larger herbs and plants, we usually tie them into a bunch and hang them over the pole we use for crisp bread that hangs above the fire so that it gets both heat and air. This works well for lemon balm and mint. Find an airy place in your home and make sure the bunches aren't too large or dense. Avoid placing them in sunlight as, just like heat, it can make them lose flavor.

For smaller leaves, plants, and flowers we use an herb drier with woven baskets that are stacked on top of each other. Spread the items out in the basket so they have space in an airy place to dry.

We also use an electric dryer, but only for things that contain a lot of moisture such as mushrooms, fruit, and berries.

Store your dried herbs in a dark, cool place in a glass jar. Though they've been dried, herbs are still fresh produce and will, in time, deteriorate in quality.

Raspberries & Blackcurrants

Sometimes, the easiest thing you can do is creep outside, barefoot in the grass, with some scissors, and just harvest a few leaves for your morning tea. Our favorites are the raspberry and blackcurrant bushes. Raspberry contains oxytocin, which has a calming effect, while blackcurrant is one big smell and taste sensation, its distinct aroma hitting you even as you pick it. Brewed together, you will get a green herby and aromatic tea.

Pick the small, young leaves; around 10 leaves from each plant is enough for around 4 cups (1 l.) of tea.

Clean the leaves to ensure no insects remain and then place them in a tea pot and pour boiling water over them. Leave to infuse for around 5–10 minutes.

Don't forget to dry raspberry and blackcurrant to use during the winter too.

Raspberry & Blackcurrant

HOT DRINKS

Southern Iced Tea with Mint

HOT DRINKS

Purple Coneflower Tea

Purple coneflower is a common, but beautiful addition to many gardens during late summer and makes a lovely cut flower. It also has a long history as a potent herb for healing and can still be bought in pharmacies to keep colds away. Native Americans used the plant, which is said to have healing properties, to treat snake bites among other things. We make a "cold" tea with ours, preferably after we have enjoyed them in a vase. It's a tea that is more for the body than your tastebuds, so add herbs rich in taste such as mint and lemon balm and make sure you brew up a mug as soon as you feel a cold coming on.

You can make tea by using fresh or dried flowers. If you are using fresh, make sure to double the amount. You can use the whole plant, so dry the leaves and stalks as well. You can also use the roots, but as this is a perennial, we leave them be for the next season.

3½ oz (1 dl) fresh purple coneflower, equal to around one whole flower, is enough for a large mug of tea. Leave it to infuse in a tea pot with around 1–1½ cups (3–4 dl) water for around 15 minutes.

GROWING PURPLE CONEFLOWER This is a hardy perennial which, once established, can cope with heat as well as dry or cold weather.

Sow the seeds indoors during late winter. The seeds need light, so cover them very lightly, for example using sand. Make sure to keep a constant level of moisture and leave them somewhere slightly cooler than room temperature. After about a month you can repot them and harden them off before planting out in the spring. They prefer a well-drained soil in a sunny, warm space, preferably south facing. It is hardy down to zone 3 or 4.

Southern Iced Tea with Mint

During the balmiest of summer days when we lie in the shade under a tree, we like to make a thirst-quenching iced tea, just like the ones from the American South. Even our kids like this tea.

½ cup (1 dl) honey
1 large bunch of mint leaves
3½ pints (1½ l) water
1 large lemon

Boil the water and pour over the mint leaves and honey. Leave it to cool down. It can be stored in the fridge for a day or two.

When you are ready drink it, cut the lemon into wedges, squeeze some into the tea, and add lots of ice.

Honey Tea

An easy and tasty way to store some of the tastes from summer for the winter is to make flavored honey. Honey absorbs the flavors from the herbs and can then be used as a warming, tasty tea, preferably with some frothed milk.

It's simple to make—just mix fresh herbs with a jar of honey. It's easiest with raw, runny honey but you can also use solid honey that you can gently warm to make it liquid.

Fill half a glass jar with fresh herbs and flowers and fill with honey. Store the jar in a dark place and turn it once a week. You can strain the honey to remove the herbs or leave them. If the honey has solidified, you can gently warm it in a water bath before straining it.

All types of herbs and flowers that give flavor can be used. We usually make honey tea from lavender, rose leaves, mint, lemon balm, and rosemary.

Boil some water and fill a large mug. Add 1–2 tbsp honey tea and dissolve in the water. Add frothed milk.

Honey Tea & Purple Coneflower Tea, page 213

HOT DRINKS

Coffee

Legend has it an Ethiopian shepherd by the name of Kaldi discovered the coffee bean. After one of his goats had eaten berries from a special tree, it stayed awake all night. The rest is, as we know, culinary history the whole world over.

Unfortunately, there is a large part of the coffee industry that for both human and environmental reasons we are not willing to support, and we try to skip as many steps of the production chain as possible by buying large packets of raw beans from small, organic farmers who we know by name. This means we roast and grind our own beans, which not only means we skip the middle men, but we also get a better tasting and fresher coffee.

Coffee Beans

There are over 100 types of coffee, but within commercial coffee production, three main types are used: arabica, liberica, and robusta. The best quality coffee is arabica, which grows at high altitudes, and the higher it grows the more aromatic the beans. For this reason, arabica beans are harder to grow than other lower growing types such as robusta and liberica.

We try to buy arabica beans from small Ethiopian growers as we think it makes the best coffee, but coffee, just like all plants, is affected by its unique environment such as weather, water, and the local conditions, so it's best to try different beans and growers to find one you like.

Raw Coffee

For a lot of people, coffee is just a powder and the long process that made it isn't even considered. In its raw state, the coffee bean has a grey-green hue and is smaller than a roasted bean, but even in this state, the coffee bean has been through a process from coffee berry to bean. There are two main processes, the wet and dry method. The latter, and the original, involves drying the berry in the sun until the beans emerge. The wet method means washing the coffee and removing the fruit flesh by scrubbing it. After this, the beans go through a fermentation process that adds flavor and complexity to the beans. Washed coffee is often higher quality but as it needs water it is less environmentally friendly, especially in hot countries where coffee usually grows. These days there are more environmentally friendly alternatives that combine both these methods.

The great thing about raw coffee is that apart from roasting your own coffee, it has a much longer shelf life as it is not until you roast and grind the coffee that it becomes fresh produce. Raw beans stored in a dark, cool, and airy space can keep for several years, whereas freshly roasted coffee is best used within a few days to a few weeks if stored correctly because roasting it starts the process of releasing the aromas that can quickly deteriorate.

Roasting Coffee

Roasting coffee is a magical process that turns a small, hard, green raw bean into a crisp, black coffee bean. Not until you have roasted the coffee will you know what it really tastes like as the roasting process chemically transforms the bean. The first stage occurs at around 220°F (104°C) when the bean starts to shrivel as it loses liquid and starts to turn yellow. It then swells to about twice the size and, at around 383°F (197°C) it starts to change color and turn brown.

The important part as a coffee roaster is when the beans start to crackle and pop, which means they are nearly finished. The popping sound happens when the beans' outer silvery membrane cracks due to expansion. At the end of the roasting process, the sugar in the coffee bean caramelizes. Generally, a light roast is slightly more tart, a medium roast is sweeter, and a dark roast more bitter.

During the roasting process, the sugar reacts with the amino acids that release over 100 aromatic substances, and once the roasting is complete, the coffee bean contains over 700 different flavors that combine to make the taste we know as coffee.

Roasting Coffee in an Oven

You don't really need any special equipment to roast your own coffee—a basic oven works perfectly. Remember that different ovens work differently and the roasting times can vary, so you need to find what works for you. Use a perforated oven tray for a more even roast, as some ovens can have uneven heat. You can stir

Coffee is roasted according to the brewing method. For a faster brew, use a bean that has been roasted hard and fast with a fine ground, and vice versa.

the beans around a few times if you notice that they are not roasting evenly.

Roasting coffee can generate a lot of smoke when you open the oven, so keep the kitchen fan on and open a window. You might want to turn the smoke alarm off temporarily too if it's close by.

One alternative to roasting in the oven is using a coffee roaster that can be placed on the hob. You can get ones that are also used for popcorn and are basically a pan with a lid and a spinner, which means you constantly circulate the beans, giving a more even roast. You can also use a dry frying pan, but only do small amounts at a time.

Apart from this you just need a sieve or a colander.

Method:

1. Turn the oven to 437°F (225°C), fan assisted if possible.
2. Place an empty tray in the oven to heat up.
3. Remove the tray and add a layer of raw beans, thinly spread for an even roast.
4. Return to the oven and wait for the "pop" which takes around 6-9 minutes. Once they pop, reduce the temperature to 392°F (200°C) for an even roast.
5. It's the popping that decides what roast you get; the longer you leave the bean, the darker the roast, but be cautious as there are just a few minutes between each roasting level.
6. Remember that roasting continues for a short while even after you have removed the beans, so place them on a cold tray to stop the roasting and cool the beans as quickly as possible.
7. The beans continue to expand during roasting until they reach a peak. If you carry on roasting they will go through a second "pop" and turn black and oily. Any more than this, a French roast, is not recommended.
8. When you roast your own beans, you retain the silvery membrane. We usually leave it, but you can remove it by mixing the beans in a sieve or colander and removing the shell. It's best done over a sink or outdoors.

Coffee Roast Levels

There are several roasting levels depending on the type of coffee you want to brew and which beans you have. Some beans are aromatic and suit a darker roast, while others are fruity and tart and work best as a light roast. In an oven, you can achieve the following roasts in under 10–20 minutes usually.

BLOND Remove the beans as soon as you hear the first pop and they have a light, milk chocolatey color. A light roast works best as a pour over coffee or a cold brew.

NEW ENGLAND A light to medium roast with a light brown bean that is both tart and nutty.

CITY This is similar to a classic Swedish medium roast. It has rich, nutty, and sweet notes. A darker variety of city is known as full city.

WIENER This is the next level when the coffee bean loses its fruitiness and takes on a more chocolatey note and the bean turns black and glossy.

ESPRESSO This is the classic Italian roast. For the best espresso roast, lower the temperature and roast the bean slightly longer. The higher roasting grade is due to the fact that a light roasted bean gives a more bitter tone, which manifests when the espresso is brewed.

FRENCH ROAST This is considered to be the classic dark roast as the bean has changed from brown to black. The beans have also turned oily from the fat that has seeped to the surface.

Storing & Grinding Coffee

Freshly roasted coffee lasts a few weeks, but we usually drink it up in around 10 days. For the first 24 hours after roasting, you can store the coffee in an open jar as it is still emitting gases. After this, store in a jar with a lid in a cold, dark space. If you want to store your beans for longer, you need a vacuum sealed jar. Don't store coffee in the fridge as moisture and large temperature changes are bad for the coffee.

In theory, you could throw some coffee beans in warm water and end up with coffee. The problem is that it would get cold long before it was done, so grinding coffee is simply to speed up the process. Grinding coffee also affects the taste, which is why different coffee cultures have different sizes when it comes to grinding. It's really a question of physics—the finer the grind, the more water gets to it, meaning a finer ground gives a stronger and more intense flavor in a shorter amount of time. This is why the espresso bean is ground finer than classic Swedish or American coffee and you should adapt the grind to how you want your coffee.

Grind your coffee when you want to use it. This applies to all grinding, from wheat in bread to malt in beer, as this gives you the most flavor when you brew it. A ground coffee is sensitive to air (oxygen) and quickly loses its flavor.

Invest in a decent coffee grinder where you can adjust the grind. Try not to use the cheap electric ones as they both grind unevenly as well as heat the coffee. You can get a good, expensive coffee grinder but a good quality manual grinder works just as well and is cheaper. Obviously, how you choose to brew your coffee is entirely up to you, so happy brewing!

From Raw Bean to French Roast

HOT DRINKS

Storing & Prepping

As fall comes to a close and the harvesting is done, exhaustion can set in and the desire to complete the to-do list diminishes. Just because you have finished harvesting, doesn't mean that you are done. The same love and care you put into growing should also be put into taking care of your harvest. An important part of being a modern homesteader is storing your produce properly, but also prepping. By prepping we mean processing and enhancing the raw goods, which is often needed, by for example preparing food for storage or to be used in cooking.

To avoid the stress of dealing with everything at once, we harvest regularly during a longer period of time.

Leafy greens and beans are par boiled in batches and frozen, tomatoes and berries are thrown into various freezers (several freezers are good if you have the space), which are then used to make ketchup, jam, and squash during fall and winter.

Another great thing to have around are glass jars, and every trip to a thrift store results in at least five clip-top glass jars to add to our large collection. The jars are filled with colorful vegetables, fruits, and berries that adorn our open shelves in the kitchen during the fall, creating an air of beauty and calm. In time we move the jars into the pantry or the root cellar.

CONSERVING

In order to enjoy your homegrown products for longer, you need to protect them against bacteria, yeasts, and mold that can ruin the food and give rise to toxic substances. You can do this by changing the environment for the bacteria, for example fermenting to lower the pH levels to reduce unhealthy microorganisms and support the healthy ones, or even just halt or kill any activity. Cold halts activity while drying, salting, and sweetening reduces the microorganisms' access to water.

Many microorganisms can't survive without oxygen, but a glass jar is worth nothing unless it is cleaned and sterilized before use to extend the use-by date and more importantly kill any dangerous bacteria and spores. Never touch the insides of the jars or lids when you are prepping them for conservation. Turn the jars upside down while the content (e.g., warm jam or stock) cools down as this sterilizes the lid and your food will keep for longer.

Method:
1. Place the bottles or jars in the oven without the rubber seals but with their lids.
2. Heat the oven to 355°F (180°C) and leave for 30 minutes.
3. Turn the oven off and leave the bottles and jars to cool down.

Drying

During summer and fall we dry lots of vegetables, mushrooms, herbs, fruits, and berries. We use three main ways to dry food: at room temperature, in a fan assisted oven, and in a dryer. We use all three ways as different foods behave differently during the drying process. For example, mushrooms, apples, and onions work perfectly on a wooden rod and left to dry in the kitchen, preferably near an open fire, wood burner, or radiator. Apple rings hanging to dry are decorative and smell lovely, but they are also tempting and disappear more quickly than we can dry them in our family.

Foods with a low water content can be dried in a fan-assisted oven on a low heat with the oven door ajar. A food dryer is a great investment as the drying time is much shorter, it uses less electricity, and it is easier to control. Drying time depends on the method, water content, and thickness of the food you are drying. Store your dried foods in airtight glass jars in a cool, dry, dark space and don't forget to write the contents on the jar!

Fruit & Berries

Dry fruit and berries until they are chewy but not too hard. Many berries need to be mashed or sliced first due to their high water content, otherwise they turn rock hard. Fruit should be sliced into equally thick slices or they risk not cooking at the same rate. Drying intensifies flavors, especially berries with a tart flavor such as raspberries and lingon berries, which can turn very sour when dried and are best placed in syrup when dry. We dry fruit and berries as candy for the kids but also for muesli and desserts.

Vegetables & Mushrooms

When drying vegetables, the faster the process, the better they taste and look as they are always best straight after harvest. To keep their taste, leafy greens and legumes should be parboiled before they are dried, in the same way that you do before freezing them. Shred, chop, or slice larger vegetables and mushrooms in a nice even size. If you are drying mushrooms in an oven, spread them out sparsely to avoid them turning moldy during the long drying time. Both mushrooms and vegetables need to be dried completely with no liquid remaining,

making them hard and crispy. Root vegetables should be able to be broken off and leafy greens and mushrooms should crumble between your fingers.

Lavender Syrup

Herbs & Flowers

We dry a lot of herbs and flowers to make, among other things, salt, teas, and beauty products. First, we pick and remove the leaves from the flowers and twigs and then we spread them out in a dryer, which is a great little invention that consists of a wooden stand and plaited trays at different levels that can be removed so you can flatten and store the dryer. We always dry herbs and flowers at room temperature.

Some favorites of ours to dry:

Black currants	Apple rings	Carrots
Sea buckthorn	Rose hips	Mushrooms
Strawberries	Chili	Tomatoes
Raspberries	Kale	

Herb Salt

There are two quick and simple ways to make an herb salt: you can dry the herbs first and then mix them with salt, or mix fresh herbs with salt and then dry the mixture. We prefer the latter as we find the salt absorbs an herbier taste in this way. We have lots of different herb salts in the cupboard and we often forget what's what and tend to sniff our way around them. To make things easier, the recipe below is for a good, versatile salt.

2 cups (5 dl)
1.7 cups (4 dl) sea salt
2 cups (5 dl) chopped herbs, e.g., savory, sage, thyme,
    chives, and oregano

Turn the oven to 122°F (50°C), clean and roughly chop the herbs. Pour the herbs and salt into a mixer and blend.

Spread the mixture as thinly as possible on parchment paper on a baking tray and dry with the oven door slightly ajar until it is bone dry and can be crumbled with your fingers.

Mix by hand or use a pestle and mortar and place in airtight glass jars with lids.

Lavender Syrup

The first time we made lavender syrup was to make lavender-flavored ice cream. It was so good that we made another batch to pour on top of it. These days we use it for desserts and summer drinks but also in tea.

1¼ cup (3 dl)
¾ cup (2 dl) water
¾ cup (2 dl) white sugar
2 tsp lavender flowers, fully bloomed
Blueberries or currants (optional)

Tie some twine around a bunch of lavender flowers and leave to hang upside down to dry for at least 3 days indoors.

Boil water and add the sugar, stirring until dissolved.

Add the lavender and some berries if you want to add color (lavender gives no color), stir, and leave to cool down.

Sieve the syrup through a fine sieve and pour into a glass bottle. Stored in the fridge it will last a few months.

Rose Sugar

This flowery sugar is perfect for summer desserts.

1 part fragrant rose petals from red or pink roses
3 parts white sugar

Remove the rose petals and layer them with sugar in a food processer. Mix until you have pink sugar.

Spread the sugar on a tray and leave to dry overnight. If you want it even finer, you can mix it again. Store in an airtight sterilized jar.

Rose Sugar

STORING & PREPPING

Pumpkin Marmalade

STORING & PREPPING

Sugar

Sugar has three properties: it gives flavor, gives texture, and stops the food fermenting or turning moldy. Using sugar to preserve food is an old method, just like salt. We usually use honey to add sweetness when baking or in food, but when preserving fruit and berries we use sugar.

We either boil sugar and water with berries or fruit to make cordials, jam, marmalade, jellies, and purees (in order to effectively preserve fruit, you need a sugar concentration of around 68 percent), or we boil a syrup with 2 cups (5 dl) sugar per 2 pints of water. The syrup can be poured over berries or fruit in a glass jar.

Pumpkin Marmalade

The first time we tasted this marmalade I thought it was quince cheese. The taste is very mild and buttery yet complex and goes perfectly with sheep's and goat cheese with that tangy barnyard flavor.

2.2 lb (1 kg)
2.2 lb (1 kg) pumpkin (we use uchiki kuri)
Peel from one orange
1 cardamom pod, seeds only
2¾ cups (6½ dl) white sugar

Cut the pumpkin into pieces and grate the orange peel. Grind the cardamom seeds and mix with sugar.

Place the pumpkin, orange zest, and cardamom sugar in a pan and simmer on a low heat for around 1 hour without a lid. Mix into a smooth marmalade and pour into clean glass jars.

Salting

In the old days, salt was a more valued commodity than gold, mainly due to its use as a preservative. Salting is a method that draws liquid out of raw produce and in this way increases its shelf life. Food is placed in salt or brine and the water moves to where the concentration of salt is the highest, which is around the food, which in turn dries out. Bacteria can't survive without water, which means they can't break down the food.

For salting meat, use sodium nitrite (curing salt) to stop the growth of microorganisms.

Pickled Egg Yolks

This is a great way to utilize egg yolks and it also tastes good. Some people find the salted egg yolks' umami-like taste is similar to Parmesan or a mature gruyere cheese and we can certainly see similarities both in taste and texture. We grate them over pasta or slice them and add to meals that need more depth and saltiness.

6 egg yolks
6 eggs
2 cups (5 dl) salt
3 tbsp apple cider vinegar

Pour salt in a bowl and make a small well for each egg yolk.

Crack the eggs and separate the whites from the yolks (save the whites to make pasta dough, meringue, or drinks). Gently pour the egg yolks into the wells and carefully cover with the salt.

Cover with a loose-fitting lid or beeswax cloth and leave in the fridge for a few days.

Remove the egg yolks, gently brush the salt off, and wash them in apple cider vinegar. Dry them until they are completely dry. This can be done by hanging the eggs in fabric in the fridge for a week, overnight in the oven at 120°F (50°C), or in a food dehydrator for an hour. If you store the egg yolks in a sterilized airtight jar they last for up to a month.

Fermentation

Lacto fermentation of vegetables means creating an environment for the lactic acid bacteria to transform (ferment) carbohydrates to lactic acid. Man has fermented foods since time immemorial as a way to preserve produce, and these days we know that fermentation also enhances flavor as well as being nutritionally good for us. For example, lactic acid bacteria are good to establish a healthy gut.

Lacto fermentation, like all types of fermentation, is about creating the best environment for good bacteria to thrive. This usually happens gradually over a period of time as the bacteria compete and become more dominant as the pH levels sink. Finally, only the Lactobacillus plantarum bacteria can survive in this acidic environment and the bacteria only produces lactic acid.

Lacto fermentation begins at room temperature and after a few weeks is moved to the fridge. It's important that no vegetables lie above the surface as these can turn moldy. We use a flat stone (find one outdoors and wash and boil it) to weigh down our vegetables. Once the vegetables are done fermenting they should still be crunchy and their flavor enhanced by a mild acidity.

A shortcut to achieving the lacto fermented taste is pickling, which is when an acidic brine (vinegar) and carbohydrates (sugar or honey) mix from the start. While lacto fermentation has living bacteria, this method aims to preserve by killing bacteria.

Fermented Red Onion

Our two-year-old adores whole, fermented red onions and eats them like apples. The taste is mild and rich, but make sure you use the right amount of salt; it should be 2 percent of the total liquid volume. Too much salt means lactic acid can't form, so always weigh the ingredients (including water) to calculate the salt content.

2 lb (900 g)
Around 1 lb (400 g) red onion
2 cups (5 dl) water
18 g salt (no iodine)

Boil water and salt and leave to cool.

Peel the red onions (place in warm water first to loosen the skin) and place in a tall, sterilized glass jar, packing them as tight as possible.

Pour the salty brine over, covering all the onions. Leave at room temperate and add more salt brine when needed (it will bubble over). After a few days the jar should be active and bubbling.

After 2 weeks at room temperature, you can move the jar to the fridge and leave for at least 6 weeks before opening. Unopened, it lasts for around 1 year.

Pickled Green Tomatoes

At the end of the tomato season (October/November) there are often lots of tomatoes that haven't quite matured. They won't ripen indoors either and instead stay green, so we pick them to avoid the frost killing them off and either fry them or pickle them according to the recipe below.

2 lb (900 g)
1 lb (½ kg) green tomatoes
¾ cup (2 dl) water
¾ cup (2 dl) apple cider vinegar
2 tbsp salt
1 tsp mustard seeds
1 tsp celery seeds
1 tsp coriander seeds
½ tsp black peppercorns
½ tsp herb salt

Boil water and vinegar, add salt, and stir until dissolved. Leave the brine to cool down and slice the tomatoes into ½-inch-thick slices.

Layer the tomato slices and herbs in a tall glass jar. Turn the cut side towards the side to make it more attractive. Fill the jar all the way to the top as it reduces as the pickling starts.

Add the brine to cover the tomatoes, add the lid, and place upside down to cool.

Pickled Tomatoes

STORING & PREPPING

Cleaning & Housekeeping

Avoiding chemicals that are dangerous to health and the environment might seem an obvious choice for your home, but in a society dependent on plastics, it's not always that easy. As parents we have bought into the hype of plastic diapers, diaper bins, and perfumed diaper bags. We've cleaned our home with products with the skull and crossbones stamped on it and reams of warnings in tiny writing on the back. We never considered the methods, tools, and products of what we used as long as they smelled and looked clean. As modern homesteaders, however, our focus is to be healthy and toxin-free.

It's a way of life that has gradually spread to all areas of our life—including how we wash clothes and dishes and clean—with the philosophy that we don't use anything that can't decompose in our garden. These methods are not new. In fact, they're mostly traditional methods that have been tried and tested. Of course, some of them still need the invaluable help from modern machinery, but you can get quite far with cleaning products using natural materials, vegetables oils, and acidic liquids.

Cleaning

We want cleaning to be simple and effective and prefer to clean little and often rather than spend all day Sunday doing it. We also believe that you don't have to be too thorough—a bit of dirt in the corner is good for the soul and we'd rather hang out with friends than be constantly cleaning. Allergies and hypersensitivity have increased in line with our cleaning obsession as a society. Research shows that children who grow up on a farm are much less likely to develop allergies, so don't be too thorough with your cleaning and make sure you keep some animals.

The Cleaning Cupboard

Your cleaning cupboard should contain acids and alkalis as well as fats. There are some things to think about before you become a household chemist as some of the substances can cause burning or skin irritations, so you need to be careful with your measurements and exercise caution.

Alkali substances, such as soap, dissolve fatty stains while acidic substances, such as vinegar and citric acid, can't dissolve fat but are good for removing chalk, rust, and patinas. They also have a bleaching effect, which can sometimes be useful, but at other times unwanted.

Acids can hide bad smells, but in order to be effective they should not be mixed with alkalis (even mild alkalis) and vice versa. For example, if you mix baking soda with vinegar, you get a chemical reaction where carbon dioxide gas is formed but any cleaning effects are cancelled out despite all the bubbling!

Cleaning Cupboard Basics:

Acids	Alkalis	Fat and wax
Lemon	Bicarbonate	Lanolin
Citric acid	Sodium carbonate	Beeswax
Vinegar 12%	Linseed oil soap	Rapeseed oil
Apple cider	Olive oil soap	Essential oils
vinegar	Gall soap,	Linseed oil
	Caustic potash	Coconut oil

Salts
Coarse salt

Useful tools:

Washcloths and floor cloths in linen
Wooden dish brushes with removable brushes
Metal or wood pot brush or scouring brush from flax
Glass bottles with lids and nozzles

Soap

In the world of cleaning, soap is the magic potion. It doesn't just clean surfaces but also rehydrates them. Concentrated soap is produced by the saponification of fat with the alkali caustic potash. Caustic potash (Potassium hydroxide, KOH) is used for liquid soap and caustic soda/lye (Sodium hydroxide, $NaOH$) is used for solid soaps. In the old days, animal fats were used to make soaps and lye was made from birch ash. These days, vegetable fats are used, with linseed being one of the fattier oils with a high saponification value. Saponification value tells us how much lye is needed to saponify one gram of any type of fat. Linseed oil is a drying oil, meaning some oil remains even after saponification. This gives a so-called super fat result, which is nurturing and hydrating.

LINSEED OIL SOAP

You need to stir throughout the process; adding some alcohol speeds up the saponification.

40 parts linseed oil
32 parts caustic potash
8 parts concentrated alcohol (99%)
20 parts boiling distilled water

Method:
1. Heat up oil and lye while stirring, but do not let it boil. Use a water bath or thick-bottomed pan.
2. Leave to cool and add spirit, then add water.

Unfinished Floors

A large part of our house consists of old-fashioned, unfinished wooden flooring. These are usually made from fir or pinewood and are easy to care for, age beautifully, and last for generations. In older houses you might find wooden flooring under Masonite or linoleum that can be transformed into beautiful unfinished floors through sanding and washing.

For this type of floor, wash with linseed oil soap and cold water twice a year (before summer and Christmas). Over time, the floor will get a smooth, oily surface that repels dirt and protects from wear and tear.

Fir flooring lightens in time while pinewood, with its red heartwood, darkens into a rich golden red color. If you want to keep pinewood floors light, you can use white pigmented linseed oil soap.

Method:

1. Start by wiping the whole floor with cold water to saturate it.
2. Add 1–2 cups of concentrated soap per 2½ gallons of cold water.
3. Use a scrubbing brush with a long handle, working along the length of the wood. Work the soap thoroughly into the wood until it feels saturated.
4. Use a large cloth to soak up any excess water that appears, to avoid any dirty water causing stains. You can use an industrial vacuum cleaner and vacuum up the water, apparently, although we have not tested this ourselves yet.

Stain Removal

Bicarbonate of soda (baking soda) is a classic cleaning tool that can be used for lots of things including removing stains from walls, floors, and fabric. On fresh stains we sprinkle some over, vacuum, and then either wash them or air it out. For hard to remove stains, we prefer a paste, which we make by using 1 part water and 2 parts baking soda. Even mold in the bathroom can be rubbed off with baking soda and water. Fatty stains are best removed with dish soap, and limescale in the kitchen and bathroom are best tackled with lemon or citric acid.

Descaling

To remove or prevent limescale, vinegar, lemon, and citric acid work best. A coffee maker is best descaled by pouring 1 part vinegar and 1 part water into the water reservoir and letting it percolate. Then use clean, cold water, to rinse through a few times. The process is the same for kettles.

Removing Blockages

Baking soda and vinegar work great in unblocking drains. First, pour down around 3½ fl oz baking soda and then the same amount of vinegar. Wait for around 10 minutes and then pour down some hot (but not boiling) water.

Oven Cleaner

For an easy clean, fill a baking tray with water and squeeze a lemon into it. Put in the oven and heat to the highest temperature. Leave to cool and clean the oven with a cloth.

For ovens that need more work, mix together a baking soda paste and smooth over the surfaces to remove stains. Spray with vinegar so it starts to dissolve. Leave for at least half an hour and then wipe with a wet cloth.

Washing Up

The first mechanical dishwasher was invented by Josephine Cochrane. Cochrane was married to a wealthy man and they often hosted big dinner parties. She didn't want the staff to handwash her valuable fine china so chose to do it herself. Eventually, she got fed up with this time-consuming task and decided to invent a machine. On the U.S. Patent and Trademark Offices website you can read her own words: "If nobody else is going to invent a dishwashing machine, I'll do it myself." True to her words, Cochrane drew up a blueprint of her design and with the aid of a mechanic, built the machine at the back of the house. In 1886 Cochrane received the patent for her invention, which went under the name, "The Cochrane dishwasher."

We went without a dishwasher for a long time and doing the washing up by hand was a given ritual after each meal. We still remember that ritual with rose-tinted glasses, but in reality, we would struggle returning to our handwashing days with young children. We still wash lots of things by hand though, such as ceramics, cast iron, wood, and older porcelain.

Take Care of Your Kitchen Utensils

Wood and water are not a good long-term combination, and kitchen utensils made from wood need to be cared for if they are to last. Oil them regularly with rapeseed oil, for example. An oiled dish brush can be placed bristles down in a bowl of vinegar for a few minutes to kill bacteria.

Washcloths and linen floor cloths can be boiled with some dish soap for a few minutes or washed in a 140°F (60°C) wash, but you should not tumble dry them.

Cleaning the Dishwasher

Place 3 tbsp citric acid in the powder compartment and run the dishwasher without any dishes in it. Then run it for a second time with only dishwasher tablet/powder. If you have half a squeezed lemon, you can pop it in the plate rack and run a wash.

Vinegar Instead of Rinse Aid

Tenside, petrochemicals, phosphates, preservatives, enzymes, and synthetic perfumes are examples of the contents in rinse aid, which we prefer to avoid. Instead, we use vinegar.

Washing Cast Iron Pans & Cutting Boards

Cast iron pans should only be cleaned with warm water and preferably as soon as they have been used and are still warm.

Cutting boards can be rubbed with half an onion and salt, then dried with a sponge or damp cloth. Regularly treat the board with oil or wax.

DISH SOAP

⅝ cup (2 dl) water
½ cup (1 dl) organic olive oil soap (grated)
2 tbsp squeezed lemon juice
A few drops essential oils (optional)

Method:
1. Heat up water in the pan but do not bring it to a boil. Add the grated soap while stirring. Mix at a low temperature until it melts.
2. Leave the soap mixture to cool and add the lemon juice. Use a blender if you like and add some water if the mixture is too thick.
3. Leave to cool completely before placing in a bottle with a pump dispenser, adding a few drops of essential oils if you like.

DISHWASHER LIQUID

½ cup (1 dl) washing soda (sodium carbonate)
½ cup (1 dl) baking soda
½ cup (1 dl) salt (non-iodized)
Squeezed lemon juice (optional)

Method:
1. Mix washing soda, baking soda, and salt in a bowl.
2. If you want tablets instead of powder, you can add lemon juice and place the mixture in an ice cube tray.

CLEANING & HOUSEKEEPING

Laundry

When you have kids, washing clothes can seem like a full-time job. We veer between wading through the dirty laundry to swimming through piles of clean clothes that we don't have time to sort. The bottom line is that washing has to be done regularly and continually to avoid reaching a monstrous mountain of laundry.

Get into a habit of washing at low temperatures apart from when you wash items such as towels, cloth nappies, face flannels, cloth sanitary towels, and bed clothes—these should be washed in 140–194°F (60–90°C) to kill bacteria.

Clean Your Washing Machine

Once a year you need to clean your washing machine with citric acid. Measure 3½ oz (100 g) citric acid in the powder compartment and run a wash at 194°F (90°C) without a prewash. Then run an empty cycle to remove any dirt that has been dislodged. Wipe the rubber parts of the machine with soap and a wet dishcloth and remove the powder compartments and wash them with dish soap. If you need to, you can place them in water with some citric acid or vinegar to dissolve the worst dirt. If you can, keep the door open between washes to avoid trapping moisture that can result in bad smells.

Fabric Softener

People started using fabric softener in the mid-twentieth century when the use of synthetic materials increased. Softeners contain surfactants that are water-repellent, which means clothes made from polyester and acrylics retain some moisture, so they don't completely dry. This means they don't become staticky and feel softer. Natural fibers naturally absorb moisture, which is why clothes from cotton and wool don't become staticky. Vinegar doesn't have any effect on static electricity, but it does make clothes softer and cleaner as chalky residue from the water is rinsed away and off your clothes.

When wool gets washed, it loses some of the natural fat (lanolin) that makes it soft and hardy against dirt and water. Sometimes you need to re-fatten your wool with a wool treatment, which can be mixed together when needed.

Mangling

We have tried all sorts of mangles (laundry wringers) during our student years in apartment block laundry rooms all over Sweden. Everything from small electric ones to huge wooden structures that are driven by foot power.

When we moved to our farm we found a small table top one in a thrift store that now has pride of place in our laundry room. It is an automatic electric mangle with finger protectors. We mainly use it for towels, wash and floor rags, bed clothes, and linen tablecloths, as well as some other items made from natural fabric. In the old days, using a mangle was commonplace and there were even separate "mangle huts" from the seventeenth century through to the 1940s.

Once the steam iron made its debut, mangling was considered a waste of women's time, but many people are revisiting the mangle again. There are several benefits and once you've got the hang of it, it doesn't take long to use.

We usually save up a large pile of stuff to be mangled and do it all at once. Mangled fabrics take up a lot less space in the linen cupboard and do not attract as much dust and mites. It also lasts longer, has more of a shine, and has that luxurious crispy feel to it. If you've ever slept in newly mangled bedclothes, you'll know what we mean.

WOOL TREATMENT

¾ cup (2 dl) water
1 tsp lanolin
1 tsp soap flakes (e.g., olive soap)

Method:
1. Boil the water. Mix water, lanolin, and soap flakes in a bowl and stir until the soap and lanolin have dissolved.
2. When the wool treatment is ready to use, mix ¾ cup of the mixture with half a gallon of water. Once the woollen items have gone through the washing machine, soak it in the wool treatment for 8–12 hours. Rinse in cold water and hang up to dry.

LINEN WATER

When mangling (wringing) fabrics, they should be slightly damp. We use linen water with essential lavender oil.

2 cups (5 dl) water
A few drops of essential oils

Method:
Mix and store in a spray bottle.

FABRIC SOFTENER

1½ cups (3½ dl) white vinegar, 12%
¼ gallon (1 l) water
A few drops of essential oils

Method:
Store in a glass bottle and add 2 tbsp softener per wash in the softener compartment.

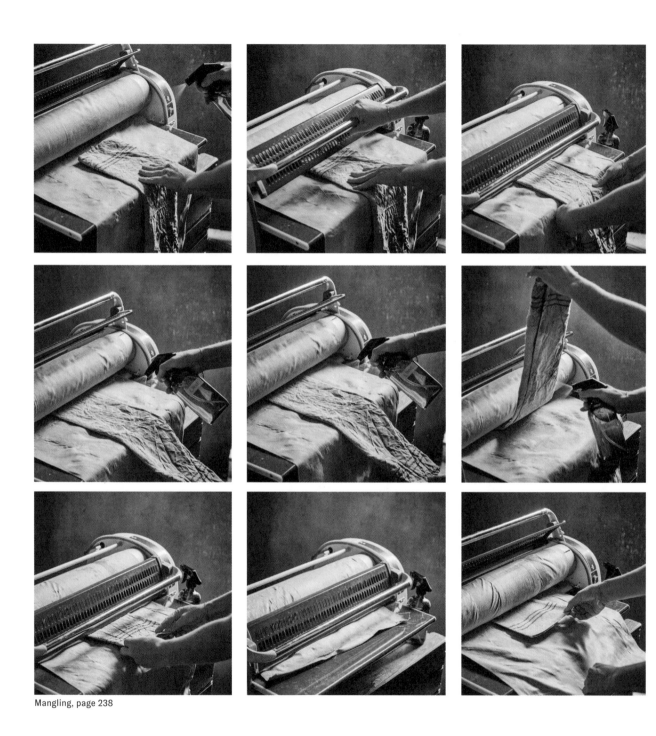

Mangling, page 238

Dyeing Clothes

Using plants to dye yarn and fabric is one of the oldest methods of adding color and has been used for 4,000 years. Plants that can be used for dyes have long been important and valued commodities.

Textiles in natural fabrics can be dyed with almost any plant and most parts of the plant can be used, for example leaves, bark, roots, flowers, and fruit. With an appetite for experimentation and some reading, there is a lot to learn about this old tradition.

All colors can be created, but some are harder to make than others. We have never tried to make a blue dye from natural materials, but a naturally blue pigment is not easy to find in nature. There are only a few plants that give a blue color, and traditionally blue dye has therefore been very valuable. It's the same with red pigments, which is why red clothes were considered high status. Black is also hard to achieve as it is made by mixing blue and red pigments.

For us, the point of using plant dyes is to give faded or dirty clothes new life. We have also attempted to dye yarn with plant color, but as of yet we have not had the time or space to actually knit anything. The results from the batches of dye we make often vary in shades. The shade we end up with depends on the temperature, fixing agent, type of vessel used, fabric, pH levels, and time. The longer your fabric spends in the dye, the darker and more intense the color. The color also depends on the plant; variety, where it grows, the season, and weather all play a part. For a stronger color, plants should be picked in early summer when it is dry and sunny.

In order for the color to absorb better and last longer and not fade, use a fixative (mordant) which makes the dye bind better and gives a more intense color than with fabric or yarn which has not been treated. We use alum as it is free from toxins, but in the past, heavy metals such as tin and copper were used. There are two ways you can fix the dye.

PREMORDANTING: Dissolve the alum in cold water while stirring until the water is clear. Add the yarn or fabric and stir thoroughly so the yarn or fabric is soaked through. Heat the water to 194°F (90°C) and leave for one hour. The yarn or fabric can be dried and then dyed within a month.

METAMORDANTING: Dissolve the alum in water and pour into the dye bath just before you add the fabric.

Examples of plants that work well for dying:

Black/grey	Purple	Brown
Iron	Red rubin basil	Walnut
Walnut/rusty iron	Dark purple hollyhock	
		Orange
Beige	Purple carrot	Sunny red
Tea	Red cabbage	Gul
St Johns Wort		Alder
Ladies mantle	Rose	Aspen
Juniper	Avocado peel	Onion peel
		Birch leaves
Red	Green	Tansy
Rose madder	Black-eyed Susan	Calluna
		Lichen
Blue	Grey green	Pomegranate
Woad	Nettles	
Chinese indigo		
	Grey brown	
	Pine	
	Fir	

DYEING WITH PLANTS

We usually do it all together rather than a separate process, although pre-mordanting your fabric or yarn gives you more control.

Use ¾ oz (20 g) alum per 3 ½ oz yarn or fabric

Method:
1. Boil some water (around 1¼ gallons (5 l) per 3½ oz yarn or fabric) in a large pot and add the plants. Turn off the stove, add a lid, and leave overnight.
2. Next day: Add the textile you want to dye and simmer on a low heat for an hour. Rinse the fabric with cold water and hang up to dry.

Waxes

Beeswax is one of nature's super products. Bees produce wax with the help of glands underneath their bodies, which is a time-consuming process. For every 2.2 lb (1 kg) beeswax, bees need almost ten times as much energy in the form of honey. For a modern housekeeper, beeswax is a miracle substance that can be used for all sorts of things including creating your own wax mixtures. Beeswax consists of myriocin, cerotic acid, and hydrocarbon and has a fantastic ability to retain water as well as antibacterial properties. Beeswax is not affected by water and doesn't oxidize as it doesn't absorb oxygen from the from the air. It doesn't turn rancid so can be stored for as long as you want really. In Germany they have found completely intact beeswax candles in 1,500-year-old graves.

We use our beeswax as a base for lots of other waxes. If you don't have your own bees, then buy your wax from a local beekeeper or an organic local apiary. Imported beeswax can contain toxins and be mixed with paraffin, for example.

TOOLS When you make wax, it's good to have tools that you are not going to use for cooking. Buy an old pan in a thrift store or invest in a wax melting pot, which is good to have if you are making waxes and creams. If you are making smaller amounts, you can melt the wax and oil in the jar that you will be storing the wax in. Use jars with a wide opening so you can easily access the wax when you come to use it. Using fabric to apply wax works well but remember you won't really be able to use the fabric for anything else afterwards, so use worn-out towels or clothes.

FIRE HAZARD Some oils, especially linseed oil, become fire hazards when exposed to air, so always handle linseed oil with care. There is no risk that the finished product in the jar will catch fire but the paper, brushes, or rags that have been used to wipe the oil or wax should be soaked afterwards and stored in a safe environment, such as outdoors.

CLEANING Beeswax can be hard to remove for the same reasons that make it a great product. A good habit to get into is to wipe containers and pans straight away with some paper towel while the wax is still warm. If you have used linseed oil, remember to soak the paper before throwing it away.

Treating Leather

To increase the life of leather it needs to be regularly treated with wax and oils, especially shoes. Our leather wax contains lanolin that is secreted by the sheep's sebaceous glands and is extracted from sheep's wool. It is very sticky and has a wonderful ability to cover cracks in clothes. Oils and fats soften the leather while wax acts like a protective and water-repellent layer. This recipe also includes castor oil, which gives the leather an extra shine.

LEATHER WAX

½ oz (15 g) coconut oil
¾ oz (20 g) caster oil
1 oz (30 g) rapeseed oil
⅓ oz (10 g) lanolin
½ oz (15 g) beeswax

Method:
1. Warm the oils and lanolin in a pan or in a tin jar in a water bath.
2. Once the oils are warm and the lanolin dissolved, add the beeswax and let it melt. Once melted, stir thoroughly to mix all the ingredients.
3. Pour the warm wax into a tin or glass jar with a lid.

USING LEATHER WAX When you use the leather wax, first clean the leather and leave it to dry. Next thoroughly rub in the wax and leave for a while. Wipe off any excess wax with a rag and if you want a shiny finish, you can buff the leather. Remember that wax can change the appearance of leather.

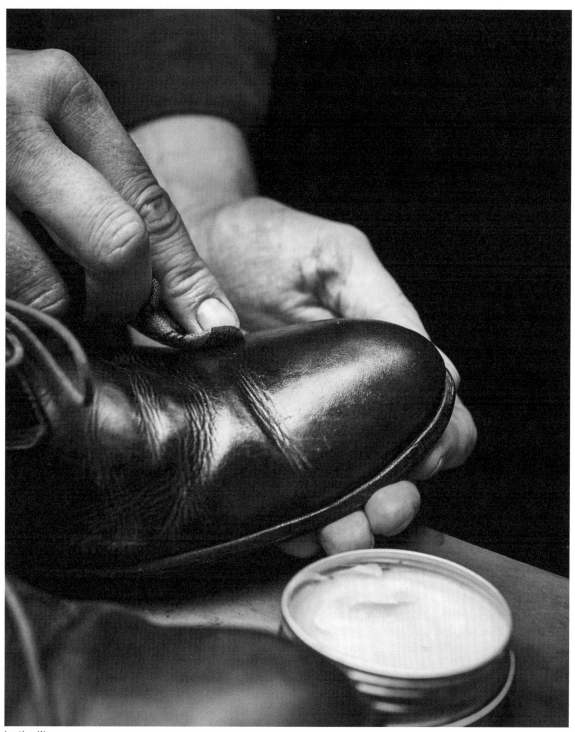

Leather Wax

CLEANING & HOUSEKEEPING

Waxing Clothes

Waxing clothes is a natural way of creating a strong and water-repellent surface without having to dress in plastic or other synthetic materials. These days many clothes are treated with substances that can damage the environment such as fluorocarbon. Unfortunately, many of the waxes you can buy in stores also contain paraffin, which is extracted when raw oil is refined and it is nothing you want to rub all over your clothes. Making your own fabric wax from beeswax and coconut oil is thankfully very easy.

Waxing fabric increases its durability and creates a surface more tolerable to water and dirt. Fabric wax works best on cotton and can even be used on cushions and other fabrics that you may use outdoors. The more wax you use, the more durable the fabric becomes, although it will also turn stiffer.

FABRIC WAX

2¾ oz (80 g) beeswax
¾ oz (20 g) coconut oil

Method:
1. Melt the beeswax in a water bath. Once dissolved, you can add the coconut oil. Stir until completely blended.
2. Pour the mixture in a prepared mold; for example a simple cast can be the bottom of a large soda bottle to make a disk shape. A silicon mold for large ice cubes also works.

USING FABRIC WAX Use the wax by rubbing it against the fabric, which will leave the surface yellowish. If you want to make it easier to iron, you can briefly heat the disk with a hair dryer. Put an extra layer on areas that are exposed to a lot of wear and tear like elbows, knees, and backsides.

Once you have finished rubbing it in, you need to melt the wax so it goes into the fibers. Use a hairdryer or iron and warm the fabric until the wax absorbs into it. It usually happens around 140°F (60°C), but if it gets too hot, the wax can start to melt and run.

If you are outdoors, you can melt the wax in front of an open fire, but you need to be careful. Hold the fabric around 12 inches (30 cm) from the fire and wait for the wax to melt. Be patient and don't get too close—also avoid large flames. In time, the protection rubs off. To remove, wash the item 2–3 times in 105-degree water.

Treating Wood Surfaces

1 + 1 = 3. Combine two amazing things and get something even better. Linseed oil and wax not only smell good but when combined become something of a magic potion. Linseed oil wax can be used to treat all sorts of wooden surfaces that you wish to protect, and when the wax solidifies, it makes for a durable and water-repellent as well as glossy surface. You can also use linseed oil wax to treat almost any absorbent surface such as brick flooring, concrete, slate, tile, metal, tabletops, and stone flooring. You can even use it on painted surfaces to give them a new finish.

Like all waxes, linseed oil wax changes the surface on different materials, often making them darker. Exactly how it changes depends on the material you put it on, for example type and age of wood, but also the color of the wax. It can be hard to know how previously treated wood might react to the wax, so if you want to know what the finished product might look like you can try and rub some wax in a less visible spot.

LINSEED OIL WAX

1 part beeswax
3 parts linseed oil

Method:
1. Melt the beeswax in a water bath. One dissolved, carefully add the linseed oil, a little at a time, stirring continuously until blended.
2. When the linseed oil and wax are mixed, pour into a glass jar or tin with a wide opening.

USING LINSEED OIL WAX Clean the surface of the item you are going to wax, removing dirt and dust. If it is wood, you can wash it with soap. The surface needs to be dry before the wax can be applied. Use a thick rag or even better, a sponge to rub the wax into the surface. Wait for around 30 minutes and wipe the excess off with a thick cloth. Wipe off enough so that it does not leave marks when you touch it or walk on it. After around a week the wax will have hardened and you can clean the surface with a pH neutral cleaning solution, such as soap for wood or a gentle dish soap, as needed.

Treating Cutting Boards

Well-used chopping boards can quickly dry out and need to be treated with oil so that they last longer and don't crack. This simple wax for chopping boards both rehydrates and protects the wood, as well as filling in small cracks. We use an organic rapeseed oil, but other organic vegetable oils can be used as well, such as olive oil or walnut oil. Different oils can give different color to the wax. Avoid using paraffin or mineral oil as these can be harmful to the environment. This wax is kind to both the environment as well as your skin so, if you want, you can give your feet a treat at the same time.

CUTTING BOARD WAX

2¾ oz (80 g) rapeseed oil
¾ oz (20 g) beeswax

Method:
1. Heat the oil and beeswax in a water bath until the wax has dissolved into the oil. Stir the mixture to blend it and pour into a glass or metal container.
2. If you want a softer wax, adjust the amount of beeswax; the more beeswax in relation to the oil, the harder the wax.

USING CUTTING BOARD WAX First, clean the cutting board thoroughly and leave it to dry.

Use a cloth to rub the wax into the board, making sure you work it properly into the wood.

Leave it to dry for a few hours and then repeat the treatment until the board is saturated.

Remove excess wax.

Protect Outdoor Wood

This wax can be used both to clean and protect various wooden surfaces. Balsam turpentine is a natural product which is extracted by distilling oil from pine trees. Turpentine is a solvent and has cleaning properties while at the same time increases absorption in wood.

It is primarily used outside, for example on wooden benches, tables, and work surfaces. If you do use it indoors, make sure you ventilate at the same time.

WOOD BALSAM

2¼ oz (60 g) beeswax
1½ oz (40 g) balsam turpentine

Method:
1. Melt the beeswax in a water bath. Remove the pan from the stove once the wax has completely melted and stir in the balsam turpentine.
2. Pour into a glass or metal jar before it solidifies.

USING WOOD BALSAM Rub wooden surfaces with the balsam, using a cloth or sponge. Remove any excess balsam. Make sure the room is properly ventilated.

Remember that turpentine is flammable and has a flash point of 95°F (35°C), so avoid handling it around a gas stove, and any cloths that you use should be soaked in water and stored outdoors.

Egg Tempera

These days when you enter a paint store you are overwhelmed by the range of modern paint. The problem is that modern paints are not particularly good for people, houses, wood, animals, or the environment. However, there is one paint that is environmentally friendly, goes on anything, and can easily be mixed at home. It consists of only eggs, linseed oil, water, and color pigment. Egg tempera, as it is known, has been used in Europe since the middle ages. A testament to its durability can be seen on the paintings in medieval churches.

Egg tempera is an emulsion paint which means you use an emulsifier (egg) to make two otherwise insoluble substances mix together (linseed oil and water).

It's not only free from toxins (unless you use a poisonous pigment) but you can use it on almost any material. Egg tempera sticks to wood, stone, metal, and concrete and you can paint roofs, floors, walls, and furniture with it. Once dry it is incredibly durable and a polished surface that has been painted with egg tempera can last for hundreds of years. It is also perfect for splash painting walls or using stencils.

Egg tempera works through the linseed oil and egg oxidizing in the air and binding together. The color is matte, but if you polish it with a semihard brush you can make it glossy.

EGG TEMPERA

1 part egg
1 part linseed oil
1 part water
Pigment

Method:

1. Whisk the egg in a container such as a metal bowl. Add the linseed oil and whisk it together thoroughly. Add water, a little at a time, while whisking until you get a creamy, gruel-like emulsion.
2. Mix the color pigment in the emulsion. When you come to test the colors, use a small amount of emulsion but make sure you write down the amounts so you can recreate the same color.

PAINTING WITH EGG TEMPERA Egg tempera is a thin paint which gets thicker the more pigment you add. If you want lots of coverage you need to paint at least three layers, waiting a week between each layer. Remove splashes immediately as the color is almost impossible to remove once dry.

As the color contains linseed oil, cloths and paper that have been used need to be stored safely. Egg tempera is fresh produce that needs to be stored in the fridge where it will last around 2 weeks.

Egg Oil Tempera

CLEANING & HOUSEKEEPING

Ducks

According to Greek mythology, the Greek Prince Icarus had a daughter instead of a son and threw her in the sea. The daughter was saved by a family of ducks, which Icarus saw as an omen and christened her Penelope, after the ancient Greek for duck. For thousands of years ducks have represented virtues such as loyalty and faithfulness and it is easy to see why once you have your own ducks—few animals are as nice to keep in your garden or as sociable. At times a flock of ducks appears to move as one in a highly synchronized maneuver. Rarely do they move more than a few feet from the rest of the flock.

When our ducks are hungry or want fresh water, they stand by our deck and call us; they like to stay nearby. When we first decided to get ducks, we had one clear goal: to combat snails, which they did. However, in time we have come to appreciate their presence in the garden in more ways than one and they are lovely animals that we really don't want to be without.

Why Ducks?

For the modern homesteader, ducks can be very handy and can easily live in a smaller garden without disturbing the neighbors too much. They are not as versatile as chickens but fill other roles as part of your eco system. Chickens take care of food waste, for example, while also contributing with fertilizer, which ducks struggle with.

Ducks are ill-equipped to break down food scraps and it's not really worth collecting their waste as it tends to spread everywhere. On the other hand, ducks don't have the same requirements when it comes to housing and they are great at foraging for food with bills that have evolved specifically to gobble down snails and insects. Another benefit of ducks is that they give more meat than chickens as they grow faster and bigger than

chickens. Within two to three months, they are almost fully grown. Many varieties of ducks also lay eggs at the same rate as chickens, and some would say the eggs taste better.

Ducks are social animals that can roam freely and mostly return to their home in the evening. Neighbors also seems to prefer ducks quacking over roosters crowing.

We also find that ducks don't cause the same amount of damage to our plants as chickens as they don't scratch the ground, although there is mixed opinion around this. Ducks do however love greenery such as grass and lettuce, so in the same way that you do with chickens, keep ducks away from new and young plants.

All Ducks Eat Snails

It's important to know that it is not only the muscovy duck that eats snails, but all ducks, although the appetite for snails is highly individual. Some ducks love snails while others will only eat them in certain circumstances. If you keep ducks to fight slugs you should remove any ducks that are not eating snails and replace them with new ducks. Our ducks (Swedish blue) are known as "the snail patrol" after they literally cleared the whole garden from killer slugs.

Ducks & Breeds

The first ducks are believed to have been domesticated in China more than 2,000 years ago. Ducks are basically tame mallards, except the muscovy duck, which has a different heritage.

It's not surprising we think ducks originate in China as there are few places that appreciate the duck as much, and the large white Pekin duck with its yellow beak is the most popular breed in the world today.

Pekin Duck

This is the true original with its white down and yellow or red bill. It is a large breed that is primarily known for its meat. Ducks are important in Chinese cuisine, and the famous Peking duck from Northeast China can be traced back to the Yuan dynasty in the thirteenth century. The breed lays around 80 to 120 eggs per year.

Size and appearance: White feathers, yellow or red bill. Weighs 9–13 lb (4–6 kg).

Indian Runners

This is an old breed from Indonesia which is characterized by its special walk and erect stature. Instead of waddling, they "quickstep" or run. They are highly regarded for their egg production, producing between 150 and 300 eggs a year.

Size and appearance: Brown and white in color, often speckled. Weighs around 4 ½ lb (2 kg).

Swedish Blue

At the start of the 1900s, blue-colored ducks were gathered together from farms along the west coast of Sweden, which became the basis for the Swedish local breed Swedish blue. The breed most likely originates from a blue breed that has long existed in the coastal area around the Baltic Sea, and these days a Swedish organization is working to preserve the breed. They were first imported to the United States in the late 1800s. They lay around 100 eggs and have traditionally been kept to provide meat.

Size and appearance: Deep blue-grey plumage with a white bib. The breed is of average size and weighs 4½–9 lb (2–4 kg).

Buff Orpington

Buff Orpington ducks originated in the United Kingdom and are very sociable and excellent foragers. They lay around 180 eggs a year and gain weight quickly, making them good meat birds, too.

Size and appearance: tan-colored with long, graceful necks. They weigh 7–8 pounds (3–3.6 kg).

Muscovy

The muscovy duck is native to North, South, and Central America. Domesticated ducks were kept by Native Americans before the Europeans arrived and brought the breed back to Europe in the sixteenth century.

The muscovy duck is different from other ducks both in appearance and behavior as they can fly and they don't quack. Muscovy ducks are also appreciated for their appetite for snails!

Size and appearance: A red warty mask on the face and black and white plumage. Weight is 6½–9 lb (3–4 kg).

The Flock

Ducks are flock animals and so to keep a solitary duck is considered cruelty to animals. You can choose to just have drakes or hens, but if you want a mixed flock, you should have one male to a group of 3–6 females. During mating season, the males are active and often violent so it can cause problems if one or two females are targeted too often.

It can happen that drakes drown the hen during mating and any drakes that are too violent towards hens or ducklings should be removed.

The Duck House

Ducks need some type of shelter, both to protect them from predators and also to keep them warm in the winter.

You can keep a limited number of ducks together with chickens but it's not great if you don't have a large space.

Ducks are water animals that make a mess, while chickens prefer a dry environment. Too much damp in a chicken coop can create an unhealthy environment and breed disease.

A duck shelter does not need to be the same size as a chicken coop with perches, nests, and feeding stations. Ducks sleep on the ground and often lay their eggs where they sleep.

Design the duck house so that it is easy to clean with a floor that can withstand liquid, like a plastic mat. Place shavings and straw on top that can be changed regularly.

As the ducks make a mess (they sieve the food through their bill) its preferable to keep the feeding

Swedish blue ducks. The second to last duck on the right has the typical blue grey plumage the breed is known for.

station outside. To avoid attracting other creatures, don't give the ducks more than they can eat over a few minutes. Alternatively, build a small, enclosed yard if they can otherwise roam freely.

Ducks have subcutaneous fat and down, making them resilient to cold, but you can still insulate your duck house if you want to give them a bit of extra comfort. Muscovy ducks have a thinner layer of subcutaneous fat than other ducks and therefore need more heat. The most important thing is that where they rest is dry and free from draft. Ducks have a heat exchange system in their legs and feet, meaning they have cold feet that can tolerate ice and snow, although if it is really cold it can be good to offer a dry surface to rest on. Spreading some straw in the snow in front of the duck house is always appreciated.

Our Duck House
We have built our insulated duck house on a pallet, which means that two people can move it, for example, into a tunnel green house in the winter. The roof can be removed, which makes cleaning the house easier, and the floor has a plastic rug that goes up a few inches along the walls so it is quick and easy to clean. We have also built a small yard with a food and watering station, and we can also keep the ducks here for short periods of time if there are predators in the area.

DUCKS

Environment & Access to Water

Ducks are domesticated mallards and prefer to live near water. It's best to have running water or a pond in your garden, but it is not vital. It's enough to have some sort of water bath where the ducks can swim. The water levels need to be deep enough for the ducks to dip into and the water should be changed once a week. During warm weather, ducks use water to cool down, so it is especially important to keep an eye on the water supply in the summer. In some cases, a water bath is better than a smaller, immoveable pond as ducks can quickly turn a pond into an overflowing muddy puddle, meaning long-term, a pond needs a pump for oxygen levels.

Apart from being near water, ducks prefer environments that are a bit wild with tall grass, blackthorn bushes, and fields. In these slightly "damp" environments, ducks can both find shelter as well as forage for food. Ducks also love fruit trees and berry bushes. A group of ducks can devour an entire blackcurrant bush in an afternoon, so cover any bushes you wish to protect. If you keep the ducks on the lawn, be prepared for the fact that they poop a lot, but at the end of the day you have to weigh the benefits; would you rather step on duck poop or killer slugs?

Food

Most ducks forage for their own food and will find snails, worms, insects, and weeds on their own. In the summer, especially if it rains, ducks can manage on their own, although they should have access to some sort of basic food. The best options are crushed seeds like oats, corn, and wheat. You can also give chicken feed and layer feed when they are laying eggs, but it is not vital. Fodder should be given next to water as they like to wet their food.

Ducks won't eat leftovers in the same way that chickens do, but you can give them corn, boiled potatoes, and breadcrumbs that have been soaked.

Predators

Ducks have the same predators as chickens: foxes, hawks, martens, eagles, and other predators will gladly grab a duck if they get the chance. The best protection is to have a secure duck house which you can close at night and open again in the morning.

Eggs

Most duck breeds lay between 100 and 200 eggs per year depending on the season. Duck eggs are usually larger than chicken eggs and weigh around 2½ oz (70 g) depending on the breed. They have a different shell which is more porcelain-like and they are smooth to touch. Duck eggs also have a tougher and more durable shell, but they taste similar and are used in similar ways. You can eat them as is or use them for baking or other dishes.

Meat

Thanks to its thick layer of fat and tasty meat, ducks have long been considered a delicacy.

A large advantage over chickens is that ducks grow faster and often reach 80 percent of their size within three months. It makes it possible, for those that want to, to keep yearly ducks that are bred in spring, chomp away at snails in the summer, and are slaughtered in fall.

Even if you want to keep a permanent flock of ducks it may be necessary from time to time to slaughter one of the animals, for example if it's been injured, is too aggressive, or too old. You should also remove young male ducks.

Slaughtering Ducks

Before you slaughter ducks, you should avoid feeding them so that there is not too much food in the gut. A good time of day to slaughter a duck is in the morning just as you let them out.

Just like with other animals, ducks need to be killed as quickly and painlessly as possible. Catch the duck and stun it with a hard smack to the back of the head using a pole made from hard wood or metal. Place the duck on a block and remove the head with an axe. A large duck can spasm quite strongly so hold on to it while it bleeds. If you want to keep the duck blood to make soup from, place a bucket underneath.

If you are slaughtering an older duck, it can be wise to hang the duck before you move to the next step to give you more tender meat. Hang the duck for 3–5 days in a room that keeps between 35–50°F.

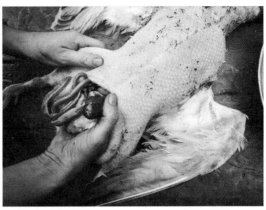

Plucking

Due to their lovely, fatty skin, ducks should always be plucked, although you can still skin them. You should pluck the duck straight after slaughter and if you are slaughtering young ducks you should do this no later than 12 weeks old as after this they get thicker feathers that can be harder to remove. You can also wait until they have grown their full plumage at around 6 months old, but don't wait until it gets too cold as it is much harder to pluck them.

It's easier to pluck a newly slaughtered duck. If the duck has thick feathers or has been hung, the easiest way is to quickly scald it, in the same way as when plucking chickens. Quickly dip the duck in a pot or bath with 160–175 degree water (70–80ºC). Small bits of down can be burnt off with a blow torch.

Cleaning

Cut off the feet and wing tips in the joints with a sharp knife or shears. Place the bird on its back and cut a hole from the bottom upwards, large enough to fit your hand. Place your hand inside and carefully, but with determination, remove the intestines. Be careful so that the bladder does not burst; if it does, rinse the bird immediately under cold water. Make sure you get the kidneys and lungs that sit along the backbone as well. Remove the windpipe from the front. Cut off the throat, although you can leave the skin.

Keep the neck, liver, gizzard, wing tips, heart, and the yellow fatty bits that sit around the bottom, which is well worth saving.

Cut the gizzards in the middle and turn inside out, remove the membrane on the inside and rinse away any grit. Then rinse the gutted bird in cold water and leave to drain before cooking or freezing.

Breeding Ducks

Just like chickens, ducks can be bred in two ways. Either you hatch them in an incubator or you let the ducks brood and create ducklings. The latter is the best option, but it doesn't always work, either for biological or practical reasons. Not all ducks are willing to brood, and if you want to start a new flock it is necessary to hatch the eggs in an incubator or buy ducklings.

Using an Incubator

Ducks need slightly longer than chicken eggs to hatch and the ducklings appear after 25–28 days. Otherwise, the procedure is similar. Make sure you get hold of large, fresh hatching eggs that have been treated correctly. Before you put them in the incubator they should be stored in the fridge and turned daily. The eggs should not be washed to retain the waxy surface. If the eggs have been transported, they need to rest for 24 hours before being placed in the machine to stabilize the yolk.

In the Incubator

Duck eggs need slightly higher humidity than chicken eggs. Around 50–60 percent. Use an incubator that automatically turns the eggs. Towards the end, the humidity needs to be as high as possible for the egg shells to become porous and allow the ducklings to break out. You can spray the eggs with a spray bottle now and again. After hatching, leave the ducklings in the incubator until they are completely dry and the other ducks have either hatched or you are clear that they are dead. To open the incubator during this time is risky as the membranes in the eggs can dry and make it impossible for the unhatched ducklings to get out.

Ducklings

During the first three weeks, ducklings should be kept separately in a box with a heat lamp. In the first week they need around 91°F (33°C), which you then gradually reduce (week 2, 82 (28°C); week 3, 72 (22°C); week 4, at least 61 (16°C). If they constantly huddle under the lamp, it's too cold and if they make a ring around the light, it is too warm.

Ducklings need access to fresh water and food. They don't need access to bath water yet as their feathers have not yet fully developed. Ducklings that get wet can get chilled down and die.

In contrast to chickens, ducklings cause a lot more dirt and damp in their environment, so it is not good to keep them in a cardboard box. Preferably you should keep them in a warm shed or duck house and clean it at least twice a week. From around 6 weeks, ducklings can live outdoors in the summer months.

Leaving the Duck to Brood

Different duck varieties have different attitudes to brooding, but if you do have a broody duck in your flock you should take care of her. A brooding duck should be disturbed as little as possible while she broods, which takes around 25–28 days.

Preparations

If you have a broody duck and you want ducklings, you can make life a bit easier for her. If the duck house is open, you can make a nest for her by adding a box

giving her peace and quiet from other ducks. You can also give her snail shells in her feed before she starts to brood to give her strong egg shells. Ducks do not eat a lot while brooding but make sure there is water and food outside her nest.

Eggs

If you have an active drake, you don't really need to do much to get ducklings. If you have fertilized eggs you want the hen to incubate, quickly swap some of her eggs for these. For most breeds 8–10 eggs is enough. Brooding ducks can be a bit grumpy and aggressive and should be disturbed as little as possible.

If you don't want the duck to brood, you need to break her habits. Remove eggs daily and if she still doesn't stop you may need to block her entrance to the nest or the duck house during the day. Eventually she will lose interest.

Ducklings

Ducks are usually very attentive parents and ducklings will faithfully follow their mother everywhere the first

few months. To give them the best start in life give them chicken feed the first 4–8 weeks. You can't stop the hen from eating too, although she will need it after her fasting.

Sexing Ducks

It's not easy to sex ducks, especially not when they're young, but in time the drake in most breeds will get larger and have a broader breast that separates him from the hens. The bottom area will also change as drakes have a curled feather. Another distinction is that the drake often has a lighter bill than the hens, even though it can be hard to spot.

A safer way is to listen to the sounds the ducks make. The classic quack comes from hens, while drakes make a raspier sound. If you check for these differences, you should soon be able to identify the sexes.

HOMEMADE FOIE GRAS

From killer slugs to foie gras, it's quite a transformation. Foie gras is one of the most luxurious things you can make while at the same time being easy and tasty. Duck liver from force-fed ducks is something you should avoid, but make sure you keep the livers from your own free-range ducks.

1 duck liver
Duck fat from the bottom and neck
Splash of cognac
Salt and freshly ground pepper
Small glass jar with clip top and rubber seal

When you gut the duck, carefully separate the liver and make sure that it is nice and shiny and free from marks. Remove the blood vessels from the liver by carefully pulling them while holding the liver in the other hand. Try to keep the liver intact if you can.

Keep the fat in the bottom and around the neck and rinse it to make it nice and white. Melt the fat in a pan with a bit of water. Keep an eye on it so it doesn't burn once the water has evaporated; you'll notice a slight hissing sound when it's time to remove the pan from the heat.

Place the liver in a small glass jar with a clip top and rubber seal. Season with salt, pepper, and a splash of cognac.

Spoon the melted duck fat over the liver until it is covered. Close the lid and place in a water bath in the oven at around 212°F (100°C) for 60 minutes. Store in the fridge (it lasts a long time unopened) and serve with toast.

Beer & Hops

On a warm summer evening, there is nothing more magical than the heady scent of a handful of ripe hops cones. These days, a lot of what we think of as beer is actually hops and hops is so much more than just beer. The range of smells and tastes that are contained in a hops cone is unbelievable.

It's spicy, peppery, grassy, fruity, and herby all at the same time with everything from black pepper to sweet mango, and of course that bitterness that transforms beer from a rather sickly, grainy drink to liquid gold.

Beer and hops have not always gone hand in hand. For thousands of years, they had separate stories; beer in different forms was brewed before the advent of farming and was often flavored with honey, fruit, spices, and different herbs to make it more palatable and also to make it last longer. Sometimes an herb mixture known as gruit was used, which can still be found in some heritage beers today.

In Scandinavia, bog myrtle, labrador tea, yarrow, and juniper were common ingredients in beer. The Gotland drink is a good example of a traditional beer, flavored with common juniper and full of character, and it's still brewed today.

Hops has been grown for thousands of years for completely different uses. A hops cone contains over 500 chemical compounds and was used for its healing properties as well as considered calming and thought to induce sleep. Drinking hops tea or placing hops cones in a pillowcase is meant to make you sleep better, a cure that that has also found some support in modern research.

Carl von Linné suggested hops could also be used against tooth ache by, "boiling the hops in rancid butter." On the other hand, if you boiled it in sweet milk, it could be used as insect repellent, as flies that drank from the brew would become "dizzy, drunk, and dead."

Early on, hops were also used as a vegetable, especially the young shoots which were eaten like asparagus, and the similarity has given rise to the name wild asparagus or poor man's asparagus, with the Romans actually calling the hops shoots asparagus. Hops shoots are still something of a forgotten delicacy that we believe should be grown in every kitchen garden.

It was probably in the Middle Ages somewhere in central Europe that hops started to be used in making beer, a unique combination that would change the course of drink history. The first documented use comes from Hallertau in Bavaria in the eighth century.

However, hops wasn't actually added for its taste but for the bitter acid called humulone which inhibited the growth of bacteria, thus preserving the beer. It meant that beer could be stored, exported, and produced in larger volumes. The flavor that hops added was actually secondary, although these days we consider it a necessary part of beer. Adding hops to beer would also change a huge part of the European farming landscape.

Biological Make-Up of Hops

Hops is a perennial vine that in the right environment is very hardy and can also grow very old. It has for a long time been an ornamental plant in gardens, and if you have ever seen one you will know its growing power.

It's not surprising, with its sedative and aromatic effect, that hops is a close relative to cannabis. It is part of the Cannabaceae family that contain the genus Cannabis and hops.

The hops plant is what is known in botany as a unisexual; i.e., there are male and female plants. A hops farmer is only interested in the female plants that grow the cones, and as pollination seems to affect the cones composition of bitter substances, male plants are kept away.

Male and female plants are easy to distinguish between. Male plants have small flowers that grow clusters while the female plants grow the clusters of cones hops is known for. When the hop cones are ripe, they emit a sticky, yellow flour from the glands inside the leaves. This is the lupulin where the hop acid and essential oils are found.

The Hop Cones' Composition

The hop cones' chemical composition is fascinating and contains oils, resin, tannins, growth hormones, choline, and estrogen. For modern brewers, the two that are of most interest are resins and hop oils. The former contributes the characteristic bitterness through water soluble alpha acids; the bitter taste develops as the cone ripens, so it is important not to harvest too early.

Hops can be divided into two categories depending on what they contribute in terms of bitterness and taste: aroma hops and bitter hops. Aroma hops contains more aromatic oils and less bitterness while bitter hops is the other way round.

BEER & HOPS

In modern beer making there are also types that don't fit into either category with a higher level of fruitiness and notes of tropical fruits, for example Cascade and Citra.

If you brew beer, the way the hops is handled plays an important part in the brewing process. Hops that is added early on to the beer emits acids, resulting in higher levels of bitterness, while the aromatic oils become less tangible.

If you add the hops at the end of the process, the bitterness is reduced and the aromatic notes are intensified. This is why different varieties of hops are mixed at different points to create different flavor combinations.

Apart from flavor, hops also has preservative qualities, although once we learned the art of pasteurization this became less important. More specifically, hops prevents lactic acid fermentation (stops the beer turning sour) and releases proteins that increase longevity and clarity.

Hops Varieties

These days work is being undertaken to preserve old heritage varieties of hops. Growing older heritage varieties is a revival of old knowledge, even while new varieties are constantly discovered and studied. It's an exciting adventure where old and unique flavors are brought back to life and tested in beer brewing. The advantage of planting local heritage varieties is that they are usually well adapted to the climate. Hops needs both sun and warmth to thrive and it is obvious that hops that is usually grown in Southern US or central Europe do not fare as well at northern latitudes where the biggest threat to crops is frost during spring and fall.

There is nothing wrong with growing classic hop varieties to be used for brewing beer, and they are often cheaper to buy while the local heritage varieties can be harder to find.

Classic Hop Varieties

HALLERTAUER MITTELFRÜH One of the classics from mainland Europe together with Saaz, Spalt, and Tettnang. This aromatic variety is known for its floral and spicy taste and is mainly used to make lager.

CASCADE One of the most well-known varieties in America, Cascade is fresh and floral like the aroma hops but can also be used as a bitter hops as it has notes of grapefruit.

GOLDINGS In contrast to mainland Europe where lager became the dominant beer, the British isles retained their tradition of ales, which also affected the cultivation of hops. Goldings is a British heritage variety that goes back to the eighteenth century and it can be used both as bitter or flavor hops and is enjoyed for its delicate spicy notes.

Growing Hops

If you plan to grow hops, the fact that it grows upwards is a huge advantage and while it can grow over 30 feet tall (9 meters) it doesn't actually need much space. It's still a good idea to plant your hops in a secluded space and not in the middle of your kitchen garden as it can start to take over and can be hard to get rid of.

Location

Hops likes to grow in a sunny and sheltered spot. It's good if it can be in an airy place to avoid fungi attacks, but it shouldn't be too drafty. A slight hill or a south-facing wall is best. The soil should be damp and nutrient rich, and as hops tend to grow a large root system in time, you should not plant them too close together. Each plant needs around 11 square feet (1 meter squared) of space. It takes around three years before the hops plants give a full harvest.

Support

Hops needs some kind of support for optimal growth and control. It can grow against a fence or trellis and its powerful growth makes it the perfect plant to create a green wall for privacy or to create a better microclimate in your garden.

A classic trellis has many advantages apart from looking good. It is easier to remove and harvest the plants. Traditional hops supports are often made from fir trees with the bark still on, which gives the plant a natural support to grow. The hops has thorny hooks that it uses to attach itself with. Other woods work as well, but if the surface is too smooth it can be scratched or wrapped with a coarse string to give better support. Wrap the string anticlockwise. The trellis should be 13–20 feet tall (4–6 meters) but can be as big as 26 feet (8 meters).

You can place the trellis straight into the soil if you can with the help of a soil drill. Alternatively, a thicker pipe placed in the soil can also be used. Make sure the trellis or pipe are placed 24–28 inches (60–70 cm) into the soil. The most important thing is that they feel steady and can be removed at harvest time. You can also attach the trellis from the top with two lines, which gives extra support in the ground as well as for the hops.

Once the hops starts to grow during late spring, bind the shoots around the trellis. Otherwise, they can easily fall out and find something else to grab hold of.

Fertilization

The hops plant needs a lot of fertilizer and water during the early stages of growth, which usually goes on until midsummer. Hops prefers a nitrogen-rich fertilizer and should be fertilized early on in the season, so start with fertilizer as soon as in March/April with chicken fertilizer, for example, and then keep going until the start of July with either nettle fertilizer, gold water, or grass cuttings.

Water regularly and make sure the plant does not dry out. A stressed plant is more at risk of being attacked by pests or disease. It is most important for the young plants, as an established plant with a well-developed root system doesn't need to be watered as frequently.

Care

It is important to keep weeds away from newly established plants. Make sure the surface around the plant is

Hops shoots are a spring primeur that taste lovely fried in some butter.

completely free from grass and other plants. Mulching with bark or straw will help keep the weeds away.

When the first shoots appear, you need to prune them. Remove the early shoots that are weak and keep 3–6 of the stronger shoots on each plant. The removed shoots can be eaten as a "spring primeur."

In the fall you need to cut down the plant, leaving the roots to winterize in the soil. Younger plants often die over winter so you can protect the plants by patting some soil around the plant and covering it with leaves that both offer insulation and provide nutrients. Keep an eye out for frosty nights during the spring and cover up the shoots with soil, grass, or straw to protect them before the frost comes.

Pests

Hops can be affected by a host of pests and diseases that often appear during the summer. One of the most feared is the buttoned snout, a moth that lays small green larva on the plant, which can quickly turn a flourishing hops plant into a skeleton. If you discover larva, remove any afflicted leaves and place a cloth under the plant, shaking it vigorously so the larva fall off. Make sure to kill the larva so they don't end up going through pupation. You can even treat it with natural pesticides such as the bacteria Bacillus thuringiensis, which kills the larvae.

Harvest

The highlight of the year is naturally harvest time, which for us takes place around the end of August, but of course is dependent on location and variety. Some hops are ready to harvest at the end of July whereas other varieties are not ready until the beginning of October. Most of the time harvest takes place in August or September and it is important to harvest before the first frost.

It's a bit of a science to work out when the hops are ready to harvest. In the old days there were different thoughts and traditions surrounding harvest—some harvested when the cones were green while others waited for them to turn yellow. Larger producers of hops often use technology and advanced analytics to work out when the cones are fully mature.

The hops should be harvested once the cones emit a strong smell and have released the lupulin. If you rub one of the cones it should leave yellow marks on your fingers. It should feel like touching silk but at the same time feel sticky. Another sign that it is time to harvest is when the cone has got some light yellow patches on it; if they turn brown and the bracts have opened its gone too far.

Once you have decided the cones are ready to harvest you need to do it fast and all at the same time. If you have grown the plants on a trellis, lay them down to more easily pick off the cones. In order to be able to handle a large number of cones at once, you should start work during a sunny morning. Don't start too early as you don't want any morning dew on the cones, and avoid harvesting in damp or rain. Handle the cones carefully as the lupulin powder can disappear if you are not careful and shake the cones. Store the cones in an airy basket or bucket until they are ready to be dried. They should be left in a cool place and not in the sunshine.

Drying

If you are planning on storing the hops you need to dry it the same day as you pick it as they are fresh produce that can quickly deteriorate in quality. Drying hops can be done in several ways, for example by spreading them out sparsely on baking trays and drying them in the oven. Make sure the cones are not lying on top of each other. Dry them at 120ºF (50ºC) and leave the oven door open. You can also dry the hops in a fruit or mushroom dryer.

Hops contain around 80 percent water and should be dried at a humidity level of 7–12 percent. It's important to not dry them at too high temperature as anything over 140ºF (60ºC) reduces the quality.

The hops are ready when they're dry but still have some elasticity; they should not be so dry that they crumble. This usually takes 4–7 hours depending on your oven, the size of the cones, and how ripe they are.

Once the hops are dry they can be placed in freezer bags, labelled, and placed in the freezer where they will last for around a year. You can freeze the hops fresh, but it doesn't retain the flavor as well. Of course, you can also brew beer using fresh hops.

Brewing Beer

We were so proud when we brewed our first beer at home a few years back, although it was more surprise that the dark, sweet brew that we'd poured into an old demijohn a few weeks earlier actually tasted of beer. In fact, it tasted even better than store-bought beer! And since then we have continued brewing beer with just as good, if not better, results.

In the past, brewing beer at home for personal use was common. The actual brewing was usually overseen by the housewife and was surrounded by various rituals to keep away evil spirits and ensure the beer tasted good and wasn't infected. During the nineteenth century homebrewing decreased, initially due to an increase in availability of strong spirits and later the industrialization of breweries offering cheap beer.

In recent decades, homebrewing and microbrewing has become more popular, especially in America, as a way to challenge the bigger beer companies' flavorless industrial beer.

The most important thing the recent development of beer brewing has taught us is that it is neither difficult, nor do you need any advanced equipment to brew beer. In addition, you can create an almost limitless variety of beers as well as a better tasting product at the end. Also, beer is not that time-consuming compared to winemaking.

From boiling the wort to enjoying a freshly brewed beer only takes a few weeks.

Traditionally, beer consists of four simple ingredients: grain, water, hops, and yeast. They each contribute in different ways to the unique taste of beer. In order to transform these ingredients to beer, the following four steps need to be followed:

Malting

A process whereby grain is transformed into malt. By soaking the grain, it starts to sprout and enzymes are released that can transform starch into sugar. The process is stopped once the grain is dried.

Mashing

By crushing the malt and mixing it with warm water in different temperatures and draining it you extract the sugar from the malt and the resulting liquid is known as the wort.

Boiling the Wort

Boil the wort and add the hops. The sooner you add hops, the more bitterness it adds to the beer.

Fermenting

After being boiled, the wort is cooled down to start fermentation when yeast converts the sugar in the wort to alcohol, which results in beer.

Larger breweries include several extra steps like filtering and pasteurizing the beer. In other words, processes that both remove particles for a clearer beer as well as heat up the beer to pasteurize it.

Ingredients

Malt

The most important ingredient in beer is malt. There's a wide variety of malts you can buy and it depends a bit on what type of beer you plan to brew as to what you get. Choose organic and locally grown malt if you can as this will make your beer taste better. What you brew beer with is known as base malt and are usually types such as lager malt, pilsner malt, or wiener malt, and in addition to the base malt you can add a smaller amount of special malt whose purpose is not to add sugar but flavor, color, and complexity.

A common malt is a caramel malt that is roasted and caramelized.

If you're a beginner you can also start with a so-called "spray malt," which is a powdered malt. It is a good way to learn the process and produce your first tasty beer, something which is important as you take your first wobbly steps towards becoming a home brewer.

Hops

The best thing is to use your own hops, but if you plan to brew a lot of beer you may not have enough, and there are lots of different types of hops to buy depending on what beer you plan to brew. If you can, support local producers. Bittering hops is added early on to the wort to add bitterness, while aroma hops is added at the end of the wort being boiled to add aroma and flavor. You can also use aroma hops for dry hopping, which means that the hops is added during fermentation.

BEER & HOPS

Yeast

The type of yeast you add is important when you brew beer as the yeast doesn't just turn the sugar to alcohol but also adds flavor and character to the beer. Simply put, you can divide the fermentation of beer into three different categories: bottom fermentation, top fermentation, and spontaneous fermentation.

Bottom fermentation is the most common type, such as pilsner and lager. Bottom fermentation occurs at a lower temperature and takes longer, meaning the yeast sinks to the bottom.

Top fermenting is the most common among home brewers and means you use a yeast that ferments at room temperature whereby the yeast cells are carried with the bubbles to the surface. In this category you can find ale and wheat beer.

Spontaneous fermentation basically means you let nature decide which airborne yeast determines the fermentation process. You can't really control the result and it can turn out great, or terrible. This is the traditional way of brewing beer, in a spontaneous fermentation, bacteria contributing to the process, for example lactobacillus and eventually Brettanomyces. A spontaneously fermented beer will eventually become a sour beer, which is becoming more popular. To control the development of sour beer you can add your own bacteria, for example the sediment from a Belgian lambic.

You can also reuse yeast, which brewers have done throughout time. To keep buying new yeast is unnecessary. Once you have poured your beer you can pour fresh wort straight away onto the old yeast layer and start a new fermentation. You can also store the yeast in the fridge until you are ready for the next time.

Water

Water is important when it comes to brewing beer and there is a reason that certain towns and places around Europe have historically become connected with good beer as it is due to water quality. As a beginner, you don't need to consider water, but if you want to refine your beer brewing skills, water treatment is necessary.

Other Ingredients

The four ingredients above are the bases of making beer and usually they are enough, but you can also add almost anything you like from the kitchen, your garden, or the forest to contribute flavor and unique character to your beer. You can use almost any type of fruit, as well as berries, herbs, root vegetables, and flowers. Why not brew a spicy pumpkin beer, a tangy sour apple beer, or a smooth honey ale? The only limit is your imagination.

Equipment

If you plan to brew a lot of beer as well as plan to make more advanced beer you will, in time, need to get more professional equipment. A brewing system will mash and boil the wort and can be set to different temperatures in order to finely adjust the process, but before you spend money on expensive technology, you can simply start with a saucepan.

SAUCEPAN In order to brew beer you need a large pan. Even if you only plan to brew with a one-gallon (5 l) demijohn, it is worth having a large pan as wort often boils over. Four gallons (15 l) is better.

FERMENTATION VESSEL A good demijohn in glass will last a lifetime. However, if you plan to brew larger amounts, 6½ gallons (25 l) or more, you can buy plastic fermenters that are easy to use.

CAP & AIRLOCK If you use a demijohn, you will need a stopper or an airlock. Make sure you buy a stopper in the correct size so it doesn't let air in or fall into the fermenter. There are different types of airlocks available, but a simple plastic one works fine. Its main task is to stop air from getting in while at the same time releasing CO_2 that's created during fermentation. The airlock also gives a reassuring indication that the fermentation process has begun.

MASH TUN You can use a saucepan if you wrap some towels around it for insulation. Even better is to use something that is already insulated, like a cooler box.

HYDROMETER A hydrometer measures the density of the wort, which is basically the sugar content of the beer, and it will tell you how successful your mashing has

Drained malt can be used to make bread or provide a feast for ducks and chickens.

been. By measuring before and after fermentation you can calculate how much sugar has been consumed by the yeast, thus giving you the alcohol content of the beer.

SIEVE A larger fine sieve is needed when brewing beer, preferably one that can be hung or supported by the pan without you holding it. The sieve is needed for the sparging as well as to drain away the hops after you have boiled the wort.

SANITIZER Keeping things clean stops other microorganisms, apart from the ones you added, to infect your brew. Unfortunately, an infected brew has to be discarded. You can buy approved sanitizers at brewery stores.

SIPHON A siphon is a tube that is usually attached to a u-shaped plastic tube that can be used to move the beer between different vessels and eventually into a bottle. A siphon uses pressure, meaning the vessel that is being filled should be at a lower elevation.

BOTTLE CAPPER You don't need to cap your beer—you can store it in a keg or cork it—but if you want to cap it you will need a bottle capper. If you are not planning to fill thousands of bottles of beer you don't need an advanced capper.

WORT CHILLER OR BATH When the wort boiling is done the wort needs to be cooled down as quickly as possible. There are different ways to do this but the easiest is to use a wort chiller that you spray cold water through. You can also use a bathtub with cold water to cool it down.

OTHER TOOLS Tools that are useful to have when mashing and wort boiling are a good set of scales to weigh the malt and hops, a large ladle, and a kitchen thermometer.

The Brewing Process

Brewing beer is not especially technical but it does require some planning. It has been said that beer is liquid bread and that's not entirely wrong. In the same way making a sourdough starter needs some planning, brewing beer does too. To suddenly start brewing beer late at night might be a nice idea, but you run the risk of falling asleep during the wort boil. Brewing beer usually takes a day to plan ahead, but you can obviously do other things at the same time.

Crushing Malt

The first step in brewing beer is to crush the malt. You can buy ready crushed malt, but as with most things, it's better to do this step yourself. Dried malt is hard, so use a flour grinder or a specific malt crusher. You can use a food processor but it will wear on the equipment.

In beer terms, crushed malt is known as grist.

While you are crushing the malt, work out how much beer you want to make. 2.2lb (1kg) base malt yields just over a gallon (5 l) of beer. You can obviously use more or less malt if you want a stronger or weaker beer.

Mashing

Next you need to mash the grist to extract the sugar. This occurs at different temperatures (rests) so the grist can go through different processes. The easiest way to mash is to do it in a large pan, 4–5 gallons (15–20 l)

Apart from this you need a smaller pot with warm water (around 176°F (80°C)) that you use to regulate the temperature. During the mashing, keep the ratio of malt to water to about 1:3. The amount of mash rests and time vary depending on the end results you want, but there are two main mash rests:

PROTEIN REST Heat the water to 131°F (55°C) and add the grist. After this keep the temperature at 118–126°F (48-52°C) for 30 minutes. You can cover the pan and wrap it in a towel so it retains the heat better.

Regulate the temperature with warm water from the smaller pot; during the protein rest larger proteins are broken down.

SACCHARIFICATION REST This is the more important rest that turns starch to fermentable sugar. Usually several rests are conducted, one at a lower heat around 145–147°F (63–64°C) and one at a higher heat, around 158 (70°C). The lower rest results in a more alcoholic and drier beer, whereas the higher rest makes a weaker but more full-bodied beer. This is due to the different enzymes that are activated at different temperatures, although it can be

hard to keep the rests exact without a brewing system. You can conduct a rest at 145°F (63°C) for 30 minutes, followed by one at 158°F (70°C) for the same amount of time. An alternative is to try and keep the temperature between 151–154°F (66–68°C) for an hour to activate the enzymes in both intervals. To mash at one temperature is called an infusion mash.

Sparging

Once the mashing is complete you end up with a wort. If you taste it, it should be sweet with a sugar content of 10–12 percent. Sparging means removing any malt remnants. Use two large pans and a sieve that can rest over the pan. Pour the wort and malt remnants through the sieve into one of the pans. Move the sieve to the second pan and repeat this process several times. Work slowly and methodically making sure everything gets rinsed thoroughly. When you pour the wort over the malt you remove malt remnants as well as extract as much sugar as possible from it. Once you have done this you have your wort.

Wort Boil

Next comes the wort boil when you leave the wort to boil anywhere from 30 minutes to 1 ½ hours to sterilize the wort and remove any unwanted substances, which is why the wort boil takes place without a lid. It's mainly to remove dimethyl sulfide (DMS) which gives an unpleasant taste to the beer.

Traditionally you add the hops during the wort boil to give the beer its bitter taste. By adding different hops at different points you can change the end product, but be careful, especially when adding hops, as wort can easily overboil. It is not always necessary to boil wort though, for example if you are making sour beer.

Cooling

After the wort boil, it's important that everything that comes into contact with the wort is disinfected. Get into the habit of spraying or washing tools in disinfectant. To avoid infecting the wort it is important to chill it as quickly as possible to a temperature where the yeast can be added. Cooling the wort quickly also reduces the presence of DMS.

The quickest way to chill the wort is to place it in a bathtub with cold water, but an even quicker way is to use a wort chiller. Alternatively, a more environmentally friendly method is the no-chill method that comes from Australia in an attempt to save water. Instead of chilling the wort, it is poured into a disinfected plastic container which is filled all the way up without leaving any air and is then sealed until it has cooled down.

Fermentation

Fermentation is the most important process in beer brewing and what transforms a sweet wort into hopefully a tasty beer. The type of yeast and temperature during fermentation has a big effect on the end result. It is vital that fermentation takes place at a stable temperature and is not exposed to sunshine. For example, a dark wardrobe usually works for a top fermented beer while for a bottom fermented beer you need to find an area that holds a temperature lower than room temperature over time, such as a garage or root cellar.

It is important that the fermentation vat, cap, and airlock are properly sanitized before the wort is poured. Yeast can be bought both in liquid and dry form and it is really just a matter of taste what you choose. After you have added the yeast, it is a good idea to aerate the wort. You can do this by holding your hand (making sure you disinfect it first) over the opening and shaking it for a few minutes. Never fill the fermentation vat to the top but leave a small space as there is a risk that the beer may spill over.

The most important thing is that the fermentation process begins, which you notice by the fact that it starts to bubble in the airlock. If you find the fermentation process doesn't start, you can try to place the fermentation vat in a warmer spot and add a new batch of yeast.

YEAST STARTER Sometimes the fermentation can be slow to get going, for example in colder temperatures or if the wort is very sweet. In this case you can make a yeast starter, which is basically where you start a small scale fermentation process a few days before. Boil some water (around 2 pints per 5 gallons of beer (1 l per 20 l) and mix in 3½ oz (100 g) spraymalt. Chill down to 60°F (20°C), pour into a glass container, and add yeast and cover the container with aluminum foil. The fermentation process gets going because the yeast starter is exposed to the air and it should be ready to use within 1–5 days.

MEASURING ALCOHOL LEVELS Before you start the fermentation process it can be good to measure your beer with a hydrometer. Measure the density of the liquid before (OG) and after (FG) fermentation and you can calculate the strength of the beer. Fill a measuring jug with wort and put the hydrometer into the liquid; the wort should be a stable 60°F (20°C). Make a note of the OG value which is measured in °oechsle. Repeat the process post fermentation and use this formula: (OG-FG)/7.62=alcohol volume percentage.

Bottling

Compared to wine, beer ferments fairly quickly, often within one or a few weeks. You will notice that the bubbling in the airlock starts to decrease. Once this happens it's time to bottle your beer.

CARBONATING The beer is flat, so to make it carbonated you need to add some sugar. Most people add half a teaspoon of sugar per bottle, but we think you get a more even result with a primer, which is a sugar solution. 6–7 grams of sugar per 2 pints (1 l) of beer is a good starting point. Calculate how much sugar you need and dissolve it in some boiling water in a pan. Leave it to cool down and add to the beer as you bottle it. It can be worth bottling the beer first to avoid stirring up the bottom layer.

POURING Make sure to disinfect the bottles, caps, and siphon first, then place the fermentation vat at a higher level than the bottles, for example on a stool on a table. Then fill the bottles in one go and add the caps. It can get quite messy so cover up anything you need to protect.

Now it's time for the carbonation process, so make sure your bottles are not anywhere too cold but place them in a dark, warm space for a few days. How quickly it starts to carbonate depends on how active the yeast is. You can open a beer to check it. If you want more carbonation, leave them for a few extra days, but if you like the result you just need to chill the bottles and then enjoy. A normal light beer usually lasts around 9 months and the higher the alcohol level, the longer it will last.

Bottling, page 275

BEER & HOPS

Harvest Ale

One of the best ways to use your hops is to make fresh harvest ale—in this case a saison ("season" in French). Originating from the Wallonian countryside, the saison yeast has a peppery and spicy character which we think works well with many heritage hops varieties. The taste will vary depending on what hops you use. To make the most of our harvest we also add hops during fermentation. This beer can only be made during August and September and remember that the hops quickly deteriorate in quality after they've been picked.

2½ gallons (10 l)
4.4 lb. (2 kg) pilsnermalt
1 lb (500 g) wheat malt
1¾ oz (50 g) dried hops
3½ oz (100 g) honey
7 oz (200 g) fresh hops
1 packet saison yeast, for example Belle Saison Lallemand

Crush, mash, and lauter the pilsner and wheat malt together using around 2 gallons (7½ l) water.

If you want to do a quick version, you can swap the malt for 2 bags of light spraymalt and half a bag of wheat malt.

Add around 1 gallon (3½ l) water and cook the wort for 60 minutes. After 30 minutes, add the dried hops, then 5 minutes before the end, add honey and then water until you have 2½ gallons (10 l) wort in the pan.

Chill the wort to 68ºF (20ºC) and sieve to remove the hops into a clean fermentation vat. Add the yeast to start the fermentation. It should ferment at room temperature, around 68ºF (20ºC). Wait for the most intensive fermentation to pass before adding the fresh hops, then go outside and pick the hops and add to the fermentation vat. After 5 days, pour into a new vat and remove the hops using a sieve.

After around 2 weeks, add the sugar solution to carbonate the beer and pour into bottles, wait another 2 weeks, and then drink.

Honey Beer

Honey and beer might not sound like a great combination, but honey is a fantastic flavor to add to beer and adds floral notes and body. We usually make a honey beer when we wash honey wax and get a sweet honey water. Apart from flavor, honey also makes for a stronger beer, which is worth remembering. The strength of the beer depends on the honey water, but you can also add regular honey. Choose a late summer local honey if you can.

2½ gallons (10 l)
4.4 lb (2 kg) pale ale malt
7 oz (200 g) caramel malt
7 oz (200 g) flaked oats
1.4 oz (40 g) dried hops
Around 6–8½ pints (3–4 l) honey water or 14 oz (400 g) honey dissolved in 6–8½ pints of water
1 packet of ale yeast, for example Fermentis Safale US-05

Crush, mash, and lauter the malt and oats together using around 2 gallons (7½ l) water.

If you want to make a quicker version, swap the malt for two bags of spraymalt and make a small mash with oats and caramel malt.

Cook the wort for 45 minutes. Once the wort is heated up, add ¾ oz (20 grams) of dried hops. Add the rest of the hops and honey water when there is five minutes remaining.

Chill the wort to 68ºF (20ºC) and sieve to remove the hops into a clean fermentation vessel. Add the yeast to start the fermentation. It should ferment at room temperature, around 68ºF (20ºC).

After around 2 weeks, add the sugar solution to carbonate the beer and pour into bottles. Wait another 2 weeks and then drink.

BEER & HOPS

Sour Ale

Historically speaking, most beers have more or less been sour beers and the clean, filtered, and pasteurized beers of today are a result of modern breweries. Before people realized that it was yeast that caused the beer to ferment, beer brewing was a magical process. People saved yeast in different ways and then started a new brew and it was commonplace to use a yeast ring, which was placed into the fermentation vat.

The yeast got caught in the ring and would then be used in the new brew. In this way, the beer would not only be exposed to the yeast but to different types of bacteria which would take over.

While lager became popular on the continent and ale on the British Isles, it was mainly in Belgium that sour beer was being made and refined, so it is not surprising that this is where most sour beer enthusiasts head to rediscover this fantastic beer.

Basically, sour beer is an infected beer, but infected in the right way. The right combination of yeast and bacteria add flavors from bubbly acidity to strawy, farmyard. Pure traditional sour ale, such as a Belgian lambic, are fermented through natural exposure to yeast rather than adding it. Usually, the windows are opened and the night air sweeps over the shallow basins, called cool ships, to add the right bacterial culture.

When you come to make your own sour beer there are different methods you can use, from a traditional, slow fermented beer that takes several years to mature, to a quick soured version that can be drunk after only a few weeks.

Bacteria & Yeast

There are several yeast and bacterial strains that are sought after by those who brew sour beers. The most common is the lactic acid bacteria that gives it its characteristic sour taste, which berliner weisse and gose are known for. Lactobacillus contributes lactic acid that is mild but also the sharper vinegar taste. The quickest and easiest way to make a sour beer is to add lactobacillus and it is a relatively controlled process where you can stop the souring when you have reached the desired result. In contrast to regular brewers yeast, these bacteria do not produce alcohol when they eat the

sugar but instead produce acid, which has an effect on the strength of the beer. The easiest way to get a strain of lactobacillus is to buy it from a specialist store.

The most sought-after yeast culture for making sour beer is brettanonmyces, or brett for short. Brett gives a more complex taste that often develops over several years and it's commonly associated with notes of farmyard and ripe fruit. To make a spontaneously fermented Belgian beer with brett is similar to the process of making wine rather than traditional beer brewing. Many Belgian sour beers are stored in barrels for a period of time to allow the complex flavors from brett to develop.

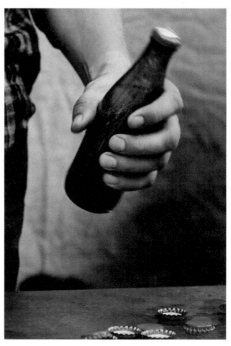

CONSIDER YOUR TOOLS When you make soured beer it is good to have a separate set of tools like a yeast brink, stopper, and a siphon as otherwise there's a risk that you infect the next beer you make with some of the bacteria you made for the soured beer. Of course, you can just clean everything, but it's easier to have a separate kit for sour beer to avoid contamination.

If the beer is souring for a long period, it is better to use a glass vat such as a demijohn, as plastic buckets can allow air in over time, which can promote acetic acid bacteria.

Quick Soured Beer

This is a recipe for soured beer that can be drunk within a month. Hops and soured beer is a complex relationship that doesn't always work well as acidity and bitterness does not make the best taste combination.

In this recipe the hops doesn't add any bitterness as it is not included in the cooking, just through aromas by dry hopping. If you want to add some fruitiness to your soured beer you can use redcurrants or raspberries instead of hops.

__2½ gallons (10 l)__
3.3 lb (1½ kg) pilsner malt
2.2 lb (1 kg) wheat malt
14 oz (400 g) oats, malted
3 capsules Probi Mage (Lactobacillus plantarum)
1 packet of yeast, preferably a strong variety such as French Saison yeast 3711 or Fermentis Safale S-04
1¾ oz (50 g) dried hops (preferably fruity)

Crush, mash, and sparge the malt and oats together; use around 2 gallons (7½ l) of water.

If you want a quicker recipe, you can swap the malt for spraymalt (1½ bags) and oat malt extract (1 bag) and make a small mash with the oats.

Add another 5 pints (2.5 l) of water and chill to 104°F (40°C). Pour into a fermentation vat.

Open the capsules with the lactobacteria and add to the mix. Add an airlock and leave it in a warm space, for example on underfloor heating, for 2–4 days. It should be around 86–104°F (30–40°C) but if you don't have this, leave at room temperature for a few extra days.

Taste the brew and if you want more acidity, leave it for a bit longer. Remember that this is beer with a living bacteria, so it will get more bitter as time goes on.

Add the yeast.

Once the first fermentation is over, add the dry hops, preferably in a bag that you can remove after a few days.

After around 2 weeks, add liquid sugar (priming sugar) to carbonate it and pour into bottles. Wait another two weeks before you drink it.

Slow Soured Beer

Making proper soured beer is not an exact science as you are dealing with different bacteria and yeasts that can develop and react in different ways, so it's more about trial and error. Simply put, the process of making slow soured beer is the opposite of making quick soured beer where you first make the beer and then infect it. You can buy cultures to make soured beer from larger manufacturers, but we prefer to make the base from the soured beer that we like the taste of—just make sure the beer isn't pasteurized.

This beer can be varied in a multitude of ways and you can start with your own favorite beer recipe. Just don't add too much hops and make it too bitter. For simplicity, this recipe is based on the quick soured beer with a few variations.

__2½ gallons (10 l)__
3.3 lb (1½ kg) pilsnermalt
2.2lb (1 kg) wheat malt
14 oz (400 g) oats, malted
Base beer from three unpasteurized soured beers with brett
1 packet of yeast, preferably a strong variety such as French Saison Wyeast 3711 or Fermentis Safale S-04
Fruit (such as blackcurrants or raspberries) or 1¾ oz (50 g) dried hops

Crush, mash, and sparge the malt and oats together; use around 2 gallons (7½ l) of water.

If you want a quicker recipe, you can swap the malt for a bag of spraymalt (1½ bags) and oat malt extract (1 bag) and make a small mash with the oats.

Add 7 ½ pints (3.5 l) water and boil for 30 minutes.

Cool down to 68°F (20°C) and pour into a clean yeast brink. Add the yeast and make sure the mixture starts to ferment. Leave to ferment in room temperature at around 68°F (20°C).

Add fruit or hops (if you want) once the first fermentation starts to reduce. Sieve and pour into a new glass jar.

Once the fermentation starts to reduce after a few weeks, drink 3–4 sour beers and add the base to the beer. Wait for 6 months and test it—if you are happy you can pour it into bottles and drink it, or wait another few months.

Winemaking

According to an old Iranian saying, the art of wine making was discovered by a Persian Princess who had fallen out of favor with the king. Overcome by sorrow, she tried to take her life by drinking the juice from a plate of rotten grapes. She didn't die of course, but instead experienced a euphoric sense of intoxication that lifted her sorrows. With the help of this discovery, she was able to regain the King's favor.

The key message from this story is that the discovery of wine probably did happen something like this, and the first yeast used by man was probably the skin from grapes.

The fermentation process that results in alcohol is completely natural. Yeast breaks down sugar to alcohol and carbon dioxide, but a whole range of other substances are also produced during fermentation that contribute unique flavors and smells in wine, beer, bread, and anything else we ferment.

Saccharomyces cerevisiae, or brewers yeast, was the yeast most commonly used in both baking and brewing in the past, but since the French chemist Louis Pasteur found, at the end of the nineteenth century, that the fermentation process is caused by microorganisms, people started to produce different strains of yeast that not only break down different sugars but also produce different tastes.

The oldest remnants of wine making have been found in Caucasus and Iran. For thousands of years alcoholic drinks have been made with almost any fruit available. The reason the grape dominated the making of fruit wines early on is simple—it is the easiest one. The grape contains all the ingredients that create a well-balanced wine with sweetness, acidity, and tannins. The grape also contains enough natural sugars, as opposed to many other fruits, to ferment a strong wine.

Because the grape has taken center stage in wine making over the last decades, wines made from other fruits have been somewhat forgotten and even completely dismissed. Fruit wine is something that is often met with distaste as it is considered sour or sickly. Truth is that a good fruit wine can be compared to a full-bodied red wine, a refreshing glass of rosé, or a dry sparkling wine, although comparing it to other wines doesn't do it justice either as fruit wine has its own unique flavor.

One of the reasons fruit wines have a bad reputation is that the ones that are offered for sale have often been of lower quality, too sweet, and with different additives, and many consumers consider fruit wine as an alcoholic juice.

What makes fruit wine even more tricky is that most fruits don't have the grapes' natural balance of ingredients, meaning you need to compensate for it in some way. However, transforming the fruits in your garden—berries, flowers, and crops—into wine is one of the best things you can do.

What Is Fruit Wine?

In reality, all wines are fruit wines, but wine made from grapes is usually excluded as well as cider as these make up their own categories of drinks. Wine can pretty much be made from any berries or fruits, but some have better properties to make a good-tasting wine than others. In northern climates, where making wine has not always been possible or worth doing, there has been a tradition of making wines from fruits other than the grape. In eastern Asia wine has been made from plums since time immemorial, and in the United Kingdom, there is still a strong tradition of making wine from different fruits. The fruits and berries that make the best wines are usually those that have a natural acidity such as rhubarb and sea buckthorn, or blueberries, blackcurrants, and elderberries that offer both asperity and tannins. To balance the wine and add sweetness, you can use sugar, honey, lemon, or citric acid.

Alcohol

Alcohol is created through a process whereby sugar is broken down by yeast. When this happens in an environment that is low or completely deprived of oxygen, ethanol and carbon dioxide are produced, ie alcohol. If, on the other hand, oxygen is present, only carbon dioxide and water are produced, which is why the fermentation process takes place in an oxygen deprived environment.

In many fruit wines and recipes, a lot of sugar is used to make a sweet wine with a high alcohol content. Historically, there has been a tendency to create a highly alcoholic beverage as the wine was usually not made for its great taste, something which has contributed to its negative reputation. Most yeasts die once the alcohol levels reach 16–20%, which is why this is usually the maximum level in alcohol. In our opinion, there are few fruit wines that taste good at that strength as they can easily be overwhelmed by the taste of alcohol, and a wine needs to be very full bodied to carry off a high alcohol content. In addition, highly alcoholic wines don't last long enough to be stored, which would make them taste milder.

In our experience, most fruit wines are best drunk as a light seasonal wine with an alcoholic content of around 8–12%. Think of them as French table wines; ones made from red berries often lean towards a fruity French Beaujolais.

Most fruits and berries don't contain enough sugar to reach a higher alcohol content naturally. For example, apples must contain 10–15% natural sugars that ferment cider to an alcohol content of 4–6%. For a stronger wine, sugar needs to be added, but at the same time you need to consider the fruit's own sugar content to get the right balance. To get the yeast to produce 1% alcohol you need to add ½ oz (18 g) sugar per 2 pints (1 l). If you add 4 lb (1.8 kg) sugar to 2 ½ gallons (10 l) water, the result is an alcohol level of 10%.

An important tool for anyone making alcohol is a hydrometer, which measures the sugar levels in the liquid, meaning you can calculate the alcohol content.

Wine Takes Time

Wine is one of the slowest things you can make at home and one of the things that will test your patience. Beer can be made from brew to bottle in a month whereas wine often takes a whole year from the start of fermentation to being able to pour yourself a glass. You can of course drink wine sooner, but it always tastes better after it has been aged for a while.

What makes wine take its time is that it needs a slow ferment, preferably for several months, and then the bottle should be aged for at least 3–6 months.

Always remember to write down the recipe as it can be hard to remember what you did a year later.

Terroir & Fruits

Within winemaking you may have heard the term terroir (from the French "terre" for land) which is used to describe the local area in terms of soil, climate, and geography that has an effect on the wine. The same goes for homemade wine too—fruit, vegetables, and berries that grow in your garden also have their unique qualities in terms of taste, smells, and ripeness.

Another important factor for the end product is variety. When we talk about wine made from red grapes, we understand that this encompasses a whole host of different tastes. Both the variety of grape and terroir add their personal stamp before the wine is even made.

Making your own wine is always a bit of an experiment, but a process that should be embraced as usually you will end up creating something entirely novel. Use our recipes as a base for your wine and then enjoy your own, unique terroir.

Yeast

The yeast you choose doesn't only produce alcohol but also contributes with taste. Different varieties will enhance different flavors contained within the fruit that in turn contribute to different nuances in your wine, and it's these unique flavors that we experience as notes of pepper, liquorish, or exotic fruits. Many aromas may not become apparent until the wine has aged for a while.

There are two ways to ferment: you can either buy yeast or allow your wine to be taken over by wild yeast as yeast exists all around us, including on the fruit's skin. In other words, if you want your wine to ferment naturally, do nothing. Wild fermentation can be a bit haphazard though—it can turn out fine or terrible, but that is all part of the charm, that you are not totally in control of the process. The drawback of course is that it can be disappointing to find out that the wine you have been working on for a year is undrinkable, so adding yeast obviously assures a better result, which is often better if you are a beginner. In our recipes we will add yeast to keep things simple.

Fermenting & Aging

As wine takes time, it's a good idea to find somewhere suitable to age and store the wine, both during the process and afterwards. When the wine ferments, it needs to be stored in a dark room with an even temperature, so avoid anywhere drafty. Most yeasts for wine ferment in a fairly broad temperature range, but it will go more quickly in a warmer space and slower in a cooler one, and this is usually how traditional winemakers control the process.

Wine that ferments at a lower temperature is usually more fruity and fresh, which works best for white wines. Red wines on the other hand usually ferment at a higher temperature, sometimes over 86°F (30°C), which gives more character and tannins.

We think that fruit wines usually work best fermented at room temperature and a cupboard or larder work well. The most important thing is that the temperature doesn't fluctuate too much.

When aging, a colder and more moist environment is preferable—for example, a root cellar, wine cellar, or wine fridge. If you are using a cork in the bottles, moisture is important so the wine doesn't dry out and spoil. A good temperature for aging wine is 46–54°F (8–12°C) and there should be no risk of frost or ongoing low temperatures in the room.

Cleaning

When making and storing wine, cleanliness is important as a wine can easily be destroyed by mold, bacteria, or the wrong type of yeast. To avoid this, tools and vessels that come into contact with the wine must be carefully cleaned and disinfected, something that can't be achieved by dish soap alone. Home brew stores often sell sterilizers that are effective, and most well-versed wine makers know that proper cleaning is half the job.

Clear or Cloudy?

Whether you want your wine to be clear or cloudy is up to you. Some prefer a crystal clear drink while others don't mind a layer of sediment at the bottom. It is mainly a matter of personal taste. You can get so-called wine fining or wine clearing agents that can help to remove the sediment, but personally we don't mind slightly grainy wine—after all, it just shows the wine in its natural state.

Watch Out for Bubbles

Fermenting wine is not completely risk-free. For one thing, there is a risk of bottles exploding if they are not handled correctly. It has never happened to us, but it is something to be aware of. The main rule is to not bottle a wine that has not finished fermenting. Make sure to stop the fermenting process with, for example, calcium sorbate. However, sometimes a new fermentation can begin in the bottle if there are sugar remnants, which is why you should preferably not use screw tops. Rather, use traditional wine corks which will pop out if there is too much pressure in the bottle. If you want to make a sparkling wine or are unsure if all the sugar has been

Red & Black, page 295

WINEMAKING

broken down, you can use champagne bottles which are made to withstand a higher pressure.

Ingredients

A good wine does not brew itself but needs the hand of a wine maker at different stages in the process. Within traditional winemaking, wine from different grapes are often mixed to give a more even quality and more uniform wine. Lesser quality wines often contain other additives and different amounts of sugar to make it drinkable. Even when you make wine at home, there are different tricks and ingredients you can use to steer the development, taste, and maturity of the wine.

Sugar

To increase the sugar levels, you need to add some type of sugar. Even sweet plums often only contain half the natural sugar of a grape. Regular white sugar contributes very little, if any, flavor.

You can buy brewing sugar, which is pure glucose, but granulated sugar works fine in our experience. Brown sugar and rock candy (crystalized sugar) can be added in smaller amounts, but as it is a "dirtier" sugar it contributes more flavor, especially notes of caramel.

Honey

In contrast to normal sugar, honey also adds a floral taste and more body to a wine, although if you use too much honey it starts to taste a bit more like mead. You can use fresh runny honey, but remember it needs to be pasteurized.

Dried Fruit

Most wines taste better if they have what we call "body." This is the fullness of the wine, which is affected by alcohol content, tannins, and aromas, so a heavy red wine usually has a lot of body. To achieve body in wine, a good trick is to add dried fruit such as raisins, apricots, and figs. A couple of handfuls of raisins in an elderberry wine can make a huge difference in the results.

Lemon & Acidity

Acidity in wine fills several functions. It gives freshness and structure but also contributes to the wine's shelf life.

When a fruit wine goes wrong it is usually due to lack of acidity. A wine with an insipid taste isn't very nice. Adding lemon during maceration is a good way to raise the acidity levels. You can increase acidity further at the end of the process with tartaric acid.

Tea & Wood

Within winemaking circles, tannins are often mentioned. These are the bitter, astringent tastes that some wines give off, a sort of harshness on the tongue. Tannin is a polyphenol, a substance which is emitted by plants to protect them against being eaten, so the bitter taste we enjoy is actually meant as a deterrent. Tannin is found in large amounts in the skin of the grape but also the skin of blueberries, sloe, and elderberries, which makes them good for making wines rich in tannin. You can also add oak cubes or oak leaves to add tannin flavors to a wine.

Sulphur

In order to control the winemaking process, for example when you want to add the yeast, you need to be able to stop any wild fermentation taking place. Boiling the brew should be avoided, so instead you can add sulfite, or sodium metabisulfite, which stops the growth of wild bacteria. The easiest way is to use it in tablet form, known as Campden tablets. When you want to stop fermentation at the end of the process you can use a mix of potassium sorbate and sulfite, which will inhibit oxidation in the wine and help to preserve it.

Yeast Nutrients

In order to thrive, yeast doesn't only need sugar but also other nutrients and minerals. When making mead and wine, where large quantities of sugar are added, it is always a good idea to add some form of nutrients and minerals. Usually a teaspoon is enough. The yeast nutrients help the yeast to ferment more sugar.

Sweetener

We prefer dry wines, but some wines taste better if they are slightly sweetened. It's always easiest to convert all the sugar that is added to the wine during the fermentation process and then sweeten it afterwards. If you are using regular sugar, such as a sugar syrup, the yeast has to be dead to prevent it from fermenting again, so make sure you stop this process, for example by adding a potassium sorbate and sulfite mix. You can also use a sweetener like Stevia, which will not ferment.

Tools & Preparations

You don't need many tools to make wine, but a few things are necessary or make the process a lot easier.

DEMIJOHN One or a few demijohns are worth investing in and they last forever. A regular one-gallon demijohn can be bought fairly cheaply but you can even find old second hand ones which work fine as long as you clean them properly. The fact that they are decorative in the kitchen is just an added bonus.

PLASTIC BUCKET A large 4–5-gallon (15–25-liter) bucket with a lid, such as a plastic fermentation vat, works perfectly.

AIRLOCK It's also necessary to have an airlock and a stopper or rubber cap as fermentation needs to take place in an oxygen free environment.

The airlock has a water trap that prevents bacteria, mold, and insects from getting inside.

SAUCEPAN A large saucepan to heat up water and dissolve sugar is needed, preferably 4 gallons (15 l) or more, but you can use a smaller one if you want to heat it up in several rounds.

SIPHON A siphon is a tube that is used to move liquid from one vessel to another. A siphon with a u-bend is easy to use and will soon prove an irreplaceable tool for your brews.

HYDROMETER A hydrometer and a glass tube are two useful items in a brewer's tool box. With the help of a hydrometer you can measure the sugar levels in the liquid and thus calculate the alcohol levels.

CORKING MACHINE The only tool, apart from the fermentation vat, which is indispensable is a corking machine. To bottle your wine is the best part of the whole process as you know you are only one step away from tasting your creation. There are many different types of corking machines you can get and unless you are making large amounts of wine, a simple one will do just fine.

STERILIZER To create a sterile environment for making your wine, you need a sterilizer that is approved for use in food produce, so you are best off buying it in a specialist wine and beer store.

The Basics of Making Wine

The basics are easy, but there are endless variations, so use the advice below as a starting point for your experiments.

1. Picking Fruit

Pick and clean your fruit, making sure the fruit is ripe enough. Unripe fruit can add acidity but also an unpleasant bitterness. Make sure the fruit is not damaged, rotten, or overripe as this can affect the end result.

2. Extracting Juice

This is in many ways the most important moment in winemaking as this is the point at which you extract the flavors. There are many ways to do this including crushing, pressing, boiling, soaking, placing in a sugar solution, and so on, and of course you can just chuck everything in a steam juicer, but we prefer as gentle a process as possible. When you heat fruit over a longer period, a lot of flavors disappear, so we prefer to spend some time on this step and usually macerate our fruit, which is described in the next step.

3. Maceration

Maceration is a process where fermentation is started with whole or parts of fruits in the brew. In this way, flavor and color is extracted from the fruit, which is especially important if you want to make a wine with high levels of tannins.

The alcohol that is produced during maceration contributes to extracting the flavors from the fruit, which is why you add yeast and sugar at this point.

4. Start Fermentation

In this stage you remove the fruit using a sieve and add sugar, yeast nutrient, water, and yeast if you haven't already done so during maceration. The remaining fruit can be added to your compost. Now everything needs to ferment in a dark, oxygen-deprived space and within a day or so you should see it start to bubble in the air lock. If it doesn't, it is either too cold or there may be too much sugar, which can slow down fermentation at the start. In this case make a starter culture where you

get the yeast going in a bottle, for example, with water, sugar, and some yeast nutrient. Once it has started to really get going, you can add it to the brew.

5. Fermentation

Depending on the yeast, temperature, and sugar levels, fermentation can take different amounts of time, from a week to several months. There's no point trying to hurry it along, so place it out of sight and leave it to finish fermenting. The wine should be left in a demijohn to mature for several months.

Once fermentation is complete, you can pour the wine to another demijohn to get rid of the sediment at the bottom, which can affect the taste of the wine. Pouring the wine into a new vat can sometimes give the yeast a new lease on life, which can lead to secondary fermentation.

6. Bottling & Storing

Once the wine has been fermented and left for a period of time, you can start pouring it into bottles. Once the wine is exposed to air, oxidization starts, which can in time destroy the wine. This is why you need to pour the wine into bottles as quickly as you can, remembering to sterilize the bottles and add the cork.

Once it has been poured into bottles, the wine should be stored in a cool, dark space for around 3–6 months. If you are using traditional corks, the space should preferably be damp and the bottles lying down.

You can of course drink the wine sooner if it tastes good, but if it is astringent and has a harsh flavor it will probably taste a lot better after a period of time in the cellar. Most fruit wines should then be consumed within a year, but some can be stored for several years.

WINEMAKING

ELDERBERRY WINE   1.3 GALLONS (5 L)

Elderflowers are wonderful and so are the berries—these black, glossy little flavor bombs are one of the best things you can make wine from.

Elderberries are packed full of tannins and color and we are lucky enough to have a real old elderberry bush in our garden that is our most prized possession. Elderberry wine gets better with time and can be stored.

Elderberries usually ripen from August to October. If you have a bush, make sure you don't pick all the flowers as if you do, you won't get any berries. Only pick bunches where all the berries have ripened and it's important not to include any green berries but leave them where they are to ripen. You can then remove the berries from the bunch with a fork. Make sure you don't get any part of the stem as it contains bitter substances.

Make sure you don't mistake real elder for false or poisonous types such as red elder or dwarf elder. Red elder has red berries and the dwarf elder is a 3 foot plant, whereas real elder is a large bush with a woody stem and a unique smell of elder. If you're unsure, avoid picking the berries and ask someone with more knowledge to check the bush.

2.2 lb (1 kg) elderberries
1 organic lemon, sliced
3.2 pints (1½ l) + 5.3 pints (2½ l) boiling water
2.2 lb (1 kg) caster sugar
1 packet champagne yeast
1 campden tablet or 1 tsp yeast nutrient
Bottles

Pick the berries from the stalks and place them in a large saucepan, 2½ gallons (10 l) preferably. Remove any unripe berries. Place the lemon among the berries.

Pour 3.2 pints of boiling water over, cover, and leave for 24 hours.

Add the sugar and crush the berries with a potato masher. Add one crushed campden tablet and pour 5.3 pints of boiling water on top. Cover and leave for another 24 hours.

Sieve the liquid into a demijohn and add the champagne yeast. After a day or so the fermentation should have started. If you want to enhance this process, you can add 1 tsp yeast nutrient, dissolved in boiling water.

Leave in a dark room at room temperature for around a month. Then sieve the liquid into a new demijohn without including the sediment at the bottom. This is when the secondary fermentation usually starts. After this the demijohn can be placed in a cooler area for around 3–4 months.

Taste the wine and bottle it. The alcohol, together with the sharp and acidic notes, will soften after a few months.

Rhubarb Wine

One of early summer's first primeurs is not only great in a pie but it can also make the most refreshing drink that your garden can give. Winemakers love the natural high acidity and the rosé color of the wine. There are over 100 varieties of rhubarb, so the color and taste can vary slightly.

1.3 gallons (5 l)
8–10 large stalks of rhubarb
3 lb (1¼ kg) caster sugar
1 campden tablet
4.2 pints (2 l) boiling water
1 tsp yeast nutrient
1 packet champagne yeast

Rinse and trim the rhubarb stalks and crush the stalks with a rolling pin or meat tenderizer.

Place the crushed stalks in a large bowl or an open fermentation vat. Pour the sugar over with a crushed campden tablet. Mix thoroughly and cover.

Leave for 24 hours, stirring a few times with a ladle so the sugar doesn't sink to the bottom.

Mix and strain the stalks so that the syrup drips into a bowl.

Pour 4.2 pints warm water over the syrup and stir until all the sugar has dissolved.

Pour the brew into a demijohn and add the yeast nutrient dissolved in some boiled water. If necessary, add some cold water. Add the champagne yeast when the temperature reaches around 68°F (20°C). Leave it to ferment in a dark room at room temperature for a month, then pour into bottles, making sure you don't include the sediment.

Leave for around 3 months before you bottle it. You can drink it right away, but it usually tastes better after it has been aged for a bit.

Red & Black

A light, tart wine that is perfect for a cookout on a nice summer evening. The blackcurrants contribute color, tannin, and depth while the red ones contribute a fresh tartness.

<u>1.3 gallons (5 l)</u>
1½ lb (750 g) blackcurrants
1½ lb (750 g) redcurrants
3.2 pints (1½ l) + 4.2 pints (2 l) boiling water
2.2 lb (1 kg) caster sugar
1 campden tablet
1 packet champagne yeast
1 tsp yeast nutrient
Tartaric acid or stevia (optional)

Remove the berries with a fork and remove any stems as they contain bitter substances.

Place the berries in a large saucepan or a plastic fermentation bucket. Add 3.2 pints of boiling water, cover, and leave for 24 hours.

Add the sugar and crush the berries using a potato masher. Add one crushed campden tablet, pour over 4.2 pints boiling water, and leave for 24 hours.

Add the champagne yeast and the yeast nutrient, dissolved in some boiling water.

Mix the berries with a large ladle, making sure you have disinfected it first, and cover with a towel. Some air should be able to enter, but no vermin.

Leave for 3 days, stirring daily with a ladle. You can tell that fermentation has started when small bubbles appear on the surface.

After 3 days you can sieve the wine and pour into a demijohn. Add boiling water if needed. Leave it to ferment in a dark space at normal room temperature for about a month. Then sieve the liquid into a new demijohn without including the sediment at the bottom. This is when the secondary fermentation usually starts. After this the demijohn can be placed in a cooler area for around 3–4 months.

Taste the wine; if you want it more acidic, you can add the tartaric acid. If you want it sweeter, you can add stevia. If you are not sure if the fermentation is complete, you can add potassium metabisulfite before bottling. The astringent taste of alcohol will soften after a few months.

House Red

If you are lucky enough to have a couple of grapevines by a south facing wall, you can get a surprising amount of grapes. There is nothing better than turning these grapes into a house wine, and if you don't have enough of one type you can mix white and red grapes. It's important to make sure that the grapes are fully ripe to the point of being nearly overripe. When eating grapes, they taste better when they are slightly tart, but when you make wine you want them to be as sweet as possible. We allow our wine to ferment naturally, but you can also add cultured yeast if you don't want to take a chance.

<u>1.3 gallons (5 l)</u>
22 lb (10 kg) grapes
Brewer's yeast (optional)

Remove any debris and rinse the grapes; its fine to leave them on their bunch.

Place the grapes in an open fermentation vat, for example a fermentation bucket. Now it's time to crush the grapes, which can be done with a wine press, but it's a lot more fun doing it the traditional way. Use a fermentation vat that is wide enough for you to stand in. Clean your feet properly and step into the vat, carefully stomping the grapes and feeling them crush beneath the arches of your feet.

The benefit of using your feet is that you prevent the seeds from being crushed, as they can emit bitter substances.

Once the grapes are crushed, you are done. Place the wine in a dark, warm space, preferably 77–86°F (25–30°C), adding an airlock and bung.

After a day or so, fermentation should have started. Leave the wine to macerate for about a week. During this period, tannins and color are extracted from the skin.

When the maceration is complete, sieve away the skin and any other debris and pour the wine into a demijohn, adding water if needed. Leave the wine to finish fermenting and then pour it into another demijohn. Leave it for at least 6 months before you bottle it. It will taste better after it has been aged for a while.

Trees & Bushes

It all started with the apple trees. We first saw our house in early summer, having driven around Uppland county all day looking at houses. We were all tired, our son was crying in the back seat, and we ended up taking a wrong turn. Skidding along gravel roads, we almost gave up and went home, until finally we saw it. As soon as we entered the driveway, we were struck by the old apple trees—their thick, gnarly arms reaching out to embrace us. These ancient trees, older than mankind, with whisperings of older generations who had cared for them.

We didn't know it then, but we were about to move into an apple paradise. The manor house below us, to which our house once belonged, owns an apple orchard with 130 trees from the end of the nineteenth century, including the local variety, the Krusenberg apple. It's highly likely that our own trees come from there as the lord of the manor would have given his staff apple trees as gifts. Not too far from us some of Sweden's oldest oak trees also stand, including the 800-year-old King Oak, which apparently was the inspiration for the Swedish bank Sparbanken's famous logo.

Inheriting old trees is a huge responsibility. Not only do they give us food and shade, but hopefully they offer the same to the next generation. We have also planted many new trees such as pear, plum, apricot, quince, peach, hazelnut, and walnut. These will also stand for generations and maybe one day our grandchildren will eat walnuts or pears from these trees.

A Long-Term Investment

Creating and taking care of a garden with trees and bushes is a long-term investment. Hopefully, after a year or so, they bear fruit, but it can take decades before you are rewarded for your hard work.

Trees and bushes prefer stability, in contrast to humans who prefer change. We build, plan, chop, and change but when you come to plant a tree you have to think long-term. It is possible to move a tree, but try to plant them somewhere they can grow in peace without having to compete with a new greenhouse or pathway.

Another thing you need to consider is that trees will affect their surroundings. That tiny sapling will one day grow into a mighty tree, giving you protection but also shade, meaning it will change the eco system in its immediate environment. In time, it will affect how you can use this land and what other plants can grow here. Try to imagine the tree in 30 or 40 years and how it will look; tall bushy trees may eventually block views and sightlines so make sure you consider the size of the tree.

Bushes don't need the same forethought, but they can still affect their surrounding environment. A blueberry or hawthorn bush can quickly dominate an area, for both good and bad. Some bushes, once established, can also be difficult to remove.

There are also other aspects to consider when planting trees and bushes, for example the area you are planting in, pollination, diversity, and the type of fruit you want.

Basically, bushes and trees need long-term planning, both when inheriting an old garden, as well as when you are creating a new one.

A Woodland Garden

If you have a lot of land, a garden that borders a forest, or just a large unused piece of land, you can create a woodland garden. It can take many years, even decades, to create a productive woodland garden and we are only at the start of our journey. A woodland garden is similar to planting at the edge of a forest. You can plant edible perennials, bushes, and trees that tend to themselves. The aim is to replace the plants that normally grow in untouched areas such as different types of weeds, aspen, and blackthorn with plants that produce edible crops. It's about planting trees, bushes, and perennials that

grow in harmony and adapt to the land. Many of the trees and bushes we describe below work perfectly in a woodland garden.

Things to Think about When Planting

How do trees and bushes change the environment over time and do these fit in with your own long-term plans? What other plants and bushes will you be able to plant in the vicinity? Some trees will grow very big in time, so make sure you find out how big the tree will grow to give it space to flourish.

Bushes and trees are so much more than just the berries and fruit they yield—they also act as barriers, borders, protection, and shade. They can partition your garden and create space, so use them to your advantage. An area exposed to wind can be transformed by a hedge of red or blackcurrant bushes. Bushes and trees are, in other words, important when creating new microclimates in your garden.

Plan for Diversity

Whether you are adding trees and bushes to an existing area or creating a new orchard, it is worth planting as many species and varieties as possible in order to achieve a good level of diversity. Not only will you get lots of different berries and fruit, but you will also get a more resilient garden. Trees and bushes can both suffer from disease and infestation, but by planting a wide variety of species you can reduce this threat. Different species also yield different amounts of fruit, with some apple trees only bearing fruit every second year.

Furthermore, trees and bushes are vital for biodiversity. They provide food, protection, nourishment, and homes to a host of birds, insects, and other animals, which again makes for a more resilient garden.

Plan for Rejuvenation

At some point, the apple tree that has stood since time immemorial will die. Hopefully it will be slow and gradual, but death can also come with a swift autumn storm. Get into the habit of planting new trees every year if space allows as in this way you lay foundations for generations to come.

When Will They Bear Fruit?

When will the fruit ripen? It may not seem important, but you'll change your mind when you're left with ten plum trees all bearing fruit at the same time. When our apple trees were planted a century ago there was some forethought. They were planted in a half moon shape around the house in order of the fruit maturing, and we move our apple musting equipment around accordingly during late summer and fall. When you plan what trees and bushes you want, choose types that mature throughout the season so you have fruit and berries for a longer period, but also have the time to deal with them.

Plan for Creativity

What sort of fruits and berries do you like? And what do you plan to do with them? Choose varieties according to how you will use them, as you will be more likely to make use of the produce. If you plan to make cider, plant a few classic cider varieties, but don't forget to plant eating apples too. If you want to make jelly, make sure you have some sweet varieties of berries, but if you want to make wine, acidic berries are better. Variety means you have lots of fruit and berries for lots of different things.

Don't Throw Twigs, and Don't Sweep Leaves

During their lifecycle, trees and bushes contribute to the diversity and ecosystem in your garden. If you still sweep up leaves and burn them, or take old trees, branches, and twigs to be recycled, then stop immediately. Leaves are a natural resource and central part of a garden's life cycle; they break down and make mold, support the soil, and give food to microorganisms. By removing leaves, you remove nourishment from your own garden, so if the leaves annoy you, break them down with a lawnmower. Same goes for twigs, branches, and trees—as far as you can, leave them to reunite with your ecosystem by composting them or creating beds for planting.

Food for the Animals

Lots of animals are drawn to gardens rich in fruit and berries—insects, birds, hares, and deer. Some need to be discouraged even if their presence indicates a garden full of riches. In late spring, the trees are an important source of nectar for our bees.

It's important to protect bushes and smaller trees against animals. However, we like to be generous, so once we have taken what we need, we let our animals take the rest. Hens and ducks are mad about berries and we love watching them eat the last of the berries that we didn't have the energy to pick.

Pollination

Who pollinates what? This is an important question if you want a good harvest, or even a harvest at all. It works slightly differently for different types of plants. Some bushes and trees self-pollinate, meaning that the pollen grains attach to the stigma of the same flower it came from. However, the harvest is usually better if they are pollinated from a different flower.

Cross-pollination is often needed. This means the pollen comes from another flower of the same variety. Apples are usually best pollinated by specific types. Before planting a new tree, it's good to check if they can be pollinated by your other trees or planted together with trees that can pollinate each other.

Some bushes, such as hawthorn, have male and female plants, so you need a male plant together with several female plants.

Choosing Trees

Choosing what trees to plant is a personal choice. The benefit of trees and bushes is that they tend to yield fruit, berries, and nuts without too much effort, which is beneficial when you are trying to be self-sufficient. Here are some of our favorites.

Apples

Apple trees are great for sustainable living. They are hardy, live for many years, and in most cases yield a good crop, but the best benefit is of course the fruit. There is so much variety in what you can do with apples, which is great if you are harvesting hundreds of pounds each year.

USAGE We store the winter variety of our apples in our earth cellar and make lots of dried apple rings, cordial, jelly, marmalade, cider, wine, and apple cider vinegar.

VARIETIES We prefer older heirloom varieties. If possible, find heritage varieties that are local to your area.

ZONE Choose varieties that work where you live, preferably those that have been grown locally.

POLLINATION If you get a bad harvest, you could have a problem with pollination. Visit your local nursery to find out what types cross-pollinate with your apple trees. You can also find useful tips on pollination processes online. You don't need to own the trees yourself, so find out which varieties your neighbors have.

DISEASE There are many diseases and insects that can strike the fruit. The most usual ones are the apple fruit moth and the codling moth. They can be dealt with, but we tend not to worry about them—afflicted apples become juice, vinegar, and cider.

BROWN ROT caused by a fungus is more problematic. Make sure to remove afflicted fruits and throw them away, including rotten fruits still hanging at the end of the season.

CARE An established apple tree does not need a lot of care except regular pruning. Remove branches that grow upwards or inwards and keep the ground beneath the tree aerated.

Plums

When we moved to our current house there was one tree above all others that we missed; a plum tree. The first tree we planted ourselves was a Tuna plum, an old heritage variety from the Swedish area of Medelpad.

Plums are a stone fruit that grows well in USDA zones 4–9. The great thing about plum trees is that they usually yield fruit quickly.

USAGE We think of plums as sweets and eat them fresh, but we also make marmalade, wine, liqueur, and put them into honey and rum.

VARIETIES Different varieties grow better in different climates throughout the United States, so do a little research to see which kinds will be best for where you live.

ZONE There are varieties that will grow in USDA zones 4–9. Plums prefer sunshine in a protected area. Make sure there is good drainage and enough space for the tree.

POLLINATION Most trees self-pollinate, but if you cross-pollinate different varieties, the harvest is bigger with larger fruits.

DISEASE Plums can be afflicted by different types of bacteria, mold, and viruses. However, most people find worms the most disgusting. It's usually the larvae from the saw fly that attack the stone. You can shake the trees so these plums fall to the ground and then throw them away or burn them. This way you reduce the amount of larvae that can attack the trees the following year.

CARE Just like many other trees, plum trees need more care the first few years. Protect the trunk from vermin and make sure to water during extended periods of drought. A plum tree can grow very tall if it is not pruned and shaped, which should take place at the end of August during dry weather only. The tree can be shaped the second or third year after being planted. Remove branches that grow inwards or upwards.

TREES & BUSHES

Peaches

TREES & BUSHES

Pear

In the United States, most pears are grown in Washington, California, and Oregon, though there are varieties hardy in USDA zones 3–8, so it's possible to grow pears across the country.

USAGE Pears don't last as long as apples, so we use them primarily for liqueur and marmalade and also pickle them in sugar and alcohol.

VARIETIES The most common variety in the USA is bartlett, but there are several other varieties to choose from. Select one that is hardy in your zone.

ZONE Pear trees grow in USDA zones 3–8. Research which varieties are hardy in your zone.

POLLINATION This works the same as with apples. Look at a pollination guide before you plant. Pears are less common than apples so you may not be able to call on your neighbor for help.

DISEASE Fire blight is a bacterial disease spread by insects. Shoots and leaves wilt and the fruit shrivels up. Fire blight should be treated quickly. However, it may be the less serious fungus pear rust, which leaves red marks on the leaves. The disease spreads via the common juniper, so check during spring if any nearby junipers have got so called tongues of fire as these need to be removed if possible.

CARE Like the apple tree, a pear tree pretty much looks after itself with some yearly maintenance. Some pear trees can grow very big, so if you want to keep them small, prune them during their growth phase. Choose a pear tree with a slow growing trunk if you lack space.

Pear trees need a bit more tending when they have been newly planted as the roots can be sensitive. Dig a large hole of around 10¾ square feet (1 sq. m) and fill with good quality, loamy soil. In the first year, the tree just needs regular watering and fertilization.

Peach

A few years ago we visited a neighbor and were met by a beautiful tree full of large, yellow-red fruits. Peaches in Uppland? Would it really work? Apparently quite well. Soon after, we planted a lovely peach tree in a sheltered area. Sinking our teeth into one of our homegrown peaches has been one of our gardening highlights.

USAGE Peaches are fresh produce best eaten fresh or made into preserves, pies, marmalade, and jam.

VARIETIES There are over 300 varieties that grow in the United States. Research or ask other growers which varieties are best for your area.

ZONE Peaches grow in zones 4–9 but most varieties grow best in zones 6 and 7. If you live in a colder part of the country, try to find a sheltered and warm spot, preferably between buildings.

POLLINATION Most sorts are self-fertilizing, but cross-pollination will increase the growth of fruit. If your tree is not yielding a good harvest, it may need help with pollination. Use a soft brush to pollinate the flowers during spring.

DISEASE Peaches can be afflicted by peach leaf curl and nectria canker amongst other things. Peach leaf curl discolors the leaves that shrivel before dropping off. Remove all affected leaves and burn them.

CARE Apart from preferring the warmest and most sheltered spot in your garden, the peach tree needs well-drained soil and must not stand in water that might freeze during the fall. Planting on an elevation can give extra warmth and protection. In the early years you may need to water it regularly, especially as it bears fruit, as too little water can result in the fruit falling off.

Prune initially before planting and then during the first couple of years. Once established you do not need to prune it.

Planting Fruit Trees

Different trees have different needs when it comes to planting, but there are some basic rules. Most fruit trees require a sheltered sunny patch with well-drained soil, and not many want to be left standing in a pool of water in the fall. Make sure you avoid spots where old root systems remain, such as roses or old fruit trees. Apart from the soil being drained of nutrients, your tree needs to compete with an already established root system. If you do need to plant in a spot like this, you first need to remove the old roots and add new loamy and nutrient-rich soil. You can plant trees any time of year, but it's most practical during the spring or fall.
Method:

1. Wet the root system by placing the tree in a bucket of water.
2. Outline your space and make sure you dig a deep hole, around 1½ feet deep (50cm). If the ground is hard, muddy, or contains stone, this is even more important as the roots may struggle to establish themselves otherwise. A large hole that is loosened up will also drain better. Don't add any organic matter as the anaerobic decay can harm the roots.
3. Even more important than depth is width as the tree mustn't compete with grass or other plants for water. Dig up a layer of grass, using the tufts of grass in the hole by placing them upside down if you like.
4. Pour water into the hole, making sure it is soaked through. While you water, you can check the

drainage. Does the water drain away or remain in the hole? If it remains for too long it may be clay soil and you need to try to improve the drainage. If there is too much clay soil and only a thin layer of topsoil, you may need to plant the tree in a raised bed.
5. Push down a wooden stake for support. If it is a big tree, two or three stakes around the tree may work better.
6. Add some loosened topsoil and plant the tree. It is important that the tree isn't planted too deep as the root crown needs to be above ground. The plant will sink somewhat as the soil settles, so leave it slightly raised. Carefully loosen the roots as they may have tangled in the pot and try and place them so they point in different directions. Add some topsoil and plenty of water. Add more soil if the layer sinks.
7. Cover the area around the tree with cardboard, hay, and leaves to keep any weeds from establishing.
8. Tie the tree against the stake(s) to ensure it grows straight and is protected from wind. Don't forget to protect the trunk with a barrier to stop animals gnawing at it. If you have a lot of deer in the area you might also want to protect the top part of the tree (the crown).

TREES & BUSHES

Pruning Trees

Pruning a tree is a science and when and how it takes place depends on the type of tree. If you are planning on cutting large parts of an old tree and are unsure about how to go about it, get a professional to help you.

If you have a lot of fruit trees, you should learn some of the basics of pruning so you can maintain your orchard. Pruning has several benefits, but it's mainly about creating a healthy tree that yields a good crop and works for your needs. In old, abandoned orchards you can sometimes see trees that have been allowed to grow wild for many years, which usually results in tall, thick trees with barely any fruit.

During the first phase, when the tree is still young, pruning takes place to shape the tree; that is the time to decide how tall it will grow and the shape it will have. After this, pruning is about maintaining the shape and creating an airy crown to allow light to reach all the fruit in the tree.

A basic rule for pruning is to keep branches that stick out horizontally and remove those that stick upwards. Don't cut branches thicker than 2–2¾ inches (5–7 cm) in diameter. The thicker they are the more they are at risk of rot. Another rule is to not go too hard but to prune a little each year. This is especially important if you have an overgrown tree that needs proper pruning. It's better to do this over several years than to attack it with a chainsaw. A sign that you have overpruned is getting a lot of water sprouts on your tree, which is a reaction to the lack of leaves from the tree.

Generally, apple and pear trees can be pruned a bit harder than stone fruits where you need to be more careful. Stone fruit trees ooze sap and are also more sensitive to mold infestations on cut surfaces.

Tools

The most important tool is a good quality pair of pruning shears. Make sure they're sharp so you get nice, straight cuts. For thicker branches you need a saw, preferably telescopic. If you have tall trees, it can also be worth getting a long-handled pruner as climbing around an old apple tree is not good for either you or the tree. Lower branches can be reached using a garden ladder. Always clean your tools as disease can spread via the cuts.

Seasons

Pruning can vary among trees, but most trees are pruned during late winter/early spring or in July, August, or September. Apple and pear trees can be pruned during both these periods, whereas stone fruits should be pruned after harvest during late summer and autumn.

Formative Pruning

You can ask the nursery for help with pruning the tree when you buy it. Leave the tree to root itself for a year before you start to shape the crown. Remove any branches that are growing inwards, upwards, or too closely together. Cut young trees during the spring.

Maintenance Pruning

Cut or saw dead or diseased branches and twigs and remove any new shoots that you don't want to keep. Remove about a third to half every year, cutting off shoots and branches that are growing straight upwards, inwards, too close together, or ones that are overlapping.

The Basics of Pruning

Observe the tree and get a good overview of the crown. How is it shaped? In which way does it face the sun? Which part is thick and shady and is any part sticking out? Start with the large cuts such as big branches, if necessary. To avoid damaging the tree, cut large branches in several steps. Begin around 12 inches (30cm) from the trunk or fork and make a cut underneath the branch. Then make a second cut slightly further out on the branch until it falls off. After this you can saw the rest of the stump off. Saw just above the branch collar so it doesn't get damaged. The branch collar is a bulbous area attached to the branch or trunk; it is important to protect it as it contains substances that help the tree heal.

Next remove smaller branches and shoots. Start with removing new shoots and dead branches. After this, get rid of branches that grow inwards or are growing too closely to each other. Don't leave stumps but cut just above the branch collar.

Take a step back now and again to check the crown. Pruning a tree is both about aesthetics and a gut feeling, so don`t rush it. Sometimes you need time to make sure you are making the right decisions.

RULES OF PRUNING

Maintenance Pruning

1. Remove tree suckers growing down on the ground.
2. Remove water sprouts and one- and two-year tree suckers that are growing straight up unless you want a taller crown. Water sprouts often appear when you have been excessive in pruning and is the tree's way of compensating for a loss of greenery.
3. Remove low hanging branches.
4. When branches cross one another, remove one of them.
5. When branches rub against each other, remove one of them.
6. Remove branches that are growing inwards.
7. Remove branches that are growing too low.
8. Thin the crown.
9. Chop off branches growing straight upwards.

TREES & BUSHES

Grafting

During our first summer, we became confused over what types of apples we actually had as some of them looked different despite growing on the same tree. We soon discovered that the previous owner had grafted other varieties onto the tree. Grafting is a great way to include several types of fruit in your garden without having to plant a new tree, and it's a shortcut to more flavors and better diversity. In fact, one single apple tree can have twenty different types of apples on it.

SCION WOOD In order to graft, you need scion wood, which is the twigs from the tree you want to graft from. You can take scion wood from maintenance pruning during the spring by saving the thickest shoots. Store them in a cold and moist environment, for example wrapped in damp paper in the fridge.

GRAFTING takes place later in the spring when sap levels increase. If you want a new variety, you can also buy scion wood or perhaps swap with a neighbor.

TOOLS You need shears, a short, sharp knife (preferably a grafting knife), beeswax, or grafting wax and a rubber band.

It's also a good idea to use labels to keep track of the varieties.

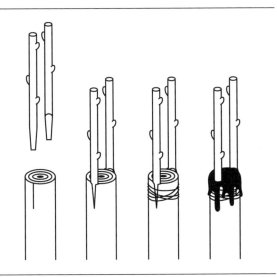

METHOD: There are many different ways to graft; bark grafting is one of the easier ones to do. The grafting takes place in late spring once buds start to appear on the trees and spring is on its way. Just remember to order any scion wood in good time.

Find a branch to graft your scion wood onto and make sure it's in a position that will allow your shoot to grow, preferably in an outer part of the crown and facing the sun.

Saw off the branch with a straight cut. The branch should be around ½ inch (1 cm) in diameter to fit two shoots. Make sure there is lots of space before the branch collar as one cut will be made below the bark.

Cut the scion wood by making a 1 inch (2 cm) long cut surface, like a flap. Then shorten the scion wood to around 4 inches (1 decimeter) retaining two to four buds.

Cut lengthways on the branch and carefully loosen the bark on either side of the cut, then carefully insert the scion.

Add at least two scions on each branch for extra assurance and tie it in place with a rubber band, raffia, or string. Now cover the scion surfaces with warmed up beeswax or grafting wax, which keeps the surface moist, aids the grafting process, and keeps mold away.

Look After Your Trees

How old your trees will get and how much fruit you get from them really depends on how well you look after them. The best ways to keep them healthy from disease, bacteria, mold, and insects is through preventative care and keeping the trees strong and healthy. Maintaining your trees by pruning dead and diseased branches is an important part of caring for your trees.

One common reason that trees get sick is drought, so during dry periods, even old trees can benefit from being watered. Don't water old trees at the trunk but further out where the roots are.

Most fruit trees don't really like to grow on lawns as they will compete for water and nutrients, so the best thing to do is to regularly dig up an area five to ten feet around the trunk and turn the tufts of grass upside down, although take care not to damage surface roots. You can also remove the grass by covering it.

TREES & BUSHES

Making Must

One of the highlights of the year and a sign that harvesting season is well and truly upon us is when we bring the fruit press out of the barn. For a few months we roll it around the garden from tree to tree and in a good year we can press several hundred liters of must. We tend to drink it as is, but we also make cider, apple cider vinegar, mulled wine (glögg), wine, cyser (something between mead and cider), and sour beer.

Tools

FRUIT PRESS A fruit press is a necessary piece of equipment when you have an orchard. Apart from apples, you can press plums, cherries, grapes, and pears and you can even use it to press honey from honeycombs.

The size and type of press you buy is totally dependent on how much fruit you plan to press. In other words, how many fruit trees you have. A 5-gallon (20 l) fruit press is enough for around five apple trees, but you will not regret getting one size up.

FRUIT CRUSHER In order to press apples and pears, you need a fruit crusher to separate the fruit, and unless you crush apples prior to pressing them, you won't extract any liquid. You can get electric or hand driven ones and it really depends on the amount of fruit and your needs.

LARGE CONTAINER Before the fruit is crushed, it needs to be washed, which is even more important if you have animals roaming around nearby. The easiest is to use a large open container to wash all the fruit. This is a task our children love helping out with.

What Apples Can Be Used for Must?

It is said that apples that have a firmer flesh work best for musting. We don't really worry about that too much and use all varieties from early, mushy apples to late crispy ones. Depending on variety, you get different flavors. After a while you will work out how to mix them to the best effect. Use the apples you have and don't be afraid to throw some other fruits into the press.

The most important thing is that the apples are ripe, and the easiest way to check is to halve the apple. If the seeds are white, the apple is still not ripe, but if they are brown it is ready to use.

Method:

1. Pick the fruit and check it over. You can use diseased fruit and fruits that have fallen to the ground but make sure to remove any parts that are rotten, brown, or diseased. You can leave the core and stem.
2. Clean the fruit in a bowl of water. It's especially important to clean the fruit if it's been lying on the ground.
3. Mash the fruit in a fruit crusher. You can press the fruit straight away but you will get a lot more must and make your job easier if you leave the crushed fruit to rest for a bit because the fruit fibres start to break down. Leave it in a cool area in 6½-gallon (25 l) containers with lids for 6–18 hours. We fill several buckets and leave them overnight.
4. Press. If you really want to, you can squeeze out a bit of extra must by pressing the crushed fruit again, which usually gives a few extra pints.
5. Apple must tastes best freshly pressed, so drink as much as you can. It will keep for 4–5 days in the fridge until it starts to ferment.

Storing Must

If you prefer to store the must, there are a few ways you can do this. The most common is to pasteurize it. Heat it in a large pan to 167°F (75°C) and maintain this temperature for 10–15 minutes. Fill large, clean glass bottles that have been in the oven for 30 minutes at 212°F (100°C), filling them all the way up. Leave to slowly cool before storing them in a dark and cool place. They will last for around six months unopened.

The method we prefer that we feel retains most taste is to freeze the must. If you have access to a large freezer, it's a great way to store large amounts of must. We freeze it in recyclable, 2-pint (1-liter) plastic bottles that are safe for reuse. Don't fill the bottles to the brim as the must will expand on freezing.

TREES & BUSHES

Hard Cider

Part of our apple crop is set aside for making cider according to the ancient laws of homesteading—well, at least in our household. The benefit of making cider is that the best apples are those that no one else wants. When it comes to making cider, it's all about the apples and your apples will create a cider unique to you. If the apples are too sweet, the cider will be sickly and not especially nice as it needs some tartness. If you have ever bitten into a really bitter cider apple, you will know that the best cider doesn't necessarily come from the best apples and if you plan to make lots of cider, we recommend you plant some classic cider varieties.

If you don't have any sour apples, there are other ways to raise the acidity in your cider, for example by adding another tart fruit or berry like sea buckthorn or redcurrants.

A more refined way to enhance your cider is to create a malolactic fermentation where the acid in the apple converts to lactic acid. Malolactic bacteria can be purchased in specialist brew stores and are added after fermentation.

To make a really good quality cider that can be compared with quality ciders from England and France is not easy and a big reason is due to our apple varieties. House cider always tastes a bit better because you make it. A house cider can also provide the basis for many other drinks, for example in the winter we make apple toddies and mulled cider with ours. If you are not entirely satisfied with your cider you can always ferment it a second time with, for example, rosehip, sloe, or blackcurrants.

House Cider

Pour freshly pressed must into a demijohn. Cover the tube with cotton wool or a piece of fabric so oxygen can enter but no insects.

Place the demijohn in a dark, warm place and within a few days it will start to ferment naturally and you can add the airlock and place the cider in a cooler place. If it does not start to ferment or you want more control over the process, you can add cider yeast.

Let the fermentation stop and then pour into a new demijohn, avoiding the sediment at the bottom.

Usually a secondary fermentation will start. Leave the cider to rest until the winter before you bottle it. Add 1 tsp sugar in every bottle to carbonate them. The cider should be ready to enjoy by spring.

Apple Cider Vinegar

One of the best things you can make from your must is your own apple cider vinegar. We consider it one of the basic store cupboard ingredients in our home that we find ourselves using daily in the kitchen but that also has a place in the bathroom and cleaning cupboard. It's a miracle cure that removes funky smells from the drains, makes hair shiny, and makes ricotta float to the surface. Apple cider vinegar made from your own apples is a natural product that will come with its own unique taste.

It's very easy to make. The apple must will eventually start to naturally ferment through the yeast converting the sugar to alcohol. Once this process is complete, other bacteria take over and convert the alcohol to vinegar as long as the "cider" is exposed to air. To make a good apple cider vinegar, you need a vinegar mother, a gelatinous disc with the right bacteria. The first time you will have to make your own vinegar mother but you can save this for future apple cider vinegars. If you are unhappy with the taste of your cider, you can use it to make apple cider vinegar.

6⅓ pints (3 l) apple must
½ cup (1 dl) organic apple cider vinegar or vinegar mother

Pour the must into a large glass jar and place it somewhere dark and warm. Cover the lid carefully with a fine net and also a towel, making sure it's secure enough to keep fruit flies away—as they can destroy the vinegar—but to allow some air to get in.

After a few days, the must will start to naturally ferment, which can be seen by carbonated bubbles and a ring forming on the surface. If the fermentation doesn't start, you can give it a nudge by adding a cider yeast.

A week after fermentation has begun, add the bottom layer of sediment from an organic apple cider vinegar, unless you have a vinegar mother, and cover carefully. Place in a dark place and wait. Soon you will notice that a vinegar mother starts to form, first like a gelatinous surface that gradually becomes thicker. Taste the vinegar now and again to see how the acidity is developing. Once it is sharp enough for you and doesn't taste of alcohol, the vinegar is ready. Sieve it and pour into clean bottles.

If you want to make more apple cider vinegar, you can pour more must straight into the jar. Just save the vinegar mother and the bottom layer of sediment. If not, you can keep the vinegar mother in a sealed jar with some of the sediment. Keep it cool in the fridge or a root cellar.

Bushes

When you examine maps of gardens from the 1800s, you are struck by the lack of lawns. Instead, you can see fruit trees, flower beds, and berry bushes spreading out across the garden. In the United States, Native Americans enjoyed huckleberries, cranberries, blueberries, and more long before the settlers arrived.

In Sweden, fruit trees and berry bushes had their hey day from the mid-nineteenth century to the second world war. People were asked to grow more fruit and berries, which was good for health as well as self-sufficiency, and at the end of the last century, nurseries would sell hundreds of different varieties of currants and gooseberries.

It is not hard to see why they have proved popular for such a long time as fruit bushes are easy to plant, grow fast, are dependable, and yield fruit full of vitamins and minerals. In addition, they are great when you need to create space, privacy, and new climate zones in your garden. In the past, berry bushes were often used as hedges, so why not replace an ugly hedge with a currant bush? We plant berry bushes all over the place, the more the merrier.

Currants

As apples are to trees, currants are to bushes, an obvious choice in many states. These white, red, and black vitamin bombs are adored by kids, adults, and animals. However, some states do not allow currants, or certain varieties of currants, to be grown due to the possibility of them spreading white pine rust. Check your state's regulations.

USAGE Currants are fantastic, not only because they usually yield a large harvest and are fairly easy to pick, but also because their usage is almost endless. We make our best wines from black and red currants, but we also make purees, jellies, marmalade, jam, and of course eat a whole load just as they are. Even the leaves can be used for teas, drinks, and pickling.

VARIETIES We tend to grow red currants (the children's favorite) and black currants (our favorite). Check to see which varieties grow best and are permitted in your area.

ZONE Currant bushes are hardy in USDA zones 3–8.

POLLINATION Currants self-pollinate but cross-pollinating them is better. Red varieties are pollinated with each other and with white ones and black varieties are pollinated with black and sometimes green currants.

CARE Currants prefer a sunny to partly shaded area with well-drained, loamy, and nutrient-rich soil. For a good harvest, pick a spot that gets warm early in the season as the bushes bloom in early spring. Fertilize yearly, preferably in the spring, for a good harvest.

Currant bushes need to be maintained with pruning, which can be done in fall or winter. Older branches stop bearing fruit after a few years so remove these. They are usually dark and thick and need to be cut right down to the ground.

DISEASE Blackcurrants can be afflicted by the blackcurrant gall mite which results in a virus in the bush. To stop it spreading you may need to remove and burn the bush. The bush can also be attacked by fungi such as brown rust, blister rust, and leaf spots, especially during damp summers.

Raspberries

There are raspberries that are native to North America and some that were introduced from Europe. Native Americans used all parts of the raspberry plant for medicinal purposes.

USAGE We love raspberries, not just the berries but also the leaves and twigs. If we have any berries left after the children have had their share, we make wine while the leaves get made into tea. Raspberry twigs are also beautiful when placed in a bouquet.

VARIETIES Raspberries are broadly divided into two categories once ripe: summer raspberries and fall raspberries. You should include both types. The difference between them is that fall raspberries crop on this year's shoots, whereas summer varieties crop on the previous year's shoots.

ZONE Raspberries are hardy in USDA zones 4–8.

POLLINATION Raspberries are self-pollinating and also very popular among insects. For beekeepers, the raspberry is one of the most important plants that attract bees.

CARE Raspberries prefer a spot with lots of sun and need well-drained, loose, and nutrient-rich soil. Raspberries need a bit of acidity in the soil, so you can add some rhododendron soil for example into your raspberry plantation. Fertilize the raspberries yearly with composted chicken or cow fertilizer.

RASPBERRIES need an even level of moisture, so water when it is dry and, if you can, mulch with straw.

Both fall and summer raspberries are pruned straight after harvest and the shoots get cut along the ground, but make sure you don't cut off any new shoots on the summer raspberries.

DISEASE Raspberries can be afflicted by bacterial disease like fire blight, which can result in dark purple patches around the new shoots. Cut them off immediately as in fall, the fungi creates spores that may spread.

Elderberry Bush

"Where the elder won't grow, there no man wants to know," goes the old saying. If we could only keep one bush, the choice would be easy: our large elder. Even in pre-Christian times, the elderberry bush was surrounded by mystery and it was considered magical and ensured that there were good spirits in your home. The Hyllerfroan or Elder tree mother was associated with the elder and was a female sprite that lived in the elder. There is definitely something magical about this bush as the creamy white flowers light up the late June nights and spread their seductive scent.

USAGE The elderberry bush has a varied flavor; in June and July when it blooms, we harvest the flowers for elder champagne, fortified wine, juice, schnapps, and ice cream. In the autumn, we collect the black berries to make jelly and red wine.

VARIETIES It's important that you can tell the difference between real elderberry and false elderberry (devil's walking stick) and dwarf elder. False elderberry has red berries while dwarf elder is recognized by the red stamens in the flower as well as being relatively small.

There are several real elderberry bushes you can choose from. Research to see which varieties grow best in your area.

ZONE Elderberry bushes are hardy in USDA Zones 4A to 10B.

POLLINATION Elderberry has to cross-pollinate, so if there isn't another elder bush in the area it is a good idea to plant two bushes.

CARE Elderberry bushes are easy to care for and can live in most places and soil types but prefer a nutrient-rich and loamy soil in sunlight.

Elderberries can grow quite large with enough space and can push into other bushes and trees. Prune the bush during the early years to give it shape, but after this prune with more caution. Remove old branches and make sure it doesn't grow out of control.

DISEASE Elderberry is fairly hardy against disease, but it is favored by aphids that hang in big bunches on the stem during flowering. They seldom harm the bush and can be flushed away if needed.

Blackberry

Grown in the wrong place, blackberry can be a bothersome weed that is almost impossible to get rid of, but in the right spot it's a faithful servant that produces some of the best and juiciest berries in the garden. There are varieties of blackberry that are native to Europe, Asia, and North and South America.

USAGE Blackberry can be used for all sorts of things such as marmalade, liqueur, and wine.

VARIETY Blackberries grow wild in many parts of North America. The varieties can cause complications as there are many hybrids being sold. Apart form "real" blackberries you can also get black cascade, sunberries, and ghost bramble, which can be hard to tell apart.

ZONE Blackberries ripen late and love heat. Most of the varieties can be grown in USDA zones 5–8 and some can grow in zones 3 or 4. The most important thing is that they are grown in a sunny spot.

POLLINATION Blackberries self-pollinate, so you only need one plant.

DISEASE Blackberries can be afflicted by the same diseases as raspberries, such as fruit worms that can be annoying. They are laid by small grey beetles, the butyridae, so remove these when you see them on the bushes.

CARE Blackberries like a warm, protected spot, preferably against a south-facing wall or fence where the berries can ripen. Water when newly planted, but they are generally tolerant to drought and do not need much fertilizing or care. Prune during the autumn after harvest by cutting down the shoots that have given harvest. Be careful where you plant the blackberries though, as they can easily take over.

TREES & BUSHES

Blue Honeysuckle

In early summer, as we long for all the berries that are still ripening, the blue honeysuckle is an early summer hero. It is a bush that is hardy and easy to grow, especially in the more northern parts of the country, and the long blue berries taste a bit like blueberries but sweeter.

USAGE We eat them fresh and they are wonderful with yogurt. You can basically use them in the same way that you use blueberries.

VARIETIES Blue honeysuckle is not found in many US gardens but is common in other more northerly countries such as Russia and Canada. Do a little research to see which varieties are best for your area.

ZONES Unlike many other plants, blue honeysuckle prefers a cold climate, preferably with a long winter. The bush is very hardy against cold and can handle temperatures as low as -40°F (-40°C). Even the flowers can deal with temperatures of 18°F (-8°C). The berries ripen early on in the season, often at the start of June.

POLLINATION To get a good harvest you need to cross-pollinate, so place two or more bushes near each other. Choose varieties that bloom at the same time, for example the Russian variety bloom earlier than the Canadian ones.

CARE Blue honeysuckle prefer the sun and can live in most types of soil, from clay to sand. It is considered easy to grow and can, in time, get quite big, so make sure you give it a lot of space. It can be pruned after a few years in early winter when you can remove old branches. In the right conditions, a blue honeysuckle can get up to 40 years in age.

DISEASE Blue honeysuckle is generally a healthy bush, but it can be afflicted by mildew. The berries are also popular among birds and a whole harvest can disappear in just a few hours, so protect them with netting.

Sea Buckthorn

These days the sea buckthorn, or sea berry, is becoming popular as something of a super berry, but the ancient Greeks already knew this. In Latin it is known as "shining horse," and it is said people in the past discovered that horses that ate sea buckthorn were healthier and more handsome than other horses. For the homesteader, sea buckthorn is a fighter that can deal with most things and can be planted in some of the less hospitable spots in your garden.

USAGE We make the golden yellow berries filled with vitamin C into juice, jam, and smoothies. Sea buckthorn is also great to add to wine as it contributes a lovely acidity.

VARIETIES Sea buckthorn grows in most of the United States. There are several varieties, including Sunny, Mary, Orange Energy, Radiant, and Garden's Gift. Some varieties are better for juicing and others for cosmetic use.

ZONE Sea buckthorn is a hardy bush that can cope with more extreme environments such as the coast with its strong, salty winds. It is hardy down to USDA zone 3.

POLLINATION Sea buckthorn has male and female plants and to get a harvest you need one male plant to around five female plants. Pollination is done through the wind, so place the male plant downwind from the female plants.

CARE Sea buckthorn has roots that retain nitrogen, meaning it does not need much from the soil. Once established it can also handle drought. The first year after planting it may need extra water if it is especially dry out.

They are best planted in a sunny spot in sandy and well-drained soil. Some varieties can grow several feet in height, so give it lots of space. It does not need a lot of pruning, but remove old, gnarly branches and cut it down if it gets too big.

DISEASE Sea buckthorn is generally a healthy plant, thanks to its thorns that protect it against animals, although young plants are vulnerable to being gnawed at.

Pruning Berry Bushes

Most berry carrying bushes only need to be pruned to continue to yield fruit. Old branches stop giving fruit after a while and through pruning you give new shoots space and keep the bush healthy and give it longevity. Pruning also prevents the bush from getting too dense or growing out of control. Bushes that are not pruned are also more susceptible to disease.

TOOLS Just like with trees, you need the right tools for pruning and a sharp pair of shears. For thicker branches and twigs, use a lopper or a saw. Some thick gardening gloves, like rose pruning gloves, are good when you are handling thorny bushes like blue honeysuckle and sea buckthorn.

SEASON Depending on the variety, the bushes need to be trimmed at different times. Many bushes are pruned in the autumn after harvest and this makes it easier to keep track of which branches and buds have borne fruit. Raspberries should be pruned yearly, but currants less frequently. Red currants have shoots on their branches that are between two and five years old, so don't leave the branches longer than this.

Renewal Pruning Berry Bushes

It's mainly berries such as currants and gooseberries that need regular renewal pruning. Bushes like blue honeysuckle and sea buckthorn can be pruned less often. Raspberries and blackcurrants can be pruned yearly, removing shoots that have borne fruit.

Method:

1. Start by removing dead branches and cut them down all the way to the ground.
2. Remove older branches—they usually have a darker bark and are thicker. If you are unsure, you can mark the old branches that bear little or no fruit during the season.
3. Prune the branches that lie against the ground or grow outward.
4. When you are done, the bush should feel airy and the remaining branches should look healthy.

Save Cuttings

When you prune your bushes, you can take some cuttings at the same time. Save the best shoots that you remove. A bunch of cuttings from currant bushes can be placed straight into a pot of soil; remove the lower leaves and keep the upper ones. Remove the cutting at an angle and you increase the chances of it establishing. Cuttings can also be taken late spring/early winter and planted in a pot ready to be planted out in the fall.

While you prune, keep an eye out for branches lying against the ground that have already grown roots—if you find these then you are one step ahead.

Raspberry & Blue Honeysuckle, page 317 & 320

TREES & BUSHES

Wood

Frost clings to the windows and there is total silence until you hear crackling, the comforting sound of sparking wood, as the warmth slowly spreads around the room. Living in a house from the mid-eighteenth century comes with responsibility. Every morning during the winter months we light the tiled stove in the dining room and our cast iron range from Husqvarna in the kitchen. This is how we wake the house and make it habitable. It is this huge chimney, several meters wide, which is the heart and lungs of the house. The fire is the pumping heart, the chimney the lungs breathing in fresh air and breathing out heat. Old houses are constructed to benefit from wood fires. Fires create a pressure that brings fresh air into the house, so an important part of our job is to ensure we have a good stash of firewood to get us through the winter. During a normal winter, we use up around 140–174 cubic feet (4–5 cubic meters) of wood.

A Natural Resource

Even at the end of its life, a tree is a natural resource that needs to be cared for. Trees, branches, twigs, and shoots fill an important, and central, part in our ecosystem. Branches from trees such as cherry and apples can be used for smoking. Large stumps and decaying logs, as well as shoots and branches, can be used to make hügel beds. Larger branches can be used to make fences, posts, and plant supports.

The largest resource for us, however, is firewood. As we don't have any woodland, we take the wood we have available, which means we use different types of wood. Each year we cut down a few trees, but we also use twigs and leftover wood. Sometimes neighbors cut down trees and don't need the wood and are usually only too glad that we come and pick it up. Producing high quality firewood is a process as wood always needs to dry. Fresh wood has a humidity level of around 50% and needs to get down to 15–20% before you can burn it.

Chimney Fires

According to some, trees such as pine and fir can cause fires as tar and soot gets stuck in the chimney and catches fire. The problem is not the type of wood but the way you make your fire and the use of damp wood. Making fire with damp wood is unhelpful for both you and the environment. Damp logs don't burn efficiently and release tar, of which some can stick in the chimney, so always use dry wood. In order to dry the wood properly, it needs to season at least one summer, preferably two.

Another reason for chimney fires is when the fire hasn't completely gone out but is still smoldering, where there is a poor oxygen supply. Your fire should always burn effectively so that basically no smoke is coming out of the chimney. When it is not burning effectively, creosote can get trapped in the chimney, which is also bad for the environment.

Get to Know Your Wood

You can use most types of wood for fires, but they have different properties that are worth knowing about. We use a mixture of woods—maple, rowan, birch, aspen, linden, oak, and pine. Once you understand the wood, you can get the most out of them. For example, pine is easy to light, but as it contains less energy it burns quickly, while oak has so much energy it needs to be mixed with, for example, pine or birch, to then move onto a harder wood type like oak or ash.

Wood also behaves differently as it burns—for example, pine and fir wood can spark a lot while it burns.

Birch

This is the wood most people prefer and it is easy to find. It's good to burn with in open fires as it doesn't spark and gives a nice and even burn. The bark also makes it easy to light as it has a porous structure and contains botulin, which is why it has been used historically to light fires.

Pine & Fir

Pine and fir have a similar energy, giving off 1,700 kWh/rm. The wood dries fast and burns well and it's easy to light. It does give off a crackling sound, and as the wood sparks it is not suitable in an open fire. But if you want to heat up a wood-fired hot tub, for example, a wood with a higher energy is preferable.

Oak

Oak has a high energy content and burns slowly, giving off a lot of heat over a long period of time, but it does contain tannins and needs a high heat to burn, so it is not good to start a fire, or to burn solely with oak wood. Oak wood needs a long time to cure, as much as two years.

Ash

Ash is great for firewood due to its high energy value, and it doesn't leave much ash. It is a very hard wood that can be hard to cut.

Beech

Beech is great to burn with to give a long, warming glow. The wood has a high density and needs to cure for a long time, preferably a few years.

Rowan Tree

Among fire connoisseurs, beech and rowan are considered the best woods to burn with. Rowan burns slowly and gives off a warm glowing ember, which lasts for a long time. Woods like beech, ash, rowan, and oak have an energy level almost twice as high as pine and fir.

Chopping, Cleaving & Storing

Caring for firewood is an old tradition and the different steps follow the seasons. The reason for this is that the firewood doesn't suddenly appear as soon as you chop down a tree but is created through a process.

Felling & Chopping Trees

It's best to fell trees during the winter as this is when they contain the least sap and will dry faster. If you fell a leafy tree during the summer, leave it to rest. Drying the leaves helps to draw out some of the moisture.

Chop the tree straight on the ground into good-size logs. It depends on your fireplace, but average length is around 12 inches (30 cm). It also depends on the type of wood. Harder woods like oak can be chopped smaller as it can be hard to split otherwise.

Splitting Wood

The wood should be split as soon as possible—early Spring is usually a good time. This is because split wood dries a lot quicker as it is not surrounded by bark, whose purpose is to keep moisture in. For smaller sticks that don't need splitting, remove the bark if you want them to dry faster.

If the wood is handled correctly from the start, it is easier to split it. Splitting wood is both meditative and a workout at the same time. A proper splitting axe from a forge makes a good companion that lasts a lifetime. A splitting axe has a wedge shape to better split the wood.

Use a solid chopping block from something like an oak tree and make sure it's the right height; it should be in line with your knees. If you miss, the axe should fall into the ground.

Use a smaller axe for chopping kindling.

Drying

When you start chopping and splitting the wood, it's a good idea to start dividing it into piles. Some harder wood needs to season for years while other wood dries faster. Smaller sticks also dry quicker and can be put aside for use in cast iron ranges or as kindling. By sorting and dividing the wood, it's easier to keep on top of the drying time.

Storing Wood

There are many ways to store wood and what works best depends on space and usage. The wood needs a place to dry that is protected from rain, and you also need a space for storage once it is dry. If you light a lot of fires it's more practical to keep this as close to your house as possible as during colder days you will need a lot of trips to the wood pile.

We have a woodshed built against our barn, which works both for drying and storing wood as it is airy and catches the sunlight. For those with space, an even better solution is an enclosed woodshed that is drafty enough to create an airy environment. The most important things for wood to dry is an airy surrounding that is free from damp.

If you lack the space for this type of storage, another alternative is to build a round wood pile (a Holz Hausen). Choose a space that is sunny, airy, and flat. Make a foundation to stop damp from seeping up, then build a grid using thick branches or planks of around 6.5 x 6.5 feet (2 × 2 meters), you can also use pallets. Stack the wood in a circle with the longest and thickest logs at the bottom. Stack them with bark facing down. Use the straightest logs to make walls and place all the uneven ones in the center. Eventually make the stack lean inwards using shorter logs to create a dome-shaped finish. Place a layer of logs at the top with the bark facing up, making sure they lean outwards to allow water to drain off rather than into the pile. If you want to further waterproof the pile, you can make a roof from old roof tiles.

Making a Fire

Apart from using really dry wood, there are a few other things to think about when preparing your fire. Take the wood in at least a day, preferably a few days, before using it. Cold wood is harder to light and also gives less warmth. In addition, the temperature indoors quickly dries up any moisture left in the wood.

If you light a fire every day, you want it to be a quick and easy process. Keep twigs, sticks, and bark, preferably from birch trees for this purpose, and store indoors. You can also make some kindling using a small axe—pine, fir, and birch trees all work well for this purpose.

Using newspaper to light the fire is not very effective as the paper burns fast, produces a lot of ash, and extinguishes the flames. Use birch bark or make your own waxed pinecone fire starters. Collect pinecones during the summer and store them in a dry place for a few months before dipping them in melted wax from old candles, for example.

Safety

Lighting a fire is an art form, even more so a craft that people have depended on for hundreds of thousands of years. To make a proper fire, you need to understand fire. To make fire, you need three things, the so-called fire triangle consisting of oxygen, fuel, and heat. If you remove any of these, you can't make fire. Making a fire quickly and efficiently means creating the best environment for each of these elements. You need air, so the logs should not be piled up or placed too close together to allow oxygen to flow through. The fuel should be placed so the heat can expand, from kindling to large logs, so build the fire step by step, starting with the smallest materials.

Using a wood burner or open fire is fairly easy as it takes place in a warm, enclosed space. Make sure you have enough air at the start to get the fire going and always follow the instructions on how to light it safely.

Chopping Wood, page 326

Indexes

Index

THANKS!

There are so many people to thank in the making of this book. Firstly, our children August and Almer, you are the reason for everything we do. A huge thanks to the children's grandparents whose help has given us space to work when it was most needed. We also want to thank our original Swedish publisher, Maria Nilsson, for helping to develop the idea of this book and our editor, Henrik Francke. Without photographer Roland Persson and assistant photographer Erik Ögnelooh the book just wouldn't have been the same. They created visual magic from our simple ingredients. A huge thanks to Lotta, Sigge, and Fabian Kühlhorn for the beautiful design. Finally, thanks to our fact checkers: Anders Stålhand, Per Jensen, Kurt Oldeskog, and Jonas Höglund. And last but not least, we thank Earth!

Visit our website at www.skyhorsepublishing.com.
Please follow our publisher Tony Lyons on Instagram @tonylyonsisuncertain

10 9 8 7 6 5 4 3 2

Library of Congress Cataloging-in-Publication Data is available on file.

Translator: Ellen Hedström
Photographer: Roland Persson. Photos on pages 58 and 264 are courtesy of Shutterstock.
Assistant Photographer: Erik Ögnelooh
Layout & illustrations: Lotta Kühlhorn, Sigge Kühlhorn & Fabian Kühlhorn
Editor (Swedish): Henrik Francke
Cover design by Kai Texel
Cover photos by Roland Persson

Print ISBN: 978-1-5107-7570-1
Ebook ISBN: 978-1-5107-7791-0

Printed in the United States of America